BRADWELL: ANCIENT AND MODERN

Faithfully yours.

THE AUTHOR.

BRADWELL:
Ancient and Modern.

————

HISTORY OF THE PARISH

AND

INCIDENTS IN THE HOPE VALLEY & DISTRICT.

BEING

COLLECTIONS AND RECOLLECTIONS IN A
PEAKLAND VILLAGE.

————

BY SETH EVANS,

MEMBER OF THE DERBYSHIRE ARCHÆOLOGICAL SOCIETY,

AUTHOR OF

"METHODISM IN BRADWELL," ETC.

1912.

© 2004 Country Books
Courtyard Cottage, Little Longstone, Bakewell, Derbyshire DE45 1NN
Tel/Fax: 01629 640670
e-mail: dickrichardson@country-books.co.uk

This is an enlarged facsimile (15%) of the first edition of 1912
printed by Broad Oaks Press, Chesterfield.

The cover illustration is from a postcard of Bridge End, Bradwell c 1904.

We are always interested to hear
from authors or societies
working on local history projects.

Printed and bound in England by
Antony Rowe Ltd

PREFACE.

This little volume has been issued in response to a desire expressed by many that the articles should not remain " buried in the files" of a newspaper. Hence, the subject matter has undergone revision, and with additions, and many illustrations, it makes its appearance in book form.

In the work of love in which he has been engaged it has been the author's desire to place on permanent record information collected during many years, so as to place this matter in the hands of those who care to interest themselves in these " collections and recollections of a Peakland village," and it is to the kind encouragement and assistance of the proprietors of the " Derbyshire Courier" that this has been made possible.

It has, of course, been necessary to consult many publications in order to procure reliable information, and to these the author has laid himself under tribute, especially the journals of the Derbyshire Archæological Society. And there are others to whom he desires to tender his sincere thanks. To W. H. G. Bagshawe, Esq., J.P., D.L., of Ford Hall, he is indebted for a great deal of valuable information relating to the Apostle of the Peak and early Nonconformity; to Edward G. Bagshawe, Esq., solicitor, Sheffield, for the loan of M.S. of his late father, Benjamin Bagshawe; to Sydney Taylor, Esq., B.A., of Buxton; to N. J. Hughes-Hallett, Esq., Clerk of the Peace, for his courtesy in allowing the inspection of county records; to the Vicars of Hope and Bradwell, and

to the authorities of the Wesleyan and Primitive Methodist Chapels, for their kindness in placing their registers at his disposal; to the Rev. R. S. Redfern, for information relating to the old chapel; and to Mr. Walter Morton, for the loan of the precious letters of his distinguished ancestor.

There are many others the author desires to thank for assistance rendered, including those who have so kindly granted him the loan of photographs, and in this connection he tenders his warmest thanks to Chas. E. Bradshaw Bowles, Esq., J.P., lord of the manor of Abney, and editor of the Derbyshire Archæological Journal, for the loan of valuable plates. The old houses, church, chapels, etc., are from the camera of Mr. H. V. Tanfield.

But especially does he desire gratefully to acknowledge the kindness and encouragement received from the noblemen, ladies, and gentlemen, whose names are in the List of Subscribers.

To those who may say that the author has overstepped the bounds of the village, it may be said that to toe a strict topographical line in these things is difficult, and he has related incidents in the surrounding villages that will cause a wider interest to be taken in the book.

With these remarks he craves the indulgence of the public for the imperfections of these " collections and recollections in a Peakland village."

February, 1912.

CONTENTS.

———

ILLUSTRATIONS.

List of Subscribers.

Adams, Samuel, Dialstone Villas, Bradwell.
Allen, Francis, Hugh Lane, Bradwell.
Andrew, Abraham, Hollow Gate, Bradwell.
Andrew, John S., Hilltop Farm, Unstone
Andrew, Robert, Victoria Villa, Totley Rise.
Andrew, Thomas, Brook View, Horner House, Stocksbridge.
Andrew, Thos. S., The Hall Farm, Totley.
Ash, Joseph, "Heatherfield," Bradwell.
Ashton, Ellis, The Kennels, Hope.
Ashton, James, Clitheroe Road, Longsight.
Ashton, Robert How, J.P,. Losehill Hall, Castleton (2 copies).
Ashford, S. J., 57, Surrey Street, Sheffield.
Athorpe, Colonel R., J.P., Leam Hall, Grindleford.
Austin, John, High Street, Sheffield.
Bagley, Mrs. Ella Victoria Norris, ex-Mayoress of Penzance, The Cliff, Penzance, Cornwall (2 copies).
Bagshaw, Dennis, Little Hayfield.
Bagshaw, W., Providence Road, Walkley, Sheffield.
Bagshawe, Edwd. G., 63, Norfolk Street, Sheffield.
Bagshawe, W. H. G., J.P., D.L., Ford Hall, Chapel-en-le-Frith (4 copies).
Bamford, Thos. S., Lord Street, Elton, Bury.
Bancroft, John, Fulham Palace Road, Hammersmith, London.
Barber, Arthur, Sherwood Street, Nottingham.
Barber, Ellis S., Manchester Road, Hadfield.
Barker, Wm. Ward, Quoit Green House, Dronfield.
Bateman, Mrs. Hannah Birley, Mildred Avenue, Watford, Herts.
Battersby, Mrs. R., Burlington Street, Ashton-under-Lyne (2 copies).
Beard, Raymond, Chapel-en-le-Frith.
Beaumont, Thomas, High Street House, New Mills.
Beeston, Rev. A. T., St. James', New Mills.
Bennett, Wm. Fox, Edmund Road, Sheffield.
Bird, Rev. George, M.A., The Vicarage, Bradwell.
Bingley, J., Grimesthorpe Road, Sheffield.
Black, W., Grimesthorpe Road, Sheffield.
Bland, George, The Hills, Bradwell.
Boardman, Joseph, Brooklands, Hope.
Bocking, Rev. John Child, M.A., Gnosall Vicarage, Staffordshire.
Bolton, H., Frickley Road, Sheffield.
Booker, H. H., Albert Road, Heeley, Sheffield (2 copies).
Booth, Mrs., Station House, Broughton Lane, Sheffield.
Boothby, Mrs. Mary Hannah, Kettleshulme.
Bonser, Right Hon. Sir John, 3, Eaton Place, London, S.W.
Boswell, Wm., Market Street, Chapel-en-le-Frith.
Bowles, Chas., Dover Road, Sheffield (2 copies).
Bowles, C. E. B., J.P., Nether House, Wirksworth.
Boycott, John Burton, Welby Croft, Chapel-en-le-Frith.

Bradbury, J. L., Attercliffe Road, Sheffield.
Bradbury, E., Attercliffe Common, Sheffield.
Bradbury, John, Stocksbridge.
Bradley, Luke, Bowden Lane, Chapel-en-le-Frith.
Bradwell, Abner, Corporation Buildings, Sheffield.
Bradwell, Alan, Netherside, Bradwell.
Bradwell, Edwin, "Netherside," Hale, Cheshire (4 copies).
Bradwell, Harvey, Kirk Oswald, Cumberland.
Bradwell, Edmund, Glencoe Road, Park, Sheffield.
Bradwell, Horace, Norfolk Road, Sheffield (3 copies).
Bradwell, John Edwy, Malton Street, Pitsmoor, Sheffield (2 copies).
Bradwell, Sidney A., Vicarage Road, Tottenham, London.
Bradwell, S. J., "Brownsville," Heaton Moor, Stockport (2 copies).
Bradwell, Mrs. Nancy, Church Street, Bradwell.
Bradwell, Mrs. Hannah, Reddish Green House, Chapel-en-le-Frith.
Bradwell, Valentine, Catherine Street, Ashton-under-Lyne (2 copies).
Bradwell, Walter, Hayfield.
Bradwell, Mrs. Sarah E., Dobbin Hill, Sheffield.
Bramall, William, Old Hall, Shatton.
Bramwell, Thos., Stocksbridge (2 copies).
Bramwell, E. C., J.P., "Ivy Dene," Grindleford.
Bramwell, Mrs. W., Windmill, Hucklow.
Brady, Chas. R., C. E., Town Hall, Chapel-en-le-Frith.
Bridge, Charles, Crookhill, Woodlands.
Brierley, Wm., J.P., Sterndale House, Litton.
Broadbent, Major John, Castleton.
Broadhurst, J. W., J.P., The Haugh, Bugsworth.
Brownhill, George Henry, White Hart Hotel, New Mills.
Buckstone, Rev. Henry, J.P., The Hall, Sutton-on-the-Hill.
Bunting, W. Braylesford, Chapel-en-le-Frith.
Burton, J. E., Main Road, Handsworth, Sheffield.
Caterer, Mrs. Florence, Newburgh Arms Hotel, Bradwell.
Chambers, Wilfred, St. Mary's Road, Glossop.
Chambers, William, Main Road, Hadfield.
Chapman, Fredk., Stanley House, Tideswell.
Chapman, Wm., Great Hucklow.
Chapman, Dr. Wm., The Rocks, New Mills (2 copies).
Clarke, Mrs. Allan, St. John's Road, Longsight, Manchester (3 copies).
Clegg, Leonard, J., Figtree Lane, Sheffield.
Clegg, John Charles, J.P., Figtree Lane, Sheffield.
Clegg, Dr. Joseph, J.P., Edentree House, Bradwell (2 copies).
Clegg, Sir W. E., J.P., Figtree Lane, Sheffield.
Cooper, Abram., Upper End Farm, Peak Dale.

Cooper, Jun., George, Nether Padley, Grindleford.

Cooper, John, The Hills, Bradwell.

Cooper, Thomas, Ford Bank, Buxton.

Corker, George, Attercliffe Common, Sheffield.

Cox, G. W., Langham, Rutland.

Cresswell, John T., Chinley.

Craig, Robert, "Rockside," Bradwell.

Cramond, James Hy., Attercliffe Road, Sheffield (2 copies).

Cutler, T. T., The Bank, Hathersage.

Dakin, Mrs. Jane, Ashopton (3 copies).

Darnley, Edwy. Maltby, Dale End Cottage, Bradwell.

Darrand, J. C., Hawthorne House, Hope.

Dearden, Dr. V. S. G., Beech House, Carbrook, Sheffield.

Derby Free Library (Sir E. T. Ann, chairman).

Devonshire, His Grace the Duke of, Lord Lieutenant of Derbyshire, Chatsworth.

Dicken, Captain, Great Hucklow.

Dickie, Matthew, "Ravenstor," Miller's Dale.

Dickinson, Edward, Woodbank Crescent, Sheffield.

Diver, H. H., Middlewood Road, Hillsboro', Sheffield.

Dixon, John, The Hills, Bradwell (2 copies).

Dixon, Robert, Brookside, Bradwell (4 copies).

Dodds, Henry, The Hills, Bradwell (2 copies).

Dormand, W., Shiregreen Lane, Sheffield.

Dyall, Jas., Carfield Avenue, Meersbrook, Sheffield.

Eagle, George, Barmaster for High Peak, Brown Street, Manchester.

Earwaker, Robt. P., J.P., Fern Lawn, Cheltenham.

Elliott, Alfred, Lord Street, Glossop.

Elliott, Allen, Smalldale, Bradwell.

Elliott, Ernest, Nether Side, Bradwell.

Elliott, Joel, Storrs, Stannington.

Elliott, Marshall, The Hills, Bradwell.

Elliott, Mrs. Martha, Ashton Road, Newton, Hyde.

Elliott, Robert, Oscar Street, Moston, Manchester.

Ellis, Jun., Joseph, Lord Street, Elton, Bury.

Evans, Alwyn, Geraldine Road, Yardley, Birmingham.

Evans, Cyril, Town Gate, Bradwell.

Evans, Dennis, Town Gate, Bradwell.

Evans, Fred, Town Gate, Bradwell.

Evans, Maurice, Attercliffe Common, Sheffield, and Upland Cottage, Bradwell (2 copies).

Evans, Josiah Barber, Horner House, Stocksbridge.

Evans, John, Peak Dale.

Evans, Samuel, Great Hucklow.

Eyre, Rev. Daniel, "Homeleigh," Devoran, Cornwall (2 copies).

Eyre, Percy, Hill Head, Bradwell.

Eyre, Jesse, Church Gates, Bradwell.

Eyre, Robert, Primrose Lane, Glossop.

Eyre, William, New Bath Hotel, Bradwell.

Eyre, V. H., Cavendish House, Castleton.

Firth, Ambrose, The Knoll, Bamford.

Firth, E. Willoughby, J.P., Birchfield, Hope (4 copies).

Fiske, Samuel, Dialstone Villas, Bradwell (2 copies).

Fletcher, Mrs. Annie, The Knoll, Bradwell.

Ford, Miss Hannah, The Hills, Bradwell.

Ford, George, New Zealand.

Ford, John, Fitzwilliam Street, Sheffield, and The Hills, Bradwell.

Ford, Joseph, Fitzwilliam Street, Sheffield.

Ford, J. J., Hayfield Road, Chapel-en-le-Frith.

Fox, Thomas, Hazlebadge Hall, Bradwell.

Fryer, C. W., J.P., "Brookdene," Thornhill, Hope.

Furness, Richard, Whirlow Hall, Totley.

Fuzzard, B. J., Chapel-en-le-Frith.

Garside, Luke, High Street, Hayfield.

Gee, John T., The Ashes, Kinder, Hayfield.

Gent, Mrs. Amanda, Idaho Falls, Idaho, U.S.A.

Gilbert, Herbert, Marple.

Gilbert, W., Mauldeth Road, W. Withington.

Goddard, Joel, Lower Lane, Chinley.

Goddard, Ernest, Ollerbrook, Edale.

Goddard, Joseph, Buxton Road, Chinley.

Goodman, Major G. D., V.D., Manchester Road, Buxton.

Goodyer, Rev. Samuel, Redland Villa, Millhouses, Sheffield.

Green, Charles, Shrewsbury Road, Park, Sheffield.

Gregory, John, The Briers, Saltergate, Bamford.

Gregory, Wilton, Post Office, Chinley.

Hagger, R. H., Newtown, New Mills.

Hall, C. W. G., Dean Street, Ashton-under-Lyne (2 copies).

Hall, Colonel Edward, J.P., V.D., Horwich Park, Whaley Bridge.

Hall, Mrs. Hannah, Bridge End, Bradwell.

Hall, Mrs. J., Gladstone Road, Ranmoor, Sheffield.

Hall, Rev. John, Swan Street, Congleton.

Hall, Michael, Greenheys Lane, Manchester (2 copies).

Hall, Jacob, Granby Road, Bradwell.

Hall, Joseph, New Terrace, Peak Dale.

Hall, Isaac, The Steep, Bradwell.

Hallam, Colour Sergeant Absalom, Little Eaton, Derby.

Hallam, Alfred, Bradwell.

Hallam, Cheetham W., The Knoll, Bradwell.

Hallam, Miss Edith, Hill Head, Bradwell.

Hallam, Ethelbert, Paradise Farm, Bradwell.

Hallam, Harvey, Hugh Lane, Bradwell.

Hallam, Harold, "Blytheswood," Sylvan Avenue, Levenshulme (2 copies).

Hallam, Mrs. Jason, Hill Head, Bradwell.

Hallam, Rev. John W., Bradford.

Hallam, Rev. Samuel Henry, Finsbury Park, London.

Hallam, William, Goosehill, Castleton.

Hampson, John, Horwich End, Whaley Bridge.

Hancock, J. S., 57, Surrey Street, Sheffield.

Harrison, Francis, "Westward Ho," Ryde, Isle of Wight.

Hattersley, Mrs., Great Hucklow (2 copies).

Haws, Frank, Freestone Place, Attercliffe, Sheffield.

Hawkins, Harold B., Stocksbridge.

Hayes, Mrs. John, Longlands Road, New Mills.

Hayward, Rev. F. M., Derwent.

Heaps, Edward Knowles, The Nook, Bradwell (8 copies).

Heathcott, Joseph, J.P., West Horderns, Chapel-en-le-Frith.

Hewitt, Mrs. John, Hayfield Road, Chapel-en-le-Frith.

Hewsoll, Geo. H., Burnside Avenue, Meersbrook, Sheffield.

Hibbs, Clarence, Paracamby, Rio de Janeiro, Brazil.

Hibbs, Horatio, Kipple Road, Chorlton-cum-Hardy.

Hibbs, Jabez, Higher Openshaw, Manchester (2 copies).

Hibbs, John, Leam, Grindleford.

Hibbs, Joseph, Yard Head, Bradwell.

Hibbs, Joseph, Clun Road, Sheffield.

Hibbs, T. Andrew, Oak Bank, New Mills.

Hibbs, Mrs. Francis, Union Road, New Mills.

Hibbert, Edwin, Market Place, Chapel-en-le Frith.

Hick, J. W., Dove Holes.
Hilton, Henry, Tunstead, Wormhill.
Hipkins, Rev. F. C., M.A., The Rectory, Bamford (2 copies).
Hill, Abraham, Manchester Road, Stocksbridge.
Hill, Henry, Norfolk Road, Sheffield.
Hill, Winfield, Norfolk Road, Sheffield.
Hill, Mrs. M. E., Shirebrook Road, Sheffield (2 copies).
Hill, Isaac, Church Street, Bradwell.
Hill, Thomas, Smalldale, Bradwell.
Hill, Rev. William Henry, Southbourne Road, Sheffield.
Hobson, John T., Main Road, Bamford.
Hobson, Walter, Bank Chambers, Chapel-en-le-Frith.
Hodkin, Edgar, Norfolk Road, Sheffield.
Hodkin, Walter, Osborne Road, Brincliffe, Sheffield.
Horobin, Thomas, Tunstead, Wormhill.
Houlbrook, Dr. W., Nether Side, Bradwell.
How, Rev. John Hall, M.A., North Bailey, Durham.
Howe, George, M.R.C.V.S., Buxton.
Hoyle, J. Rossiter, J.P., Grange Cliffe, Eccleshall, Sheffield.
Hubbersty, H. A., J.P., Burbage Hall, Buxton.
Hunstone, Advent (sculptor), Tideswell.
Hudson, W. A., Post Office, Chapel-en-le-Frith.
Hunter, E. L., "Kelcliffe," Fulwood, Sheffield.
Huss, H. P., Bank House, Chapel-en-le-Frith (4 copies).
Hyde Public Library, John Chorlton, librarian.
Hyde, Joseph, The Greggs, Chapel-en-le-Frith.
Ingham, James Anthony, Union Road, New Mills.
Ingham, Walter Gilbert, Tideswell.
Inman H., Foxglove Road, Shiregreen, Sheffield.
Jackson, Ed., Wheat Sheaf Hotel, Dove Holes.
Jackson, Henry, Windmill, near Bradwell.
Jackson, Isaac G., Union Road, New Mills.
Jackson, Rev. J. C., Tideswell.
Jeffery, Joshua G., Town End, Stocksbridge, (8 copies).
Jeffery, Robert, Hill Head, Bradwell.
Jennings, Thomas, Hartle Moor, Bradwell.
Johnson, George, Randall Street, Sheffield.
Johnson, William, Rose Cottage, Smalldale, Bradwell (2 copies).
Johnson, Miss, Rose Cottage, Smalldale, Bradwell.
Jodrell, Sir Edward Cotton, K.C.B., Reaseheath Hall and Shallcross Manor (2 copies).
Jowett, William, The Manor House, Mellor.
Kay, Mrs. John Thomas, Bradwell.
Kenworthy, Joseph, Stretton Villa, Deepcar.
Knowles, Rev. J. Lionel, R.D., New Mills.
Lacey, J., Brunswick Street, Sheffield.
Lamb, James, Steade Road. Sheffield.
Lander, Dr. H. W. Graham, Hathersage and Bradwell (2 copies).
Leighton, H. B., Mount View, Heeley, Sheffield.
Littler, Mrs. Josephine, Higher Tranmere, Birkenhead.
Littlewood, Mrs. F. L., Idaho Falls, Idaho, U.S.A.
Lloyd, Rev. G. E., Lairgate, Beverley.
Lomas, J. E., Harley Grange. Buxton.
Longden, Wm., White Knowle Farm, Chinley.
Mabbott, H. E. D., The White House, Chapel-en-le-Frith.
Macrone, A., Club Garden Road. Sheffield.
McLeod, Mrs. Fanny, "Holly Bank," Cadishead.
Maltby, Arthur, The Old Hall, Great Hucklow.
Maltby, Mrs. Clara, Chippingham Street, Attercliffe, Sheffield.

Manchester Free Public Libraries, C. W. Sutton, librarian.
Maples, Charles, Graham Road, Sheffield.
Mason, Miss, "Beaconsfield." Wrexham.
Mason, Rev. W. H., Llydan House, Welshpool, Montgomeryshire.
Maw, J., Broomhall Street, Sheffield.
Melland, Mrs., Longsight, Manchester.
Mellor, Wm., Sunny Lea, Fernilee, Whaley Bridge.
Miller, J. T., Smalldale, Bradwell (2 copies).
Middleton, Arthur Somerset, Buxton Road, New Mills.
Middleton, Archie C., Moston, Manchester.
Middleton, Miss, Chester Street, Birkenhead.
Middleton, Miss Ruth, Mill Street, Bakewell.
Middleton, Charles, Hylton Cliffe, Broomhall Park, Sheffield.
Middleton, Martin, Greenway, Hyde.
Middleton, Robert, Oakbrook Road, Ranmoor. Sheffield.
Middleton, James A., Manchester Road, Denton (8 copies).
Middleton, John, Town Clerk of Chesterfield (4 copies).
Middleton, Miss Lucy, Hawksworth Road, Sheffield.
Middleton, Thomas, The Old Post Office, Bradwell.
Middleton, Thomas, Manchester Road, Hyde.
Middleton, William, Smalldale, Bradwell.
Morris, Samuel, Manchester Road, Denton,
Moore, Colonel J. H., J.P., Castleton.
Morton, Miss Alice Maud, Town Gate, Bradwell.
Morton, Fredk. J. H., Capetown, South Africa.
Morton, Gladstone, Manchester.
Morton, Jabez, Cheetham Hill Road, Manchester (2 copies).
Morton, Leonard, Manchester.
Morton, Miles, Ellesmere Place. Longsight, Manchester (2 copies).
Morton, Miss M. H., New Mills.
Morton, Thos. M., J.P., Lister Lane, Halifax (2 copies).
Morton, Vernon, Manchester.
Morton, Walter, Pulman Street, Rochdale.
Moseley, J. E., Church Street, Hayfield.
Mosscrop, Rev. Thomas Gilbert, Pool, near Leeds.
Mower, Thomas, Torr Street, New Mills.
Mulliner, George, Albert Terrace, New Mills.
Murray, J., Burngreave Street, Sheffield.
Nadin, Dr. Joseph, Bradwell.
Naish, Frank E., Manor View, Handsworth, Sheffield.
Newbold, T. E., Grange Road, Buxton (2 copies).
Nicholson, Edward, C.C., Brough House, Bradwell.
Norfolk, His Grace the Duke of, Derwent Hall (2 copies).
Oldfield, Edward, "Ashford," Rusholme, Manchester (4 copies).
Oldham, Robert, Spring Villas, Birch Vale.
Padmore, T. H., Stanley Road, Meersbrook, Sheffield.
Palfreyman, Frank C., Horwich End, Whaley Bridge.
Palfreyman, Mrs. George, Litton.
Palfreyman, John, Horwich End, Whaley Bridge.
Palfreyman, William, Bollington.
Palmer, John, Union Road, New Mills.
Parke, Dr. T. H., Foxlowe House, Tideswell.
Partington, Oswald, J.P., Cadogan Square, London, and Easton, Glossop.
Paton, R. A., The Moor, Sheffield.
Peacock, J. W., Station Road, Hathersage.
Pearson, Robert, The Lumb, Bradwell.

Pearson, William, Myrtle Cottage, Stocksbridge.
Pearson, Vincent, Stocksbridge.
Pinder, J. T., The Hills, Bradwell.
Plant, B., Guest Road, Hunter's Bar, Sheffield.
Pollitt, J. Sumner, "Holker Lea," New Mills.
Porter, Dr. W. S., Phœbe Croft, Hope.
Proctor, Frank, The Hall, Bugsworth.
Puttrell, J. W. Derbyshire Pennine Club, 94, The Moor, Sheffield (4 copies).
Pursglove, Samuel, Hope.
Pye Smith and Barker, solicitors, 5, East Parade, Sheffield, and Bradwell (2 copies).
Rawson, Mrs. John, Huttley Cottages, Wilmington, Hull.
Redfern, Rev. R. Stuart, Leigh, Lancashire.
Reynolds, Fredk. T., J.P., Mayor of Southport.
Robinson, George, Brookfield, Edale.
Robinson. John W., Firth Park Road, Sheffield (2 copies).
Robinson, Joseph, Brooklands, Hope (2 copies).
Robinson, R. H., Heanor.
Rogerson, Rev. Thomas, The Vicarage, Tideswell.
Ross, John, Station House, Hope.
Rowarth, Miss Elsie, Freebirch, Cutthorpe, Chesterfield.
Rowarth, Harry, Freebirch, Cutthorpe, Chesterfield.
Rowarth, Mrs. Hannah, Freebirch, Cutthorpe, Chesterfield.
Rutland, His Grace the Duke of, Belvoir Castle (2 copies).
Sandeman, Edward, C. E., Bamford.
Sanderson, Mrs. Violet, Mona Road, Crookes, Sheffield (2 copies).
Scarsdale, The Rev. Lord, Kedleston Hall, Derby.
Sellars, Joseph, High Lea Road, New Mills.
Shaw, A. P., J.P., Whitehall, Buxton.
Sheffield Free Public Libraries (10 copies).
    S. Smith, F.R.H.S., F.S.A., Librarian.
Sheard, W. C., New Mills.
Shepley, Eli., The Rocks, New Mills.
Shepley. Thos., Market Place, Chapel-en-le-Frith.
Shepherd, Dr. H. R., Peveril House, Castleton.
Shipton, W. Louis, Spring Gardens, Buxton.
Shirt, Jabez, Slack Hall, Chapel-en-le-Frith.
Sidebotham, John, Market Street, Chapel-en-le-Frith.
Sidebotham, Joseph, Spring Gardens, Buxton.
Sidebotham, Joseph, Cross Street, Castleton.
Simpkin, W. F., Hyde Road, Gorton, Manchester.
Sidebottom, Major R. Bennett, J.P., Redcourt, Glossop (2 copies).
Sidebottom, Colonel Wm., J.P., V.D., Harewood Lodge, Broadbottom.
Slack, Mrs. Hannah Lax, Harvest Lane, Sheffield.
Slack, Jabez, Lawson Cottage, Tideswell.
Slack, James Handel, The Mount, Saughall, Chester.
Slack, Vandyke, Tideswell.
Slater, Thomas, Hague Bar, New Mills.
Smith, Mrs. Joseph, Stocksbridge.
Smith, Mrs. Harry, Stocksbridge.
Smith, Mrs. Rachel, Hornsea, London.
Somerset, Miss S. M., Broomhead Institute, Lincoln (2 copies).
Southall, Rev. Albert, Carbrook Vicarage, Sheffield.
Stafford, Mrs. Matilda, Whitle Farm, New Mills.
Stockport Free Library (2 copies), R. Hargreaves, Librarian.
Stevenson, John, Eden Tree Lodge, Bradwell.
Stone, Durham, Porter Street, Staveley.

Stone, Mrs. S., High Street, Staveley.
Stubbs, Philip, Sheffield.
Swain, W. H., "Ivy Lea," Roslyn Crescent, Hathersage.
Taylor, F. H., Overdale, Bakewell.
Taylor, Colonel H. Brooke, The Hall, Bakewell.
Taylor, John, J.P., Crossings West, Chapel-en-le-Frith (2 copies).
Taylor, Sydney, B.A., Buxton.
Taylor, Dr. T., Portchester House, Bournemouth
Thornley, Mrs. M. A., Union Road, New Mills.
Toler, T. C., J.P., C.C., Taxal Lodge, Whaley Bridge (2 copies).
Travis, W., Burnside Avenue, Meersbrook, Sheffield.
Tym, Nathan, Edale.
Unwin, Joseph, Laneside, Hope.
Wainwright, J. W., Wincobank Avenue, Shiregreen Sheffield (2 copies).
Walker, Aaron, Station House, Nuneaton.
Walker, Henry, Dale View, Bradwell.
Walker, John, Small Dale, Peak Dale.
Walker, Mrs. Olive, The Hill, Bradwell.
Walker, Saml., Carbrook, Sheffield.
Walker, Z., Dale View, Bradwell.
Wallworth, Mrs., Angler's Hotel, Bamford (2 copies).
Walton, H., Windmill, near Bradwell.
Waterhouse, B., Greenwood, Hope.
Waterhouse, William, Great Hucklow.
Watts, James, J.P., Abney Hall, Cheadle and Kinder (2 copies).
Watts, Samuel, Edale House, Edale (4 copies).
Watts, Henry T., Harcourt Road, Sheffield.
Ward, F., St. Mary's Road, Sheffield.
Ward, George, High Peak Hospital, Chinley.
Ward, G. H. B., Park Farm, Cricket Road, Sheffield.
Welby, E. M. E., J.P., Stipendiary Magistrate of Sheffield, Norton House, Norton.
Wells, Barton, Croft House, Aston, Hope.
Whiteway, Rev. R. W. B., "Elmfield," Lymm, Cheshire.
White, Wm. Edward, Turf Lea, Marple.
Whitehead, Robert, J.P., Hargate Hall, Wormhill.
Whitney, W. H., Deakin's Walk, Ranmoor, Sheffield.
Whittam, Mrs. Elizabeth, Walkley Road, Sheffield.
Wharmby, J. T., Longlands, New Mills.
Wilde, H. E., London City and Midland Bank, Attercliffe, Sheffield.
Williamson, Walter, Duckworth Road, Bradford.
Wilson, Henry J., M.P., Osgathorpe, Sheffield.
Wilson, Joseph, Chapel-en-le-Frith.
Wilson, Mrs., East View, Smalldale, Bradwell.
Winnard, Mrs. Bertha, Fitzwalter Road, Park, Sheffield.
Wolfenden, James, H., Manchester Road, Denton.
Wood, Mrs. Sarah Ann, New Street, New Mills.
Wood, S. Hill, M.P., Park Hall, Hayfield.
Woodroofe, Mrs. Jane, Stanley Road, Wakefield.
Wragg, Albert E., Edensor, Bakewell.
Wragg, Durham, Glen View, Bradwell.
Wragg, John, The Lumb, Bradwell.
Wrench, E. M., M.D., J.P., V.S.O., Park Lodge, Baslow.
Yates, Abraham, Stoneyford, Chapel-en-le-Frith.
Young, Albert, London City and Midland Bank, Attercliffe, Sheffield.
Young, Mr. and Mrs. A., Water Grove, Eyam (2 copies).

Bradwell, Ancient and Modern.

A History of the Parish and of Incidents in the Hope Valley.

INTRODUCTION.

The old-world Peakland village of Bradwell has a history, and a most interesting history too. Its steep winding streets—if streets they can be called—and all sorts of queer little out of the way places running in and out in all directions, break neck, oblique, skew-tilted, beginning everywhere, leading nowhere, make the stranger feel that he is living in mediæval times. Occupied by the Romans, who left their traces everywhere, recognised as one of the boundaries of the Forest of the Peak this romantic spot was never troubled with a surveyor. Every man was his own architect. He built what he liked where he liked, and as he liked, with the result that in the twentieth century there remains one of the most comical looking, beautiful, and picturesque old towns even in picturesque Peakland.

But its very name has been deplorably corrupted. The statement made in the middle of the last century that its name was derived from "a well on the verge of the village" is erroneous. It is one of those place-names which indicates the occupation and military organization of its people—Brad, from broad or spacious, and Wall, indicating a site at or near a Roman fortification. The original name was, therefore, Broad-wall, or Bradwall, for a portion of the Roman fortification still exists, and upon a portion of the wall of the ancient Forest of the Peak the town is built. Its very earliest settlers, too, who took their name from the place itself, retained its original spelling of Bradwall in the Hope Church registers right down to the year 1843, and, at least, one of these oldest of local families, now resident in Sheffield, very properly retains its name, Bradwall. Further, the death comparatively recently, of a resident of Bradwell, inscribed on the family gravestone, describes her as of Bradwall.

CHAPTER I.

"I will show you caves and barrows,
 Of a world before the flood,
When the bison and hyæna,
 Rang'd over moor and wood;
Where races of men lie buried,
 Who fought with weapons of stone,
And sew'd their deer-skins together
 With implements of bone."

J. H. J.

IN PRE-HISTORIC TIMES.
WHEN MEN LIVED IN CAVES.
Discoveries in Hartle Dale Caves.

A place with distinct evidence of its occupancy by the Early Britons, Romans, Saxons, Danes, and Normans cannot fail to be interesting. The district abounds in caves, and in many of them there are distinct traces of Pre-historic man. There are several small caves in Hartle Dale, and exploring one of these in 1872, the late Rooke Pennington, of Castleton, says that the floor consisted principally of blackish mould containing a few limestone fragments, and pieces of chert. It contained bones of the goat and pig, fox and rabbit. Two pieces of pre-historic pottery were also turned out. The ornamentations were unusually rude for such a remote period, being simply punctures made in the clay before baking, with a sharpened stick, without any regard to regularity.

In 1877 Mr. Pennington, the late Mr. John Tym, and Professor Boyd Dawkins, whilst examining other small caves and rock shelters in Hartle Dale, picked up a milk-molar of a young woolly rhinoceros, which had been thrown up to the surface by rabbits burrowing in the floor of the small cave at the mouth of which it was found. In an adjoining cavern there lay on the rock the tooth of a bear, evidently washed out of some fissure within. The first mentioned cave they dug out thoroughly, finding bones of the rhinoceros and bison, which Mr. Pennington thought had been carried to their last resting place by water. About the same time a fine arrow head was found on the Bradwell Moors.

These discoveries take us back to the days of pre-historic man who dwelt in the caves, and an examination of the many barrows, or "lows" has shown them to be burial-places of long forgotten races who once lived in Britain.

Stone Circles Explored.

The author of the same work says that one of the most interesting barrows ever explored was on Abney Moor, near Bradwell, but it was destroyed to build a wall. Upon a rampart of earth, by which it was surrounded were ten upright blocks of stone each about three feet high, and placed at equal distances round the barrow. When the mound was dug into, Mr. Pennington and his party found in the centre of the tumulus a large flat piece of sandstone upon which was a mass of burnt human bones, deposited with considerable care. There were also flint flakes, some jet beads, some amber beads, and an arrow head. The beads had evidently formed portions of necklaces. There were pieces of burnt gritstone and sandstone, found, evidence that the funeral fire had been lit upon the spot.

Two other barrows on the same moor had been previously explored and human bones, urns, heads of flint, etc., found in them. In the immediate vicinity were a number of pit dwellings which Mr. Pennington says were no doubt once covered with some sort of thatch such as heather would supply.

About a mile distant, in the direction of Hope, is The Folly. This is a small circular entrenchment, about 75 feet in diameter, with a slight elevation in the centre. On one occasion a celt was found here, and it is probable that this circular rampart originally had a stone circle.

Travelling along that portion of Bathamgate, which is best preserved, separating the Bradwell and Tideswell Moors, will be seen on the Tideswell moor side of the road an almost perfectly circular enclosure or camp within a now very low rampart, the whole having a diameter of 300 feet. A small part of the north-west arc of the circle has been cut off by the old Roman road, which is a proof of the early or pre-Roman origin of this circular camp.

Deposits of the Flood Found in a Lead Mine.

In a book on "Darbyshire," printed in 1660, there is the following record of a curious discovery:—

"Near Bradewalle were dug up in sinking a lead-grove, a piece of a bone, and tooth of wonderful proportions, namely, the tooth (though a quarter of an inch of it was broken off) was 13 inches and a half in compass, and weighed three pounds ten ounces and three quarters; and with this, among other pieces of bones, a very large skull which held seven pecks of corn. The con-

jectures of the learned upon them are various, some supposing the tooth and bones to be a man's (and why not when a skull so monstrous was found with them); but others have thought it the den molaris of an elephant, and for this opinion they produce some elephants' bones found near Castleton. The most probable conjectures about these phenomena are that they are the exuviæ of those creatures brought hither by the general deluge, and deposited by specific gravitation in the earth, then rendered as fluid as mud." This strange discovery was made in the Virgin Mine at Hazelbadge, which was worked for lead at least five hundred years.

Ancient Barrows Explored: Human Remains Found.

About the year 1867 a great deal of interest was taken in discoveries of pre-historic man on Hazlebadge Hills, about midway between the Hall and Bradwell. On this field, close to Hill's Rake there is a large barrow, which was explored by Mr. Benjamin Bagshawe, solicitor, Sheffield, a gentleman well versed in local lore, and an antiquarian, and local archæologist of repute, whose ancestors had for many generations been located in the Grindlow and Foolow district.

Having obtained permission from the Duke of Rutland's agent, Mr. Bagshawe secured the services of two reliable miners, Robert Evans and John Bancroft, who went about their work with the greatest care. They had not been at work long, when only about a foot beneath the sod they came upon a stone cist, which on being opened was found to contain the skeleton of a man, not lying down, but seated upright, with his elbows on his knees, and his head on his hands as if he had been shut up in the tomb and buried alive. By the side of another man was the skeleton of a horse, and altogether fourteen skeletons of both sexes were found, in addition to many burnt bones, and a number of flint arrow heads. Only about half the barrow was explored, and the explorers believe that if the other portion was searched many interesting discoveries would be made. There does not seem to be any doubt that these bodies had lain there two thousand years, having been deposited by the ancient Britons long before the Romans came to the Island.

In the winter of 1891 some workmen getting out the foundations for a kitchen at the rear of a house belonging to Mr. John Ford, on Bradwell Hills, facing what is known as "The Green," made a discovery which went to prove that the house itself was built upon an ancient barrow. Only about two feet below the surface of the ground, three skeletons were discovered. Two were lying on their sides, with the knees tucked under the chin, and were within a wall of flat stones placed on edge, which formed three sides of a square. The third skeleton was found lying at full length on its back with a square stone standing at the head and another at the feet. Near the two skeletons within the small cist a very rough flint flake was found. The skeletons were terribly broken by the workmen, and an official of the British Archæological Association who visited the place and took away the flint, and as many of the bones as he could get, tried to put together the fragments of two of the skulls, but was not very successful. One skull seemed to be of a very low type of man, the forehead was very shallow, the bone projected over the eye, and at the top of the nose the bone was very wide and thick. The remaining part of the barrow had quantities of human bones mixed up with it, which were supposed to be early burials disturbed for the later interments. Probably if a search was made there would be many similar " finds " in the immediate locality. In 1897 workmen excavating foundations of new houses for Mr. T. Cooper, in " Nether Side," opposite the Newburgh Arms Inn, discovered a sepulchral cist of gritstone slabs containing male adult bones (supposed to be pre-Roman), leaden " spindle whorl," iron spearhead, about seven inches long, copper button, and a Roman coin. The spearhead and whorl were placed in the Buxton Museum. A week or two later the workmen found a copper coin of 1738, and a three shilling bank token of the reign of George III., 1815. The spindle whorl was one inch diameter and about quarter of an inch thick, and its upper surface was decorated with five raised fillets, and the button consisted of a disc of copper about quarter of an inch in diameter with a small ring attached to the back. It was decorated with small hollows, inlaid with gold.

Grey Ditch, a Monument of the First Century.

One of the most interesting features of Bradwell is the long strip of defensive earthwork known as Grey Ditch, which one authority declared is " the most important remaining fragment of the Limes Brittannicus of the first century, in its third stage between Templeborough and Brough."

Grey Ditch shows itself plainly, telling without doubt of early tribal resistance to onslaughts up this valley. Standing on the high road at " Eden Tree," near the New Bath Hotel it may be seen stretching along to Micklow on one side, and to the summit of Bradwell Edge on the other, right away up " Rebellion Knoll " to the mountain road leading to Abney and Brough 1,100 feet high. One writer of the 17th century (Mr. Bray) said it was carried from the camp on Mam Tor, and was a fore fence of the Romans, crossing Bathamgate and Bradwell water, but subsequent authorities doubt whether it ever was connected with Mam Tor. Its elevation is about 10 feet, and its total average width about 35 feet. It is a rampart thrown up to resist attack from the Brough side, and well known archæologists are of opinion that it was possibly once a boundary, of the ancient kingdom of Northumbria or Brigantes.

There is no doubt that it was for some military or defensive purpose, and probably there is a rich reward for the future explorer of such an interesting spot. More than a century ago pieces of swords, spears, spurs, and bridle-bits were found on both sides and very near it, between Batham Gate and Bradwell water.

GENERAL VIEW OF BRADWELL.

CHAPTER II.

THE ROMAN OCCUPATION OF BRADWELL.

THE ROMAN ROAD, BATHAM GATE.

Discoveries at the Roman Station Anavio (Brough.)

Bradwell is built on the Roman Road from Buxton baths to Brough Fort, the most famous of the Roman roads in Derbyshire, Bathgate, or as the natives call it, Bathamgate, which ran from Buxton over Fairfield Common, crossing Peak Dale, Small Dale, and over Bradwell Moor, where it is in a splendid state of preservation, in fact, almost in its original condition, to-day. Passing through the gateway at the bottom of "Bathamgate," the road crosses the Moss Rake between the Upper and Nether Cross Mines, again enters the moorland and stretches along right down Small dale (a portion of Bradwell), Gore Lane, and "Streetfield" (so called from the Roman street) where it entered the military camp at Brough, or Anavio. From thence it continued along through Hope, over the ridge which divides Edale from the Woodland Valley, along the Doctor's Gate to Cold Harbour and so on to Glossop and the Roman Fort of Melandra, where interesting excavations have been made within recent years. Built on this important road, and being also on one of the recognised boundaries of the King's Forest of the Peak, Bradwell was a place in the very earliest times, of considerable importance. These were declared to be the bounds of the Forest at an inquisition in 1274. "Beginning at the south end of the River Goyt, and so along that river to the River Ederowe, and so by the River Ederowe to Langley Croft near Longdendale Head, and so by a certain bye-way to the head of the Derwente, and from the head of the Derwente as far as Mittenforde (Mytham Bridge) and from Mittenforde to the River of Bradwall, and from the River of Bradwall to a place called Rotherlawe ("Ralley Road"); and from Rotherlawe to the Great Cave of Hazelbache, and from the Great Cave to Little Hucklowe, and from Hucklow to Tideswell, and so to the River Wye, ascending to Buxton and to the Springs of Goyt."

In the Record Office there are some old maps showing the "Forest Wall," so constructed that it would keep cattle off the great tract specially reserved for the deer, whilst the deer themselves could leap it to wander at their pleasure over the rest of the forest. In ancient records the name of the place is spelt "Broadwall," a name that occurs on many Roman sites, and "Bradwall," and one part of the village is still known as "Wall Head," a continuation of the ancient forest wall from the head of the Bradwell Brook. That access was gained from every side through gates, is evident, for—in addition to the great military road

of Batham Gate—Moor Gate, Hollow Gate, Town Gate, Hall Gate, and Over Gate, all remain to-day, entrances to the town from all sides.

Built, partly, on the old Roman Road, Bathamgate, it would be of considerable importance 1700 years ago, because of its close proximity to the Roman station, Anavio, at Brough, just a mile distant. It was in the upper of two fields called the Hallsteads, where the fort was planted, close to the Bradwell Brook, low enough to be near the water, "high enough to command an outlook all over the valley, and guarded by nature on three of its four sides."

The excavations made in 1903 by Mr. John Garstang, on behalf of the Derbyshire Archæological Society, were most interesting.

The fort was a rectangular oblong with rounded corners, about 285 feet by 340 feet, and its internal area, exclusive of the defences, amounted to about 2¼ acres. The fort was defended by a stone wall six feet thick. There were four gateways, and each corner contained a turret. There was a central building, or headquarters, and a well built edifice close by, but other edifices in the fort were not then excavated, though there are indications of the bath-house near Brough Mill and the union of the Noe and Bradwell Brook.

But the most important discovery was a pit or vault, nearly rectangular in shape, eight feet long, by five to seven feet wide, and eight feet deep, walled with eleven courses of good masonry, floored with cement, and entered by eight steps.

The writer was present when this discovery was made, and during the greater part of the time the treasure-house was emptied. The walling contained a fragment of an inscribed slab dated about A.D. 158, which had been broken up and used as building material. Lower down were three other fragments of the inscribed slab, a drum of a column, a stone trough, a few corroded coins of the fourth century, Roman pottery and bones. The regimental standards and military chest were kept in the headquarters building close by, and this pit was a strong room where the valuables were kept. The fact of there being a big flow of water into the pit led some to believe it to be a Roman bath, but experts consider this to be owing to the defective drains of the fort. When the pieces of the inscribed slab were put together and the slab restored it was found to contain an inscription, which being interpreted, read: "In honour of the emperor, Titus Aelius Hadrianus Antoninus Pius, pater patrial (erected by) the First Cohort of Acquitani, under Iulius Verus, legatus Augusti pro praetore (Governor of Britain), and under the superintendence of Capitonius Fuscus, praefect of the Cohort." The emperor is Pius, who reigned A.D. 138-161. The Cohors I Acquitanorium presumably garrisoned Brough when the slab was erected.

There was also found a square block 20 inches high and 12 inches square. On the front was rudely carved in low relief a wreath or garland, with tassels, which encloses an inscription. It was placed in the Buxton museum.

Two other Roman altars were found, and were evidently once inscribed. The larger, 28 inches high with a panel for lettering, stood for many years in the village of Hope, and the other was found among the debris in the vault. There were also numerous tiles inscribed with the name of the regiments in garrison at Brough when they were manufactured.

When the excavations were suspended in 1903, the walls were covered up, but the vault, complete, was left open, being railed round for the protection of cattle.

But there had been occasional "finds" at the Hallsteads for centuries past, and it was well known to archæologists as the site of a Roman camp. Some authorities have declared that a town stood on the site, which is not unlikely, considering that the locality stretching right away to Eccles House is known as "The Breach," i.e., a gap, particularly in a fortification made by a battery. Some masons getting out the foundations of a barn on "The Breach," nearly half a mile from the camp, bared ancient walls of immense thickness.

In the year 1747 a bust of Apollo and of another deity, in stone, were ploughed up on the Hallsteads. Some years later two large urns containing ashes, were taken out of the ground in a fine state of preservation. They were found on a tongue of land between the camp and Bradwell Brook, which was doubtless a cemetery. No doubt when this comes to be explored there will be more interesting discoveries. At a still later period—about 1767—a half-length figure of a woman was found, with her arms folded across her breast and wearing a large peaked bonnet on her head. One valuable find in 1783 was a gold coin of Vespasian, and foundations of buildings have been turned up by the plough on every side, also loads of tiles, bricks, broken swords, spears, and bridle bits, and during the excavations of 1903, there were found pieces of lead ore and spar, evidently from the Bradwell mines, some of which were worked by the Romans.

A double row of gritstone pillars, between which three men could walk abreast, formerly crossed the field where the Bradwell Brook and the Noe have their confluence. It is said that the original church of Hope was built of stone from the fort. It is certain that the village of Brough was so built, in fact, it abounds with inscribed stones, and the capital of a Roman pillar is built on the wall of a field in the centre of the village by the roadside. About the year 1790, Mr. Samuel Sidebottom, a farmer, found in the Hallsteads a gold coin of Agustus Cæsar.

A Roman Pig of Lead.

When foundations were being dug for new Bradwell Board Schools in 1894, the workmen found an ancient pig of lead, which is now in the Sheffield museum. It weighed 112 lbs, was 20 inches long, 5½ wide, and 3 high. It was considerably worn, and the part which might have borne the inscription had perished. It was unquestionably Roman, and being found close to the Roman road, with so many ancient lead workings all round, it was probably smelted at the place.

Ancient Baking Ovens.

About the same time highly interesting discoveries were made in Nether Side on property belonging to Mr. John Hall, and at the foot of Charlotte Lane, just behind the old chapel. When Mr. R. Barker was taking down some old property at the latter place some curious buildings were exposed, which were, by some, supposed to be Roman ovens, used when the garrison was at Brough. It was a circular building of dressed sandstone blocks, turned red by the heat, and the top, almost flat, was held by a massive keystone of rectangular shape. The floor was composed of blocks of dressed grey sandstone, and the structure was most elaborate and skilfully constructed. It was hoped by some, that these interesting relics would remain uninjured, so as to add to the many antiquarian attractions of the locality, but they were destroyed. There is, however, very good reason for believing that they were not Roman at all, but that they were public bakehouses, of which there were many in Bradwell centuries before, when the inhabitants sent their meal to be baked, before the modern ovens came into use. As a matter of fact octogenarians could remember the one near the old chapel being used. On the top sides of the stonework was a great thickness of lime ashes, in fact, the building was covered with it. It was first heated by burning chaff which was withdrawn before the bread was put in, and the accumulated heat of the chamber would be retained for weeks. It is, perhaps, a pity that this splendid object lesson of our forefathers was not preserved.

The Battle of Edwin Tree.

The very ground which the Roman soldiers occupied was later the scene of fierce conflicts during the Heptarchy, when England was under the government of the seven Saxon kings. Derbyshire was included in the kingdom of Mercia, founded by Crida in the year 582, and ended in 874. After Crida it was in every way enlarged by Penda, and afterwards converted to Christianity by Peada. Having long endured the miseries of the Danish wars, it was, after a duration of 250 years, subjected to the dominion of the West Saxons.

Standing on the old Batham Gate, and close by the Grey Ditch is "Eden Tree."

This is stated to be the site of a battle during the heptarchy, and at the close of the engagement a king named Edwin was captured and hanged on a tree near the spot. This tree was afterwards called "Edwin's Tree," long since corrupted to "Eden Tree," and after the tree had perished the spot where it stood bore the same designation as it does at the present day. There must have been an habitation here at the time of the battle, for tradition says that the King was captured in a garden.

About 1850 Mr. John Maltby, a local worthy who was the owner and occupier of the "Eden Tree" when making some excavations there found ancient places of interment in which were many human bones. Indeed, Bradwell is built on a battlefield, and everywhere there are names of places strongly indicative of human carnage—Grey Ditch, Rebellion Knoll, Gore Lane, Deadmen's Clough, and many others. Gore Lane is close to Eden Tree, on the line of Batham Gate, the Roman road.

CHAPTER III.

IN THE TIMES OF THE FORESTERS.

The Earliest Foresters and the First Settlers.

" Beshrew his horn, beshrew his heart,
  In my forest he may not ride;
If he kills a deer, by the conqueror's bow,
  By forest law he shall bide.
Ride on, Sir Payne, and tell the churl
  He must cease his hunting cheer,
And come to the knee of the Suzeraine lord
  Awaiting his presence here.
Ride with him, sirs, some two or three,
  And bring him hither straight;
'Twere best for him to come at once,
  Than cause his lord to wait.
There are trees in the forest strong enow,
  To bear the madman's corse,
And he shall hang on the highest bough
  If thither he comes perforce."

Wm. Bennett.

It has already been stated that a thousand years ago Bradwell was a recognised boundary of the Forest; in fact, the river was the boundary line to its source, the forest wall running parallel. Consequently that part on the east side of the river was outside the forest. There was no coal in those days; the people burned turf, hence they were very jealous of their rights of turbary. In the time of Henry the Third (1216), Castleton, Bradwell, and Hazlebadge had extensive rights to turbary, and Sampson de Arcel, "lord of the town which is outside the forest," although he had common of pasture, was not satisfied, and he was fined for digging turf. The following places also took turbary without license: Hocklowe, Tideswell, Wormhill, Buckstone, Bowden, Eston (Aston), and Thornhill.

The ancient records contain numerous entries relating to the "waste of woods" in the Peak, and one of these reads: "Wood of Nunneley, wasted by vill of Bradwall, bail. Richard Daniel, and Robert le Archer, of Thornhill and Aston." The district was formerly well wooded, but it has been completely cleared, and most of the timber used up in the lead mines.

When the Domesday Book was compiled in the reign of William the Conqueror (1086)—the first account we possess of the tenures of English estates—we find that: "In Bradewelle Leving and Sprot and Owine had i.i. carucates of land hidable. Land for i.i. ploughs. There now in demesne i.i. ploughs, and VIII villeines having i.i. ploughs. T.R.E. value xx shillings; now xxx shillings."

A carucata was as much land as one man could manage and till with a team of oxen in a year. There could be no certain quantity, for an industrious man would plough a great deal more than an idle man. In the time of Edward II. (the martyr), 975, it contained about 100 acres. The tax was called hidage, which meant a payment of money to the King. The villeines were farmers, such as had goods and stock of their own, and paid rent to their lords, part in money, at this time very scarce and dear, and part in labour. They were obliged to till and plough the land, sow and carry the corn and hay, etc., for the use of the lord and his family. They took their name from Villa, a hamlet, small town, or village, where they generally dwelt, and in process of time they became copyholders.

Breaking the Bad Old Laws.

It should be mentioned that many of the offenders against the forest laws were men of position themselves. They were not passive, but very active resisters of those bad old laws, and seemed to unite in breaking them so as to bring about a better state of things, and were invariably bail for each other. As long as 35 years passed between courts of eyre being held, when sons were called upon to answer and receive punishment for something done by their fathers, long ago deceased. To kill any animal of the forest was more heinous than murder, and was visited with inexecrable torture.

If the Foresters, who were officers sworn to preserve the vert and venison in the forest, found a man trespassing on the vert, they might "attach" him by the body, and cause him to find two pledges, or bail, to appear at the next attachment court, when he was set at liberty under bail (or mainprized) until the next eyre of the justices. If offending a second time four pledges were necessary, for a third time eight pledges, and for a fourth time he had to be imprisoned until the eyre. One of the offenders within the king's demesne in the year 1242 was Galf de Bradwall. In 1272, the first year of Edward I. (Longshanks), John Gooring of Tychill was consenter to the crimes of John de Oke and Peter de Ospring, who took one doe, and one of his six bondsmen was Elias de Bradwall. The same Elias de Bradwall was bail for Roger Woodrove (probably of Hope), who harboured all night Allcock de Stones, who took one doe in Edale, in the year 1282, and in the morning took the venison to the house of William Foljambe at Wormhill.

In the year 1275 it was presented that when the King hunted at Campana in the Forest, on the Feast of the Assumption, William, son of Rankelle of Hocklow, came, and where the King's hounds had put at bay a certain stag in the park beyond the bounds of the forest, hunted and killed the said stag, together with the hounds, and when the King's huntsmen came and cried him, that he fled, and the huntsmen carried that venison to the King's larder. Those who became bail for him were William Fabre de Bradwall, Richard le Nuke (? Newwall Nook), Robert de Abeny, Alan de Wormhill, Richard de Duffield, and Henry Coteril. How this Hucklow worthy was dealt with we are not told, but if ever he was caught, doubtless he would have the most severe punishment the cruel forest laws could inflict upon him, seeing that he had not been content with shooting a stag, but actually shot the King's hounds as well.

Those Who First Enclosed the Land.

At Forest pleas the assart rolls were always presented. The word "assart" signifies the reduction of waste or woodland to a state of cultivation, and for thus cultivating the land our forefathers were fined for trespass, and always had to pay so much per acre for the crops sown on it, generally 1s. per acre for every crop of winter corn and 6d. per acre for spring corn. In a list of assarts allowed by Warner Engaine (the Bailiff) in the year 1237 at 4d. per acre, Gregory de Bradwall had enclosed 2 acres, and Galf de Bradwall was his bail. Matthew de Bradwall had also enclosed 6 acres. In another roll a few years later, there is an entry of interest showing that there must have been camps or soldiers' quarters in Bradwell, for in the list of assarts there is: "Fratees Hospital de Villa Castra at Bradwall, Thomas Bante 1a, bail Galf de Bradwall. Robert Sergeant Prior of Lenton ½ a, bail Gregory de Bradwall and Galf Quental." Another offender was Nicholas, son of William de Bradwall, who had enclosed an acre, and William, son of William de Bradwall (evidently the offender's brother), became bail for him. In the time of John de Grey (1242) William de Bradwall gets another acre.

The First Houses and Who Built Them.

Another form of forest encroachment was purpresture, which meant building a house or homestead within the forest bounds. During the first 35 years of Henry III.'s reign there was an average of eight houses a year built in the Forest, and as a fine had to be paid for each, it was a source of considerable revenue. In 1283 Galf de Bradwall was called to account for having raised three houses in the forest without warrant, and Clement de la Ford (Ford Hall) became his bail. Another offender was Magister John de Derby, Dean, the Prior of Lenton in Bradwall. In the same year the following were proceeded against, before Roger L'Estrange, for breaking the forest laws in a similar fashion: Richard Millward de Bradwall, William ad Fontein de Bradwall (twice), Richard Cruzer de Bradwall, Elias de Bradwall (three times), Nicholas the Clerk of Bradwall (twice). Galf, son of Faber de Bradwall, again turns up for building a house to the injury of the forest, and this time has to find two bondsmen, his friends Clement de la Ford and Adam, son of Thomas of Castleton, again coming forward.

At the Pleas of 1286 it was presented that "The Queen Consort of the King had a horsefold in the forest with 115 mares and young, to the great hurt of the forest, and it is found that many had horses and mares in the same campana under cover of the aforesaid horsefold, who when required to answer say that they are the Queen's." Four of these belonged to Nicholas de Bradwall.

In the Pleas, in the time of Henry IV. (1399), there is the entry: "Arthur Eyre, for demesne of Bradwall, £4 16s. 4d.," and on a subsequent roll are the following: Bradwall, Robert Eyre for Strylly's londe, Robert for Hucklow land, Robert for his land, Robert for land of John Howe, Robert for land of John Kocke, William Townsend, Thomas Woodroffe for land of R. Hunt, Elias Marshall, John Kirke, John Medalton, Roger Howe for an intacke, Roger Townsend, Robert Myddleton for an intacke, John Kocke for land of R. Greene, Johis Wryght, Ric. Kocke, Thurston Eyre, Hugh Bradwall, Henry Forness for land of John Tyme, Johis Burton, Wm. Elott, Thomas Eyre for land of R. Slacke, Thomas Wodroffe, Thomas Barley. Total villa for turbary, Total villa for pinfold. Robert Eyre for demeyne de Bradwall £6 16s. 8d., Robert Halom for one Cantabulo.

At the Old Court Leet.

The rolls of the various courts, or views of Frankpledge held throughout the reign of Henry VI., are interesting as containing the old names. A court was held at Castleton on Wednesday after the feast of St. Edmund, king and martyr (1472), when Nicholas Howe attached Nicholas Eyre, who acknowledged that he owed "one lode of ore and five dishes; "Wm. Gervis attached Wm. Morten, in plea of debt 23s. 4d., acknowledged 4d. Richard Slacke de Burgh attached Nicholas Eyre in plea of 3 lodes of lead ore. Wm. Middleton attached Thurston Hall. Robert and Wm. Elott attached William Townsend. Wm. Morton attached Matilda Wragg, because he is not responsible for distress of corn. John Donne attached Nicholas Eyre because he killed one ewe price 2s. 6d. John Gervis admitted owing Nicholas Eyre 6 lode of lead ore. Hugh Howe was fined because he did not prosecute his claim against Ernest Cooke and others in four pleas of trespass. In the same year, at a court held Wednesday, on the feast of St. Leonard, John Middleton attached Robert Elott of Bradwall, who admitted debt and " is in mercy."

There was another item of interest at a view of Frank Pledge at Castleton on Wednesday after the Feast of St. Edmund king and martyr (13th Oct., 1472), when Nicholas Eyre, Thos. Howe, Nich. Seward, Wm. Bagshawe, Roger and Wm. Townsend took of the Lord the demesne lands of Bradwall for 10 years, paying four marcs annually, and they did fidelity. Wm. Morten, son of Rich. Morten, Johanna, wife of Jo. Barbour, and Thos. Glover, were offenders at this court.

In the following year, at a great Court Leet, John Middleton attached Nicholas Halle of Cotes, and John Howe attached Robert Middleton. At another court held the same year on the Vigil of the Apostles Simon and Jude (28th October), Wm. Townsend, Thos. Bradwall, Jo. and Wm. Hall, Wm. Forness, Roger Townsend, and Nich. Howe were on the jury. At this court Wm. Forness surrendered a cottage in Bradwall near the tenement of Thomas Woodruff, to Robert Elott, fine 4d., and " did fidelity." Wm. and Thomas Middleton assaulted Nicholas Eyre. Alexander Walker assaulted Jo. Crosby. Jo. Halum, Thos. Donne, and Roger Marshall fined for offences. When the tenants of these assarts died their heirs paid double rent for the first year, and the King had also the second best beast, the first going to the Church.

For many of these extracts we are indebted to Mr. Yeatman's " Feudal History."

There are interesting references to several of the leading people of Bradwell in the Lichfield Mortuary List for the year 1399. These dues were payable on the death of a householder or his wife, to the official receiver for the Dean and Chapter. The custom in the Peak was that the second best beast was taken (horses and cattle), and when no beasts were kept the best wearing apparel of the deceased was claimed. But it was a merciful provision that no beast was taken except where there were three, so that the survivor of the deceased had always a beast left.

In the list the value of a tunic (clothing) varies from 2d. to 3s., a cow 4s. to 8s, and an ox from 6s. to 15s. But in order to arrive at the relative value to-day these sums should be multiplied by twenty.

On the death of Margarite, wife of Thos. de Bradewalle, the Church claimed her tunic, valued at 4d. On the death of Alicia, widow of Richard, son of Galf de Bradewalle, an ox, value 11s., was claimed, and after the death of Arabella, wife of Thos. de Bradewalle, her husband had to forfeit a cow worth 6s.

CHAPTER IV.

WHEN THE FOREST WAS CLEARING.

Landowners at Loggerheads.

About the year 1400 the forest was gradually getting cleared of trees, and the beasts of the forest were being thinned. The lands were getting into the possession of many small owners, and in Bradwell their descendants still remain on the spot. The Wirksworth Hundred Rolls relate how, in the reign of Henry VI. (1438), Robert Eyre and Richard Walkden, vicar of Hope, gave £20 to John Birmingham and Alice his wife; John Woodhouse, Margery his wife, 9 a. in Little Hucklowe, and the same in 26 Henry VI. gave 100 un. to Thomas Padley and Rose his wife for ¼ of 3 messuages and 50 a. land, and 10 a. meadow in Hope and Bradwell.

At an Inquisition taken at Ashbourne in the 10th year of Henry the Sixth, to ascertain the Knight's fee, etc., within the County of Derby, for the purpose of ascertaining the subsidy for the defence of the realm, one of the entries reads thus: " Richard Coke, of Bradwell, 20s. in Bradwell," and another: " Edmund de Ashenhurst, of Ryton, Notts., 13s. 4d. in Bradwell." There is a list of all the great landowners in the Peak on whom levies were made, from which it would appear that the two named were landowners here.

On the 2nd of March, 1486, in the first year of his reign, Henry VII. leased to Sir John Savage, junior, of Castleton, for seven years, the following at the undermentioned yearly rents:—The herbage or agistment in Campana in the High Peak called le Champaigne in the High Peak £40; for the herbage of Crokhill and the pasture called Rowley and Asshope, and the herbage of Westendene and the pasture Birchendever-both, and the pasture called Alport, in Crokhill £30 7s. 6d., for the messuage called Crokhill, in the parish of Hope, in Crokhill, 25s. 10d. ; for the vacarry of Eydale £38; for the demesne land called le Castel Flattes, in the field of Castelton, £4; for the lands, meadows, and pastures of Bradlowe with the herbage of Bradlowe, £10; for all the demesne lands and meadows of Bradwell, in the High Peak, £5 6s. 8d. ; for the herbage of Maynstonfeld, or otherwise called Chyneley, £10 13s. 4d. ; for the herbage of

Shelf and Combes, £4 7s. 8d.; for the mill of Maynstonfeld, 36s. 8d.; for the mill of Tynstide, 36s. 8d.; for the water-mill of Newmyll, with the meadow called Erles Medew, in Ashbourne, £6 13s. 4d.; for "lotte and cope" arising from the lead mines within the King's lordship of the High Peak, £6 13s. 4d.; for the fishery of the water of Wey, with all rivulets and waters within the precinct of the forest of the High Peak, 5s.; for passage, stallage, and advowson of the toll of the market of la Frith 33s. 4d. The said John Savage is to keep all the said premises in repair, the King finding sufficient timber for the said repairs, but the said John to be at the cost of carrying the same.

The calendar to the Pleadings in the Duchy of Lancaster contains many interesting entries relating to the litigation centuries ago. In the 41st year of Queen Elizabeth's reign (1599) the Attorney-General was plaintiff and Rowland Eyre, otherwise called Ayer, the defendant, the premises and matters in dispute being, "intrusion on the Grange called Howfeilde, grounds called Hobholmes and Fearnholmes, the demesne of Bradwall fishing of the river, and lott and cope of the lead mines."

In the same year there was another action concerning exactly the same properties, the parties being Rowland Eyre and Jarvis Eyre, on behalf of the said Rowland, plaintiffs, and John Millward and Robert Millward defendants.

But there had been actions at law prior to this, for in 1594 the Attorney-General, on behalf of the tenants and inhabitants of the Manor as plaintiffs took action against "Andrew Eyre, Hugh Bradwall, and Ellys Marshall, the defendants, the premises and matters in dispute being common of pasture for beasts and cattle on divers specified lands in Bradwall Town."

There was another suit in 1597, when Alexandra Eire, Walter Marshall, Richard Middeton, Ellis Ashton, Robert Bowman, Hugh Marshall, and William Marshall were the plaintiffs, and they contended that Thomas Eire, the defendant, was in illegal possession of demesne lands in Bradwall, and fishing in the Wye water.

There was, in fact, litigation extending over many years between the Eyres and the rest of the freeholders.

Being completely sick of the forest laws, and anxious to be freed from them, as well as from deer lying and feeding in their corn and grass, and have the wastes improved, the freeholders petitioned King Charles about 1639 to improve the wastes. In the following year the forest was disforested and the deer destroyed, and Charles II. granted his share to the Earl of Chesterfield in trust for Queen Catherine. But in 1684 Thomas Eyre of Highlow, by some grant from the Queen, obtained the lands at a yearly rent, including waste lands in Bradwall, Hope, Castleton, Aston,

Thornhill, Wormhill, Chapel-en-le-F:ith, Shallcross, Fairfield, Fernilee, and Mellor.

In Vol. xi. of the "Historical Manuscripts Commission," relating to the documents of the House of Lords, there are some interesting particulars of a case heard before the Chancellor and three Barons of the Exchequer in the year 1685, when Thomas Eyre, of Hassop, accused his relative, Thomas Eyre, of Highlow Hall, of land grabbing. It is the petition of Eyre, Henry Balguy, "and divers others, freeholders and inhabitants of the towns of Hope, Bradwell, and Wormhill, in the County of Derby." The document is dated May 26, 1685, and reads:—

"Charles I., in sight of the Duchy of Lancaster, was seized of the Manor and Forest of High Peak, in the County of Derby, and several waste grounds parcel whereof, wherein are the towns of Bowden-Middlecale, and Chappell-en-le-Frith, and divers others, besides the towns of Hope, Bradwell, and Wormhill, in which last three towns the freeholders and tenants have time out of mind had common pasture and turbary, and other profits upon the waste thereof. Thomas Eyre, of Gray's Inn and Highlow, the Relator, Respondent, upon a pretended discovery that a moiety of the waste in the said forest belonged to the Crown, obtained a lease or grant thereof, at fifty pound per annum, during the Queen Dowager's term, and interest therein (of which nothing has been paid), and one hundred yearly in reversion, and thereon exhibited two informations against the tenants of Bowden-Middlecale, and Chappell-en-le-Frith and other hamlets, and obtained decree allotting him several thousand acres, far beyond the value of the rent reserved, pretending that enough would be left for those entitled to the rights of common. Not content with that, he exhibited a distinct information at the suit of Sir John Heath, late Attorney-General for the Duchy, on behalf of the late King and the Queen Dowager, and Sir James Butler, Her Majesty's Attorney-General, and others, against Petitioner and others, Freeholders in the towns of Hope, Bradwell, and Wormhill, suggesting that in 1639 or 1640 the latter petitioned the late King to disforest the Forest of High Peak, for which he was to have a moiety of the waste there, and that the same was accordingly disforested and divided between the Crown and the Commoners by certain agreements made forty or fifty years ago, and praying to have a moiety of the waste of those three towns, containing over three thousand statute acres, and to have an execution of the said pretended agreement by decree of the Duchy Court."

The names attached to the petitions are of considerable interest at this day, because we get at the local men of note so very long ago. Those from Bradwell are in small capitals. They were:—Thomas Eyre, William Inge, Henry Balguy,

Thomas Balguy, Nicholas Thornhill, Jo. HURLER, JO. WAGSTAFFE, ROBERT HALLAM, JOHN BOCKING, ANTHONY HALL, GEORGE HALLAM, Adam Bagshawe, Nicholas Stones, Anthony Longsdon, George Bagshawe, Richard Bower, Humphry Thornhill Thomas Fletcher. There is a long report of the case in the Government records, from which it appears that Eyre, of Highlow, somehow got possession of lands which belonged to Rowland Eyre, of Hassop, but when later on, there was redistribution, fresh fences around Bradwell. Hope, and Wormhill, and when there had been purchases made, then Rowland Eyre, of Hassop, about 1687, got a fresh order from the Chancellor of the Duchy and the petitioners won their case. "In the tenth year of Queen Anne, 1711, the Chancellor decreed that the Plaintiff and all other the said tenants, freeholders, and copyholders of these several townships may for ever hereafter peacefully enjoy their moiety of the said commons, etc., and the soyle thereof."

CHAPTER V.

SOME OLD CHARTERS FOR FIVE HUNDRED YEARS.

LANDOWNERS AND INHABITANTS IN THE MIDDLE AGES AND AFTER.

Here are a number of charters showing grants and conveyances of properties and curious tenures, dating back more than 600 years.

In the 15th year of the reign of Edward I. (1287), William de Bradwall was on the jury at an inquisition, and Clement de-la-Ford was a contemporary.

On May 6th, 1298, a grant was made from Robert, son of Ellis de Bradewall, and Alice his wife, to Thomas Foljaumbe, of Teddeswell, of a yearly rent of 12d. secured upon their lands in Schatton.

On March 25th, 1305, William, son of Willhelmini Blaunchard, of Castiltone, made a grant to Peter de Shattone, forester, of a rent of 2s., with a day's reaping in autumn, price 2d., from a tenement in Burgh. Witnesses, Clement de la Ford, Ballious de Pecco, William Hally, Robert le Eyr, etc.

On August 24th, 1405, power of attorney was given by Richard de Rouworth, of Hope, to John Dean, chaplain, and Richard Bocking, to give seisin to Anabella his sister of a piece of land under Nunley.

On August 15th, 1411, William Horderon and Anabella his wife granted to John de Staveley a piece of arable land lying between " Le Greensyde " and " Le Nunnley."

In the fifth year of the reign of Edward III. (1332), John de Bradwall was witness to a Shatton deed.

In the 19th year of the reign of Henry VII. (1504), Robert Eyre, of Padley, died, seized of lands at Broadwall, 6 messuages and 124 acres, held of the King as parcel of the Duchy of Lancaster. A service twice a year at the court of Peak Castle.

In the first year of the reign of Richard III. (1483), Nicholas Eyre, of Redseats, Castleton, had lands in Bradwall.

In October, 1657, William Fitzherbert and his son Basill, his heir apparent, owned the Farcotes, in Bradwell—probably alienated about this time by them.

In 1711, Thomas How, husbandman, of Youlgrave, and Mary How, his wife, in consideration of forty pounds and one shilling, conveyed to Thomas Middleton, of Bradwall, butcher, a barn adjoining " Ye Hollowgate and Ye Gutter." The witnesses to the deed were Laurans Marshall, Hugh Bradwall, and Chr. Marshall.

In 1715, John Derneley, of the Mountains, in Bradwall, is mentioned in a Duchy deed, and Mark Furness in the same document.

In the reign of Henry III. or Edward I., Robert de Bradewell, son of Will, son of Fabiana de Bradewell, granted to Richard, his brother, half a bovate of land in Bradewell, the rent being a rose on the Feast of St. Peter and Paul (29th June). The witnesses to the deed were John Flemink, bailiff of the Peak, Will Hally, Robert Balgy, etc.

On the Wednesday before the Feast of St. John (24th June), 1376, a final concord was made in the Court of John, King of Castile and Leon, Duke of Lancaster, at Castelton, whereby John de Wetton and Elena, his wife, release to Walter de Bradwalle a messuage and nine acres of land in Bradwalle.

Under date 15th July, 1532, there is a lease for five years from James Denton, Dean, and the Chapter of Lichfield, to Nicholas Bagshawe, of Capella de by Fryth, of the tithes of hay and corn at Bradwall, and of the mill of Brugh.

Under date 1430, there is a lease from the Prior and Convent " des Preez," of Derby, to Walter Halley, of Blakebrook, Henry Joye, Hugh, son of the said Walter Halley, and William del Kyrke, of Chapel, of the pasture of Byrstallegh (Berristal Lodge, Bradwell), in the parish of Hope.

On October 5th, 1551, Henry Wyllyaves, Dean, and the Chapter of Lichfield, leased for 99 years the tithes of Bradwall, Brughmill, Offreton, Abney and Abney Grange, Upper and Lower Shatton, Overton and Hylowe, to Nicholas Bagshawe, of Farewell, co. Staff.

On November 11th, 1483, Nicholas Eyre, of Redseats, Castleton, executed a feoffment to Richard Vernon, of Hasyl Badge, Henry Columbell, of Darley, Walter Halley and Hugh Needham, of all his lands in Redseats, Castylton, Bradwall, Herdikwall.

and Sterndale, in High Peak, in trust for the said Nicholas, with remainder to his sons, Nicholas and Martin.

In 1714, Thomas Eyre, gentleman, leased to Thomas Middleton, Bradwall, clothier, his one-sixth part of a farm in Bradwall, called Little Martin's farm, namely, 3 closes of land in Stretfield, and a little Pingle under Eden Tree, one-fourth part of pasture under Eden Tree, one Bastard Rood in Grey Ditch, one Butt under Micklow, and one-sixth part of all commons to the same, on payment of £4 11s. 8d., and one fat hen yearly, and the keeping of a hound or spaniel every sixth year.

In 1742, Martin Middleton, yeoman, and Thomas Middleton, of Smalldale, weaver, granted to Thomas Middleton, for £20, a close called The Hassocks, subject to the payment of 5s. a year to the poor of Bradwell as charged by the will of Thomas Middleton, father of Martin Middleton, on the Feast Day of St. Thomas the Apostle for ever.

In 1766, Elizabeth Middleton, widow, and her son Martin Middleton, husbandman, of Bradwall, for £32, conveyed to Isaac Maltby, blacksmith, "all that housing and backside known by the name of Gutter Barn," on payment to His Majesty King George fourpence a year. The deed was signed by the vendors, and also by Thomas Middleton, clergyman, brother and heir to Martin Middleton, and witnessed by Robert Hall and Elias Marshall.

In Calendar of Deeds at Derby is: 14 July, 14 George III. (A.D. 1774), John Wagstaff, then late of Glossop, in the County of Derby, farmer, but then of Youldreave, in the same county, of the first part; Edward Timperley, of Youldgreave, aforesaid, gentleman of the second part; and Samuel Hadfield, of Newton Heath, in the Parish of Manchester, in the County of Lancaster.

Bargain and sale in fee of a messuage in Bradwell, in the County of Derby, a parcel of land thereunto belonging, one other messuage and one croft called Whortley Yard in Bradwall, another messuage, a barn and a little building in Bradwell aforesaid, and a barn called the Cock Barn, and the several hereditaments within Bradwell aforesaid, subject to a life estate therein of Olive Wagstaff.

In 1784 Adam Hallam, butcher, conveyed to John Bradwall, yeoman, a house and butcher's shop in Bradwall. In 1794 William Jacson, of Smalldale, miner, in consideration of the upper part of a croft called Offerton Croft, and five shillings in money, conveyed to Charles Andrew, of Smalldale, farmer and lime burner, a croft at Eden Tree. The witnesses to the deed were Robert Whitley and John Ellis.

In 1798 Charles Andrew, late of Eden Tree, near Bradwall, but now of Chesterfield, labourer, and Mary, his wife, for £83 12s. 6d., conveyed to George Ibberson, of Bradwall, labourer, the croft at Eden

Tree on which he had built a house and barn. This deed was witnessed by Benjamin Barber and Robert Middleton.

Even in the 16th Century the working classes were little better than slaves, for an Act of 1562 compelled all persons between the ages of fifteen and sixty not otherwise employed or apprenticed to serve in husbandry; if they left their employment unlawfully they were sent to prison, and servants leaving a parish without a testimonial were liable to imprisonment. The magistrates in Quarter Sessions fixed both the hours of work and the rate of wages, and any labourer who did not obey was liable to be fined £5 and serve a month in gaol. And no employer was allowed to give higher wages; if he did so he was liable to a fine and imprisonment. Single women between twelve and forty were compelled to work, and a workman who assaulted his master must be imprisoned for not less than a year. And in 1597 the Act was extended to weavers.

The condition of the working classes in Bradwell may be gathered when it is mentioned that in the year 1634 farm lads under twenty had to work for ten shillings a year, and a female of that age a pound, while the wages of a harvestman varied from eightpence to a shilling a day, and a woman haymaker sixpence a day, while a day labourer had sixpence a day in winter and sevenpence in summer. Those receiving these sums had to find their own food. Carpenters, joiners, plumbers, glaziers, masons, bricklayers, slaters, and plasterers had only a shilling a day, reduced by 2d. a day during winter, and the law compelled all tradesmen to work for the farmers during harvest, or be punished by being put in the stocks. In twelve years the wages had been raised about 4d. a day. No wonder that the Bradwell men preferred to work in the mines, where they had their liberty rather than be under such servitude. And at a time when wheat was 41s. 8d. a quarter.

In the 16th Century subsidies or aids were granted by Parliament to the Crown on various occasions for Royal or Imperial purposes, and were levied upon landowners in respect of the annual value of their lands at the rate of 4s. in the £, and upon other persons in respect of their movable goods, including crops on the gross value at the rate of 2s. 8d. in the £. In 1599 those who were assessed and paid this tax on their lands in Bradwell were Elliz Marshall, George Howe, and Mark Trickett, and in 1634 the freeholders were John Hallam, William Marshall, and Miles Marshall.

Seventeenth Century Residents.

From the Easter Roll for the Parish of Hope for the year 1658 we get a very fair glimpse of the condition of the people of Bradwell in the middle of the seventeenth century. These Easter dues were quite distinct from the tithing of animals. In Hope parish it was the custom to pay 2d. upon each cow, 1d. on each calf, an acknowledgement of 1d. from every keeper of sheep, and 2d. from every bee-keeper. These ecclesiastical dues were rigidly enforced.

As showing that Bradwell must have been a populous village even so long ago, the list is of value, there being over 150 who had Easter dues to pay on their live stock. Here again, many of the old family names will be found, some of whom have long ago left the soil, while others remain. The "Bradwall" list is as follows:—

	s.	d.		s.	d.
Adam Slack	0	11	Jo. Hambleton ...	0	11
Adam Wright ...	0	9	Jo. Hallowe	1	0
Adam Kirk	1	4	Jo. Wright	0	11
Adam Thornehill	1	1	Jo. Ogden	0	9
Adam Padley ...	0	10	Jo. Swinscow ...	-	1
Adam Balgay,			John Bullock ...	0	9
gent.	0	9	James Middleton	0	9
Adam Hallam ...	0	9	Jo. Lingard and		
Adam Marshall	0	9	his mother-in-		
Allen Bower	0	9	law	0	9
Andrew Smith ...	0	9	Jo. How	0	9
Andrew Hallam	0	10	Jo. Morten	0	10
Baggot Hadfield	0	10	Jo. Wilson	0	9
Eliz. Wood	0	9	Jo. Middleton ...	0	9
Edw. Slacke ...	0	6	Joseph Burrowes	0	9
Edw. Marshall ...	0	11	Lawrence Balgay,		
Edw. Wright ...	1	0	gent.	0	10
Ellis Middleton	1	0	Lawrence Mar-		
Ellis Ashton	1	1	shall	0	9
Ellis Lyderland	1	1	Matthew Thorne-		
Ellis Mellor	1	1	hill	1	4
Ellis Morten	0	9	Mark Woodriffe	0	9
Francis Yellot ...	0	6	Martin Marshall,		
George Morten ...	1	1	Bayliffe	0	9
George Eyre	2	2	Martin Middleton	1	10
Geo. Doodin	0	9	Martin How ...	0	6
Geo. Slacke ...	1	0	Martin Marshall	0	9
Geo. Wilson ...	0	10	Martin Furnesse	0	9
Geo. Bridocke ...	1	0	Matthew Brome-		
Geo. Worseley ...	1	1	head	0	9
Geo. Hunter	0	9	Michael Hill	0	9
Geo. Bradwall ...	3	4	Nicolas Sykes ...	1	1
Geo. Andrewes ...	1	1	Richard Millward	0	8
Geo. Burrowes ...	1	1	Rob. Offerton ...	1	5
Gilbert Charles-			Rob. Middleton,		
worth alias			sen.	1	7
Marshall	0	9	Richard Middle-		
Godfrey Hallam	1	0	ton	0	9
Godfrey Marshall	0	11	Robt. Clowes ...	1	4
Godfrey Morten	1	0	Rbt. Marshall ...	1	1
Godfrey Chap-			Rbt. Burrowes ...	0	10
man	0	9	Ro. Bradwall... ...	0	9
Henry Slacke ...	0	7	Ro. Hallam, fil.		
Hen. Tricket	0	10	Ellis	0	9
Hen. Bromehead	0	9	Rob. Heyward ...	0	9
Hen. How	0	9	Roger How	0	9
Hugh Taylor			Richard Ragg ...	0	10
alias Hall ...	0	9	Rob. Leech	0	8
Hugh Hill, sen.			Rob. Hall, jun. ...	0	9
Hugh Bradwall...	1	2	Ralph Cowper ...		
Humphrey Mid-			Robt. Eyre	0	9
dleton	0	10	Rich. Frost	0	9
Humphrey Mar-			Rob. Palfreyman	0	9
shall	0	9	Rob. Hallam... ...	1	1
John Downing ...	1	0	Rob. Hall	0	11
John Wyld			Rob. Middleton,		
John Hurler... ...	0	9	jun.	0	9
Jo. Case, sen. ...	0	10	Roger Smyth ...	1	6
Jo. Case, jun. ...	0	9	Steven Jackson ...	0	9
James Bagshawe	0	9	Tho. Slacke	1	0
John Wood	0	9	Tho. Armefield ...	0	7
Jo. Yellott	0	10	Tho. How, ye		
Jo. Bradwall ...	1	0	sonne of Mich.	1	0

	s.	d.		s.	d.
Tho. Ashton, alias			Uxor, John Chap-		
Quimby	0	10	man...	0	6
Tho. Dower	0	10	Uxor, Tho.,		
Tho. Morten	0	10	Padley...	0	6
Tho. Brownell ...	0	9	Uxor, Wm. Eyre	0	6
Tho. Padley ...	0	9	Uxor, Wm.Wilson	0	6
Tho. Hall	1	0	Uxor, Bradwall		
Tho. Bromehead			cum filio		
jun.	0	9	Dennis	1	0
Tho. Marshall ...	1	1	Uxor, Low	0	7
Tho. Dolphin ...	0	9	Uxor, Francis		
Tho. Bradwall ...	1	10	Heyward	0	7
Tho. Eyre	0	11	Uxor, Tho. Jack-		
Tho. Bromehead			son, sen.	0	7
sen.	0	6	Uxor, Miles Mar-		
Tho. Hallom,			shall	1	0
sonne of			Uxor, Dernelly ...	0	9
Humph	0	11	Wm. Midleton,		
Tho. Bray...	1	6	alias Wilson...	0	9
Tho. How, fil			Wm. Hunter ...	0	10
John	0	10	Wm. Jackson... ...	1	6
Tho. Doodin	0	9	Wm. Nelson	0	9
Tho. Marshall,			Wm. How, fil		
sen.	0	9	Jo.	0	9
Tho Hallom,			Wm. How, fil		
Outland	1	0	Mich ,...	1	3
Uxor, Jo.:			Wm. Burgesse ...	0	9
Barbor...	0	9	Wm. Hartle	1	0
Uxor Jo.: Nowell			Wm. Hill	1	2
Uxor Jo.: Doodin			Wm. Hall	0	10
Uxor, Tho.:			Wm. Smith	0	9
Midleton	1	2	Wm. Case	0	9
Uxor, Wm.,			Wm. Hugill	0	9
Bramhall	7	0	Wm. Downing ...	0	9
Uxor, Noden ...	0	7	Wm. Hall, sen....	1	0
Uxor, Heath,			Wm. Charles-		
Anderton ...	0	7	worth	0	10
Uxor, Rich.,					
Hallom...	0	10			

"Uxor," of course, means "widow."

The enclosure of the common lands was made in the year 1806, and the award executed in 1819. The lands thus awarded to various owners measured 718 acres 17 perches.

In "a particular account of the rents due and payable to her present Majesty Queen Anne within the Manner of High Peak for the year 1709," we have:—

"BRADWALL."

Rowland Eyre, Esq., for Brough Mill	00...07...00
Ditto for Nether Hall	00...09...00
Ditto for Thornhill	00...06...00
Ellis Middleton for Land near Brough	00...00...01½
Ellis Middleton, of Brough	00...02...00½
Hugh Bradwell, son of George ...	00...02...00½
William Bradwell	00...01...00
Edmund Greaves, for part of Ellis Bradbury	00...00...08½
Wm. Ragg for part of the same	00...00...09½
Godfrey King, for Land there...	00...02...00
Mr. Richard Bagshawe and John Hurler for part of Mr. Eyre's	00...02...00
Hugh Bradwall, for part of Mr. Eyre's	00...00...03
George Lingard for an Intack for Coppy	00...00...01
George Bagshawe for Land	00...00...01
Ditto for Land, late Revels ...	00...00...02
John Middleton for fallow land...	00...00...06
Libertys of Bradwall	00...10...00
Edward Eyre for Land, late Old- field's	00...00...04
Turbery	00...04...00
Pinfold	00...00...06

Isaac Morton for Land late Marshall's	00...00...01½
Martin Middleton for Gregory's Revil's	00...01...01½
Ditto for Land, late Ward's ...	00...00...07½
Ditto for more late Middleton's	00...00...03
John Morewood, Esq., for Land late James Middleton's	00...00...04
Edwd. Bradwell, son of Hugh, for Geo. Bradwell	00 00 01
Ditto for more, late Revill's... ...	00...00...02
Humphrey Blackwell for copp....	00...00...01
Rowland Eyre, Esq.	00...00...11½
Thomas Toft for Land	00...00...02
John Crooks	00...00...04
William Middleton	00...00...04
Thomas Howe...	00...00...04
Do. for Derneley's...	00...00...02
Thomas Thornhill	00...00...04
Mr. John Wagstaff	00...04...00
Thos. Silvester...	00...01...04
John Howe for Coppy...	00...00...01
The Heires of John Hurlor for part of Stephen Marshall's...	00...00...04
Ditto for more late Heathcot's	00...00...04
John Roe for Land late Mr. Eyre's	00...05...04
Mr. Ward for Land late Revil's	00...00...04
Joseph Ibbotson, for coppy	00...00...01½

When Voting was "Open."

At the Parliamentary election of 1734 the candidates for Derbyshire were the Right Hon. Charles Cavendish, Liberal; Sir Nathaniel Curzon, Bart.; and Henry Harper, Esq., Tories. The following were the electors of Bradwell at that time :—

Name.	Place of Abode.
John Bradwell............	Bradwall.
Robt. Burrows, sen....	Bradwall.
Robt. Burrows, jun....	Bradwall.
Joseph Burrows......	Great Hucklow.
Thomas Chapman...	Bradwall.
Thomas Duddin......	Bradwall.
Robert French........	Smalldale.
John Greaves............	Bradwall.
Godfrey Hall............	Bradwall.
Robert Hallam............	Bradwall.
Thomas Hallam........	Bradwall.
—. Ibbotson...............	Smalldale.
Benjamin Kirk............	Bradwall.
Elliss Marshall........	Bradwall.
Martin Middleton......	Bradwall.
Martin Middleton......	Bradwall.
Richard Middleton ...	Bradwall.
Richard Middleton, jun......................	Bradwall.
Thomas Middleton......	Bradwall.
Isaac Morton............	Hognaston.
Monk Morgan............	Ashover.
Philemon Pickford...	Bradwall.
Daniel Roe............	Smalldale.
John Salt.................	Bradwall.
George Trickett........	Smalldale.
Joseph Vernon............	Chinley.
Richard Wragg........	Bradwall.
William Wragg............	Bradwall.
Richard Worsley........	Bradwall.

All these voted for Cavendish with the exception of Daniel Roe, who voted for Curzon. The result was : Cavendish, 2,077; Curzon, 2,038; Harper, 1,800. Cavendish and Curzon were elected the members for Derbyshire. At the election of 1868, the following were the votes of the Bradwell electors :—Lord George Henry Cavendish (L.), 120; Sir William Jackson (L.), 124; Captain A. P. Arkwright (C.), 28.

BROUGH MILL AND APPROACH TO ROMAN CAMP.

CHAPTER VI.

WHEN KNIGHTS WERE BOLD.
THE STRELLEYS OF HAZLEBADGE AND BROUGH.

CURIOUS TENURE OF BROUGH MILL.

" I come to where the old Corn Mill
    Cast its long shadows down the hill;
Through the rent sails the wind did moan,
    The battered top returned a groan;
The canvas flapped—each creaking sail
    Bore to my ear a mournful tale;
And, listening as the breezes stir'd,
    This strange soliloquy I heard."
           —PLATTS, Eyam.

What historian, or archæologist, or anti-quarian, can pass through the Roman station of Brough and look at the old corn mill, built of the stone from the Roman camp, without thinking of the once power-ful family of Strelley? They were original owners of the place near Nottingham, from whence they derived their name, and possessed lands there long before the Nor-man conquest. And they were amongst the first in antiquity and prestige in Derby-shire.

In or about the first year of Henry II., A.D. 1154, Hazlebach, with the rest of the Peveril estates, was forfeited by its owner for poisoning the Earl of Chester, and it came into the hands of the Strelleys.

But what about Brough? It is certain that Philip de Strelley was in possession of Brough Mill before King John began to reign in 1199, because in the Pipe Rolls there is a list of those assessed for the Coronation of King John, among them being "Philip de Strelley, £4 for the Mill of Burgh." And in the Hundred Rolls of 1275 it is recorded that "the Mill of the Burgh was in the hands of the said King John, and he gave it to Philip de Strelley for the service of finding a valet for carry-ing a falcon trained to take herons in the season, and so it was held from King to King, by heir to heir, and Hugo Strelley now holds it." It was indeed a curious tenure, but a great honour to attend the King on horseback whenever he should come into Derbyshire carrying a heroner. "If his horse should die on the journey, the King was to buy him another, and to provide two robes and bouche of court."

But the office was no sinecure, because the King was often in Derbyshire, and some-times on the very threshold of Brough and Hazlebadge. King John was often in the county, Henry III. stayed at the castle of the Peake in 1264, and Edward I. visited Derbyshire in 1275, and stayed both at Tideswell and Ashbourne, while Edward II. was often here. Henry IV. was frequently in the Peak, and in 1402 tarried for a time at Tideswell, from which town he issued orders as to military preparations against the Welsh, and the Strelleys were horsemen under Henry V. at the Battle of Agincourt.

There were strange doings in those days, for we are told that Philip de Strelley paid to the King ten marks and a palfrey (i.e., a small horse fit for ladies) for the privilege of marrying Avicia, the posthumous daugh-ter and heiress of Richard FitzRogers. Sampson, son and heir of Philip, paid two marks for his relief of the mill at Brough in 1247, and in 1250 he held the manor of Hazlebach. In 1252, Adam de Langesdone and Albredo, his wife, gave to Sampson de Strelley, for a sparrow hawk, 3 oxgangs of land in Haslebach, in fee, performing all services pertaining to the same land. In 1250 William Burdett granted to Robert "Molendarins" (the miller), of Haselbache, half a vigate of land in the fields of Hasel-bache, and there are other charters of

HAZLEBADGE HALL,
where the kingly Vernons held their courts and Sir Richard Vernon lived.

about the same date confirming to Sampson two "tofts" of land in Haselbache, "pay-yearly one pair of white gloves as one farthing." Hugh de Strelley died in 1292, and in a transcript of the original inquisi-tion, held at Hazlebadge in the 20th year of King Edward I., when "Nicholas, Clerk of Bradwall, and Robert, son of William of Bradwall," were on the jury, they "say that the said Hugh on the day of his death held a certain water mill at Brough, in chief of our Lord the King, by the service of carrying a heron falcon to the court of our lord the King in the season, at the King's charge, whilst he shall dwell there, except that he shall have his own proper horse when he come to offer his service, which horse, if he die, shall be made good to him by the King. And the mill is worth £9 6s. 8d. per annum. Item, they say that the said Hugh on the day of his death had a certain manor at Hasselbach with edifices and enclosures, and it is worth eleven and a half marks per annum. Item, he had in demesne five bovates of land worth six shillings the bovate yearly. Item, he had in bondage sixteen bovates of ploughland, worth six shillings the bovate yearly. Item, in free tenants, six shillings. Item, "Loth Minerie," worth 10 shillings." (A tenure of lead-mining upon which the King claimed every thirteenth dish.) Item, profits of Court, worth half a mark. Item, herbage in a certain wood they value at 40 pence. There is a certain mill at Hasel-Bach enclosed worth 20 shillings per annum. Item, the said Hugo had from a certain freehold in Wardlow six shillings. Item, they say that the said Hugh held the manor of Haselbach of Mr. Robert de Strelley, by homage, and the service of the fourth part of a knight's fee. Item, they say that Philip, son of the said Hugo, is his next heir, and is of the age of twenty years on Michaelmas next."

The Strelleys held Brough and Hazle-badge until 1421, when Joan, widow of Sir John Strelley, Knight, granted to Richard Vernon and his heirs all their estates in Castleton, Hathersage, Brough, Haselbach, Allestree, etc., on payment to her of ten marks annually during her life, and so the estates passed into the hands of the Vernons of Haddon. The Hazlebadge mill was in what is now known as "Mill Meadow."

Bishop Littleton was here 11th August, 1743. He says: "A Roman road is very conspicuous near Braddall in this (Hope) parish, being about 6 feet in breadth, and rising about 2 feet above the line of the meadow where he first observed it. The course of this road, he thinks is from Castleton westward up the ridge of the hill called Waller Edge eastward on the summit of which I heard there were entrenchments. The road is called the Bullwark. Query if it has not a communication with the Batham Gate leading from Buxton to Burgh. At Burgh, vulgarly called Brough, the ruins of round buildings are daily discovered, and just by the town in a rough stone enclosure I met with a carved stone representing a man's head, which, though not very well executed, yet was undoubtedly dug out of the adjacent mines, and a work of the Romans. I also purchased of one of the inhabitants a fine vase, somewhat broken, with the following letters: V T A R. Between Braddal and Brough are certain grounds called the Stead Fields,

where they say a battle hath been fought, and I was told that sword blades, rings, and coins were sometimes discovered by the plough. The inhabitants have a tradition that a great town was overwhelmed by an earthquake, that one King Peveril had a palace here and one King Aiding, of Hathersage, the next adjoining par.sh, and they have the following saying :—
"When King Peveril reigned at Brough,
  Then there was gold and silver enough.
King Peveril was Robert Peveril, the great Norman Baron. As to King Aiding, I can say nothing, but by the name I should guess he was a Saxon thane."

HAZLEBADGE HALL AND THE VERNONS.

A Portion of Dorothy Vernon's Dower.

" I'll show you ancient ruins,
  Of castle, camp and hall,
  Where feudal chiefs and barons
  Once held high festival."
—J. H. J.

Bradwell has reason to be proud of one of the most historical and finest manor houses in the county, in Hazlebadge Hall, at the head of Bradwell Dale, an old home of the Strelleys. What history is there in every stone of the building ! But the Hall of the Strelleys has long ago been demolished, and the material used up in the erection of farm buildings, the present being a wing built by the Vernons in 1549. What a grand Elizabethan gable is that which fronts the road, with its magnificent mullion windows and how bold in the apex stands out the Vernon crest, a boar's head ducally gorged, and the quartered arms with the Vernon frett, and the Swynnerton cross fleury ! And the initials H.V. and the three strokes are no longer a puzzle to the wondering beholder, for they are doubtless the initials of Henry Vernon, the son of Sir John, who rebuilt this part of the Manor House, just about the time of the birth of his second son, Henry, and signalised the birth by terming the new comer Henry Vernon the Third.

And the fine old Hall has played a prominent part in the history of the district for not only did it shelter the Vernons for many generations, but was a residence of the family, and a shooting box for the lords of Haddon. But it was more. "It was dignified as a vice-regal lodge. It was the seat of judgment, for here Sir Richard Vernon, as High Steward of the Forest and Constable of the Castle, held his Courts."

The records of these courts of this high and mighty man go to show that he carried things with a high hand. On one occasion, Roger Clark, one of Sir Richard's servants, went with seven men armed with Jacks and salets, and hauled Robert Bagshawe, one of the King's tenants off to the Castle of the Peak, and imprisoned him there for three days without any cause.

And he was oppressed by various amercements being made upon him. Well might poor Bagshawe complain to the Earl of Suffolk. On another occasion William Hadfield, a tenant of the King in Edale, complained to the King's Council of the Duchy of Lancaster that Sir Richard had sued him in the King's Court for trespassing with his cattle. And Hadfield was so terrified that he declared "the said Richard is so mighty in the said county that the said ' besecher' may not abide the danger of his suit."

The mighty Sir Richard was evidently very fond of throwing his neighbours into prison, for there are many such complaints. One day in 1440, the notorious Roger Clark, with his seven armed men, collared Robert Woderofe, of Hope, one of the foresters of fee of the High Peak, hurried him off and imprisoned him in the Castle without any cause. And he did this, in spite of the fact that Woderofe and his fellow foresters had had liberty since the time of King John, Duke of Lancaster, either to occupy their claim with cattle of their own, or to agiste the cattle of other people.

In 1480, at the Court of Henry Vernon, Esq., held at Hazlebach, a large number were fined for various offences, among whom were Elias Furness, Wm. Poynton, Thos. Bytley, Hugh Howe. Robert Eyre, Uxor (widow) Thurston Eyre, Hy. Stafford, Thos. Middleton, Thomas Bradwall, Hy. Ellott, Elias Marshall, and Denis Marshall, of Bradwall. At a great Court held at Hazelbach on the 4th August, 1488, there seems to have been a regular raid on offenders against the laws, as the records contain the following :—Jo. Bradwall of Bradwall, trespassed with 20 sheep; Wm. Bradwall the like, with 20 sheep and cattle; Hugh Johnson 12; Robt. Middleton 40; Elias Marshall 40; Edwd. Bradwell 16; Hugh Howe 1 cattle 60 sheep; Richard Cox 20; Thos. Howe, 1 mare and 12; Roger Eyre, 1 mare and 3; Richard Thompson, 1 mare 14 beasts; John Donne, 1 mare 20 beasts; John Elliott the same; Wm. Elott, 1 mare 4; John Middleton 20 sheep; Richard Elott the same; Robert Halom 30 beasts; Christopher Stafford, 1 colt 30 sheep; Nicholas Seward, 4 beasts and sheep. There were about a score others fined for similar offences, those from Bradwell being Wm. Poynton, Elys Furness, Roger Bradwall, John del Hall, Robert del Hall, Denis Marshall, Henry Hawksworth, Thurston del Hall, Nicholas Marshall de Butts, and Jo. Halom, of Overtown.

But more interesting still is the old Hall as having been the property of the famous Dorothy Vernon, who brought it to the Manners family, in whose possession it still remains. It is a pity that a score years ago the fine old building was disfigured with a roof of blue slate, when it might just as easily have been roofed with grey slate in conformity with the structure. Well might the late Duchess of Rutland condemn such disfigurement the first time she beheld it.

Under date 1630, there is the following entry in Hope Church Register :—"John Manners, of Haddon, Esquire, grants liberty to install a seat in the place belonging to the House of Hazlebadge, in Hope Church, during the pleasure of Thomas Eyre, or Southwinefield, gentleman."

This is interesting as showing how the famous Dorothy Vernon brought Hazlebadge to John Manners.

<hr>

CHAPTER VII.

IN THE OLD FIGHTING DAYS.

<hr>

Petitions for Pensions.

"Can you to the battle march away,
And leave me here complaining;
I'm sure 'twill break my heart to stay,
When you are there campaigning."

Under the Anglo-Saxons all men were required to bear arms as a sort of rent for the land they held. By the Laws of Assize, in the year 1511, every holder of land was bound to produce one or more men fully equipped or capable of fighting in national defence. In 1558 an Act was passed by which all gentlemen having estate of inheritance to the value of £1000 had to keep and maintain at their own cost and charges six horses and requisite weapons, ten light horses and weapons, 40 suits of plate armour, 40 coats of plate corselets, 40 pikes, 30 long bows, 30 sheafs of arrows, 30 steel caps or skulls, 20 blackbills or halberts, 20 acquebuts, a kind of hand gun with a carved stock, and 20 morions or sellets. Those who had land worth less than £1000 had to find fewer, and all in proportion to their income, while those who had goods value £10 to £20 had to find certain weapons.

In the year 1574, Vid. Vernon de Hazelbatch presented one light horse, and the freeholders of the parish of Hope, in which Bradwell was situate, had harness and weapon in readiness for four men—two archers and two bill-men, in addition to four archers and 16 bill-men without harness.

The old Parliamentary pensioners were discarded after the Restoration, and those who had fought on the other side were put in their place. There were very large numbers of such pensioners, and for many years the Royalists had to petition the justices in Quarter Sessions. There was a petition at the Quarter Sessions, held at Bakewell in 1689, from Thomas Heathcote, of Hope, and as there are Bradwell names among the petitioners, it will not be out of place here. It reads :—

"Whereas you said petitioner Haveing formerly beene a Souldier for the late King Charles the First from the year 1642 for the

Terme of six yeares untill the end of the late Civill Warr under the Command of Sr. William Sevvile for the two years or thereabouts untill Collonell Rowland Eyre late of Hassopp, Esqr. tooke up Arms for his said Late Matie King Charles the First who then was Released from the said Sevvile and went under the Command of the said Collonell Rowland Eyre for about foure yeares longer And whereas your said Petitioner having severall wounds at diverse and severall Battells and Sieges, and beene severall times Imprisoned And now being very Aged poore and Indigent Most Humbly Craves yor Worships favour to Admitt him into p'sent pay as a Maimed Souldier within this County there being a vaccancy upon the death of Francis Rippon late of Pilsley."

"Wherefore wee his Neighbours duely Consider the truth or the premises doe hereby Certifie in behalf of yor said petition that it is an object of Charity to entertain him into the said pay And in soe doeing you will much oblige your worshipps Servants

> WILL : BROWNE
> JO : HALL
> ANTHONY HALL
> JOHN BOCKING
> MATHEW BERLEY
> RICH : THORNHILL
> HENERY ASHTON."

" I am crediby informed the contents of this petition is true

> THO : LEAGH ; SAM : CRYER, RICH : TERRY."

"Will : Browne" was the Rev. Wm. Browne, who was Vicar of Hope from 1685 to 1690, and " Sam : Cryer" was the Rev. Samuel Cryer, who was Vicar of Castleton from 1644 to 1697.

Poor old Heathcote's petition was at last granted, for we read that it was "ordered upon a Certificate read in Cort that Thomas Heathcote of Hope bee Admitted a maymed Soldier in this County in Roome of Robert Bramwall and that hee receive his Pention and due this Mich's and soe to bee continued and paid quarterly till further Order."

In 1703 the constables were, by Act of Parliament, ordered to bring before the Justices all able bodied men within their township who had not any lawful calling or employment, or visible means of livelihood, and who had no vote for a member of Parliament and these were forcibly enlisted in the army. Large numbers of men from all parts of the county were compelled to serve against their will, not only unemployed, but debtors. The latter were liberated from prison when they consented to enlist, but they might obtain a substitute to serve. There is an entry relating to one such debtor from here,—William Wragge, who although he only owed 12 li, at the suit of George White, John Wragge was listed in his room with Captain Nicholas Revell in Lord Pasten's Regiment of Foot.

When Militia Service Was Compulsory.

In the year 1638 we have " A List or Rolle of the names of all such persons as are betwixt the age of sixteen and three score yeares within every such all Townshippes of the said Hundred of High Peak as the same were delivered to the hands of Richard Greaves Chiefe Constable of the said Hundred of the Pettie Constables of every of the aforesaid Townshippes as hereafter particularly followeth."

BRADWALL.

Gilbert Charlesworth, Will. Charlsworth, Thomas Garlick, Edward Newton, Thos. Hallam, Myles Marshall, Robert Walker, Adam Marshall, George Burrowes, Robert Overton, Thos. Chippingdale, Will. Wilson, Gy. Hallam, Robert Eyre, Mark Woodrowe, Roger Howe, Thomas Braie, John Dudden, George Dudden, Thomas Dudden, Richard Brailsford, Robert Morton, Humphrey Marshall, Martin Marshall, Will Cocke, Richard Cocke, Robert Hall, Ffrancis Heyward, Thos. Howe, Robt. Morton, John Overton, Roger Smithe, Jervis Hallam, Robt. Bradwall, Ellis Bradwall, Will Bradwall, Ffrancis Eyre, Robt. Eyre, George Bradwall, Job Swinscowe, John Cave, Robt. Eyre, George Hunter, Stephen Marshell, Martin Marshall, Ellis Morton, Matthew Thornhill, Deonise Bradwall, Thomas Lowe, George Bradwall, Thomas Bradwall, Will Derneyley, Matthew Broomhead, James Broomhead, Matthew Johnson, Richard Tymme, Thomas Spencer, Richard Philips, Thomas Philips, Adam Balgie, John Heathe, Anthony Walker, James Ogden, John Ogden, John Chapman, John Bradwall Richard Ragge, Robt. Leech. Thos, Hall, Will Hall, Thos. Eyre, Thos. Ragge, John Hallam, Nicholas Howe, Thomas Hallam, Thos. Rogers, Richard Kirkman, Richard Hallam, Thos. Dove, Robt. Dove, John Bradwall, Will Hall, Will Braye, George Mellor, Richard Morten, Adam Hallam, Leonard Taylier, Thomas Bradwall, John Hadfield, Adam Marshall. Hugh Hill, Nicholas Sykes, George Morten, Godfrey Morten, Anthony Woode, Roger Overton, John Marshall, Godfrey Marshall, Robert Barber, Thomas Barber. John Ffurness, Will Bramhall. Tryamer Arnfield, Thos. Marshall, Walter Marshal, Humphrey Hallam. John Ashmore, Robert Midleton, Will Middleton, Thomas Jackson.

Drawing Lots in Church.

Parish Churches have been put to strange uses, and it is interesting to know that in some of the churches lots were drawn for those supplying the military contingent demanded from the township for the local forces.

On the second of February, 1782, the lots for the Militia were drawn in Hope Church "at a table in the ile in front of the screen." The identical copy of the Bradwell list affixed on the door of Hope Church 130 years ago, is the property of the author. It is of interest as showing various occupations followed by the inhabitants of that time. Here is the copy with the exception of the number of names.

"A true List of all the Men now dwelling or usually residing in the Hamlet of Bradwell in the Township of Hope, Between the Age of 18 and 45. Taken June 8th. 1782."

First Class Men Liable to Serve:

Thos. Hall, ffarmer.	Wm. Bocking, miner.
Thos. Andrew, miner.	Robt. Bocking, miner.
Geo. Andrew, jun., miner.	Josiah Cheetham, miner.
Robt. Morton, miner.	George Barnsley, ffarmer.
Robert Middleton, miner.	Robt. Elliott, miner.
Samuel Duding, labourer.	Thos. Cheetham, miner.
Geo Andrew, sen., miner.	George Hall, miner.
Thos.Bradwell,miner.	Mark Ashton, miner.
Geo. Bradwell, miner.	Thos. Walker, miner.
Robt. Middleton, sen., miner.	Solomon Barber, miner.
Isaac Bradwell, miner.	Wm. Ibbotson, miner.
John Jackson, miner.	Robt. Marshall, cordwainer.
Christopher Jackson, miner.	Andrew Barber, miner.
Christopher Broadbent, mason.	John Hatfield, blacksmith.
*John Broadbent, mason.	Francis Fox, baker.
John Hall, mason.	Thos. Marshall, miner.
Robt. Middleton, weaver.	Thos. Bocking, cordwainer.
Elias Burrows, miner.	Robert Whitle, miner.
Geo. Marshall, labourer.	Rowland Middleton, wheelwright.
Geo. Ibbotson, labourer.	Wm. Hobson, weaver.
Wm. Ashmore, ffarmer.	Abram Dakin, grocer.
John Birley, cooper.	Thos. Marshall, miner.
Josiah Birley, cooper.	Adam Hallam, miner.
John Andrew, labourer.	*Robt. Hallam, miner.
Jacob Eyre. baker.	Thos. Morton, miner.
Robert Bradbury, skinner.	Henry Hill, miner.
Dennis Bradwell, miner.	Robt. Hill. grocer.
Joseph Hibbs, miner.	Anthony Wright, miner.
Richard Bennett, miner.	Geo. Palfreyman, miner.
Thurston Jackson, miner.	Martin Middleton, miner.
Thomas Howe. miner.	George Maltby, miner.
Hugh Pearson, miner.	Thos. Hallam, miner.
Joseph Barber, miner.	John Hallam, miner.
John Elliott, miner.	*Robt. Hall. miner.
Robt. Midleton, miner.	Robt. Hawksworth, miner.
Wm. Wragg, miner.	Geo. Middleton. miner.
Saml. Barber, miner.	Abram Walker, miner.
Richard Wragg, miner.	Thos. Ward, taylor.
Thos. Wragg. miner.	Thos. Hallam, miner.
Robt. Bocking, miner.	Robt. Burrows, miner.
Wm. Hamilton, carpenter.	Charles Middleton, miner.
	Robt. Bocking, miner.
	Wm. Cheetham, miner
	*Robt. Barber, miner.

Second Class:

Wm. Ryalls, three children.	Emmanuel Downing. three children.
Wm. Hill, do.	Thos. Cheetham, do.
Johnson Evans, do.	Joseph Bradwell, do.
Robt. Marshall, do.	Miles Marshall, do.
Isaac Bradwe'l, do.	John Cheetham, do.
Geo. Barber, do.	Ellis Cheetham. do.

Third Class:

John Noel,	infirm.	James Morton,	do.
Wm. Bennett,	do.	Christopher	
John Cooper,	do.	Morton,	do.
Thos. Hilton,	do.	Miles Marshall,	do.
Wm.Palfreyman, do.			

Balloted Before:

Daniel Stafford.	Isaac Furnace.
Wm. Howe.	Robt. Poynton.
Elias Hall.	John Bradwell.
Elias Middleton.	Thos. Greaves.
George Furnace.	Isaac Walker.

Fourth Class.—Exempted by Law.

George Fox, Headborough.	Adam Bunting, apprentice.
John Jennings, apprentice.	

"Any man who Finds himself agreevd must Make His apeal on Tuesday the 18th inst at the sighn of the White Horse in Bakewell."

On the back of the document is written: "This list was wrote by Mr. Edwd. Fox, Schoolmaster." Those names preceded by a star (*) were evidently those whose fate the next ballot had decided.

When the Miners Rebelled.

The dread of an invasion, in 1796, brought about a more stringent Statute for the raising of extra local forces of Militia. The public rebelled against it, and in the Peak district there were riots. There was a serious riot at Bakewell when the Militia lists such as the one given above were burnt before the faces of the Justices. On the day the magistrates met, the lead miners of Bradwell, Castleton, Eyam, Tideswell, Longstone, ond other places, marched into the town armed with clubs, picks, miners' spades, and other weapons. The mob took all the Militia papers from the officers, being lists (such as the above) of men liable to serve in the Militia, went into the room where the magistrates were sitting, seized Dr. Denman, the chairman, and turned out his pockets to see that no papers were left. They then made a bonfire of the whole of their booty in front of the White Horse, and destroyed all the papers. So serious was this riot that the Cavalry attended the next meeting of the magistrates when a large mob again assembled, but were dispersed, and a number of them taken prisoners and conveyed to Chesterfield gaol. There were no Bradwell men taken prisoners.

The first Volunteer Corps in Derbyshire, was founded in 1803. The North High Peak Corps wore scarlet coat with blue collar and cuffs, and white trousers. One company was called the Bradwell, Peak Forest, Great Hucklow and Grindlow Volunteers, but nearly all the men were from Bradwell. There were 66 effective rank and file, and the officers were Benjamin Barber, captain; Robert Needham, lieutenant; and Benjamin Pearson, ensign; all gentlemen of position in Bradwell. Curious enough, Benjamin Barber was a well known Wesleyan local preacher, known as Captain Barber. He was a lead mine owner, and Benjamin Pearson (a cotton mill owner) was a church-warden at Hope. The company formed part of the Chatsworth Regiment of Volunteer Infantry, and Benjamin Barber was one of the captains.

About 1796 there were many Peakland men who were by the Act of Parliament at that time compelled or "impressed" to enter the army, a number of lead miners of Bradwell being among the number. Each parish had to find men, and some of these were married with children. One of these was Hugh Hill who became a sergeant in the 65th Regiment of Foot, who on October 30th, 1800, when his regiment was stationed at Sandown Fort, Isle of Wight, wrote a long letter to his children. It is addressed

CHAPTER VIII.

BRADWELL'S RELIGIOUS MOVEMENTS.

THE EARLIEST NONCONFORMISTS.
CHAPEL OF THE APOSTLE OF THE PEAK.

Nonconformity existed amongst the miners of Bradwell in the very earliest times of dissension from the Church. As already stated there was no church here, the inhabitants being compelled to attend the Church at Hope or take the consequences of

The ancient Chapel of the Apostle of the Peak.

to "Mr. Henry Hill to be Left at Mr. Thos. Willson's across Smith Field, Sheffield, Yorkshire," and after mentioning various family affairs he says: "We expect the French to invade England very shortly, there is a camp of the French opposite Deal. It makes duty go very strict with us. When the sky is clear we can see their camp, which is upwards of 4000 men, but they have a good deal to do before they pass our wooden walls of old England. Our batteries and forts and castles which we have three castles and two forts to do duty at. We have at No. 1 and 2 forts 12 thirty-six pounders, four long nine-pounders, besides Howitzers and other implements of war." In a postcript he says: "Pray God send a speedy peace, for everything keeps rising now as fast as ever." Hugh Hill returned to his native place, and was always known as "The Sergeant," down to his death in 1824, at the age of 54.

their neglect. Early in the 17th century the constables had to make presentments at Quarter Sessions of all those persons who had not attended church. Some of these were Catholic, some Quakers, and others Presbyterians. These recusants or Nonconformists were very numerous in Derbyshire, especially in the High Peak, and at the Sessions of 1634, Francis Eyre, the constable of Hope, presented these recusants for absence from church for two months past: "Robert Jackson, of Bradwall, mynor; Gartrude Jackson, wife of William Jackson of the same, mynor; Gartrude Yellott, wife of Thomas Yellott, of Aston, husbandman; and Joan Wilks, of Hope, widow." These, then, may be considered some of the earliest Nonconformists in Bradwell How many more there were it would be interesting to know.

But in spite of the penalties, Nonconformity continued to spread, and in 1682 over 450 persons in Derbyshire were hauled up at the Assizes on warrant either to show some reasonable excuse for absent-ing themselves from church for twenty-one Sundays past or to pay a shilling for every Sunday they had been absent, the fines to go to the poor of the several parishes where the offenders resided. Many of the offenders lived in the parishes of Hathersage, Tideswell, Chapel-en-le-Frith, Ashford, Monyash, and Hope. The Bradwell names on the Hope list were Andrew Hallam, Robert Middleton, Margaret Middleton, Laurence Trickett (Smalldale), and Hugh Fox. From this time the penal laws against Nonconformists were gradually relaxed. At this very time the Apostle of the Peak was spreading the Gospel in the Peak district, and before long he had established congregations and built chapels in about a dozen villages, the old chapel at Bradwell being one of the number.

The First Nonconformist Chapel Wrecked.

The old Presbyterian Chapel, which stands in a secluded situation hemmed in by cottages, is one of the most interesting and historical religious edifices in the county. The old building, which with its walls a yard thick, appears as if intended to last a thousand years, was built for the Apostle of the Peak, the Rev. William Bagshawe, the ejected Vicar of Glossop, in 1662, and was the first edifice erected for public worship in Bradwell. Its history would make up a thrilling story, for it sheltered the men and women of two centuries ago, who were persecuted and suffered martyrdom for freedom to worship God according to their conscience. The saintly Bagshawe visited Bradwell, and was received with open arms by the miners, in whose cottages he held meetings for worship with closed doors and windows, so as not to expose his auditors to the lash of the severe laws in force against them. But the seed was sown to such an extent that soon after the repeal of the Five Mile Act (in 1689) meetings for public worship were held, and the Presbyterian congregation formed. Mr. Bagshawe's diary contains interesting entries giving glimpses of the religious life of Bradwell at that time. Under date January, 1695, he observes: "On the 25th, I was at Bradwell, had many hearers, and divers appeared much affected." In April he wrote, "On the 7th my labours lay at Bradwell, when I spoke on the soul and on coming to Christ without money. The people continue willing, and J. Turner by presents obligeth my dear wife." The next entry is instructive as being the first to mention the old chapel. It is in August of the same year (1695), and reads: "On the 25th. I preached and prayed in the new meeting place at Bradwell, where very many heard; and I was assisted." Again on Aug. 29, 1695: "One fruit of my poor labours ye last year is ye poor people of Bradwell have prepared a more meet place to meet in, and they are more than willing

that my younger brethren should take their turns in preaching there." "August ye 25th. Flocked in." A New Year's Day visit of the fine old man is thus recorded: "1696. January 1st. After praying in secret, and with those of the family who could be got together, God favoured me this day as he had done yesterday, in that there was little wind or wineglass. Though T. Barber and I were lost in a close mist as we went towards Castleton and Bradwell we got thither in due time. Many were heeding hearers; I hope they were more. For the main mine heart was right. On April 8th the same year he writes: "I laboured at Bradwell with some help Jo. Hadfield was hurt by my mad horse, and fainted, to our affrighting, yet recovered through mercy." There are other interesting entries relating to Mr. Bagshawe's visits to Bradwell down to his death on April 5th, 1702, and it was when regularly visiting and exhorting the people of Bradwell that he wrote a little work, "The Miner's Monitor," in fact, the Apostle of the Peak was the principal religious factor in Bradwell in those days of trial.

It was a memorable time for Bradwell when the sanctuary of the Nonconformists was wrecked. Dr. James Clegg, who succeeded the Apostle of the Peak as the minister at Chinley Chapel, has this entry in his diary: 'August, 1715. A Popish mob demolished the meeting house of the Dissenters at Bradwell." Previous to this, on October 1st, 1714, the doctor writes: "I set out for Bradwell to view ye old Meeting House. It's a good building. Son Middleton and Wm. Evatt were with me. We dined at Martin Middleton's."

During the year 1715 the hopes of the Romish party were much excited by the prospects of a French invasion in support of the Pretender, and they fomented riotous assaults upon Nonconformist places of worship throughout the kingdom. The weight of the storm fell elsewhere, but the skirts of it extended as far as the Peak of Derbyshire, and the chapel erected for the Apostle of the Peak was wrecked by a mob from Hope, who smashed the windows, pulpit, and seats to pieces, and left the building in ruins. It is stated that the mob entered Bradwell during the night, otherwise there would have been bloodshed, as the miners of Bradwell were mostly dissenters.

From the death of Mr. Bagshawe in 1702 the chapel was in charge of his grandson, the Rev. John Ashe, who wrote a memoir of the Apostle of the Peak, and Dr. Clegg, down to 1720, when Rev. Robert Kelsall, a young man of just over twenty-four, took charge.

In the year 1883, Mr. C. D. Heathcott, of Exeter, a native of Derbyshire, was transacting business at a bookseller's shop in London, when he saw offered for sale a mahogany reading-stand bearing the following inscription : "This reading-stand belonged to that excellent minister, the Rev. Robert Kelsall, who was for nearly 50 years pastor of the old Presbyterian congregations at Great Hucklow and Bradwell in Derbyshire. He died 23rd of June, 1772, aged 73." Mr. Heathcott purchased this valuable article, and feeling that either Great Hucklow or Bradwell was the proper resting place for so interesting a relic, he very considerately made his way to Derbyshire, called upon the pastor—Rev. R. S. Redfern—and kindly placed it in his keeping as the representative of the congregations for the time being.

On a tombstone in Tideswell Churchyard there is the following inscription :—

"To the memory if the Reverend Robert Kelsall, who originally came from Pool Bank, near Altrincham, in Cheshire, and was Minister of the Gospel at Great Hucklow and Bradwell, which charge he fulfilled with great zeal and integrity near the space of 50 years. His life was spent in the practice of most virtues that can adorn and dignify the human mind. Of gentle manners and ingenious conversation, he was agreeable to all who had the opportunity of his acquaintance. But these were only secondary qualities; he had an unfeigned piety towards God, and was charitable and benevolent to his fellow creatures. He was a sound scholar, well skilled in the writings of the Ancients, yet free from ostentation and the love of praise. As a Minister of the Gospel he had great talents, and was, as St. Paul says, an example to his flock, in conversation, charity, faith, and purity. He has left an example not easy to be equalled, but must ever be admired, and we hope imitated. He died June 23, 1772, aged 75 years."

WILLIAM MIDDLETON,
a Presbyterian of 80 years ago.

The Chapel was destroyed by fire during Mr. Kelsall's pastorate, and the date 1754

over the door, probably denotes its restoration in that year.

The Rev. John Boult was appointed minister at Mr. Kelsall's death, and laboured here about twenty years, when he was succeeded by the Rev. Ebenezer Aldred.

An Eccentric Parson.

An eccentric man was Mr. Ebenezer Aldred, the minister of the old Chapel here, at Hucklow, and other places more than a hundred years ago, after the congregation had become Unitarian, and he had a curious history. He was the son of a minister at Wakefield, and was brought up to business there, but was unsuccessful. Hunter, the historian of Hallamshire, says: "When I first knew him, which was about 1796, he was living in Sheffield with a brother-in-law without employment. He got some commission to America from the Sheffield merchants, but this did not succeed. At last, when more, perhaps, than fifty years of age, he became a minister, and had the care of a chapel in the Peak of Derbyshire. There he lived in a kind of solitude, became dreamy and wild; laid hold on the prophecies; saw Napoleon in the Book of Revelation; at last fancied himself the Prophet who, standing neither on land nor water, was to proclaim the destruction of a great city; came up to London; drove through the streets fully laden with copies of a book, of which I have a copy, and, himself dressed in a long white robe, got into a boat on the Thames, and two claimed his commission. This, I believe, is merely a literal account of the affair. He lived some years after. He had two sons, clever youths. One was a schoolfellow of mine. The other (father of the Rev. J. T. F. Aldred, Vicar of Dore) was a partner with his brother-in-law, Dr. Warwick, and now lives at Rotherham."

The late Thomas Asline Ward, in his diary under date August 18, 1812, mentioning a walking tour in Derbyshire with Messrs. Nanson, Ebenezer Rhodes, the historian, and Wood, alludes to this remarkable man. He says: "We sauntered over the moors to Hathersage, dined, crossed the country to Tideswell, supped, and slept. Passing through Hucklow, saw and conversed with Mr. Aldred, a Unitarian minister who has the care of three or four chapels in the Peak. He is a tall venerable looking man with grey hair floating over his shoulder, and is the same who, several months ago, sailed in a boat on the Thames clothed in a white garment, denouncing woe to the Metropolis. He has also published a book of prophetic conjectures, which are so extravagant as, combined with his eccentric conduct, to induce a supposition that he is beside himself."

For these quotations we are indebted to Mr. R. E. Leader's article on Mr. Ward's diary. The eccentric parson's wife was a daughter of the Rev. Samuel Moult, who was minister at Rotherham from 1743 to 1776. Dr. Warwick, who married one of their daughters, was a physician and minister of the Unitarian Chapel, Rotherham, and another daughter was the wife of the Rev. John Williams, who was some time minister at Norton and Halifax.

The old Chapel used to be designated "The Naylor's Chapel," after the Rev. Robert Naylor, who was Aldred's successor in the pastorate about 1814. Naylor's term was a long one, for he laboured here until 1840, when he retired.

Another who occupied the pulpit regularly for 33 years, and occasionally for twenty years longer was the Rev. Robert Shenton, who came into Bradwell a mere stripling of a youth to do missionary work for the Primitive Methodists, quite a new organisation. He preached the opening sermons of the Primitive Methodist Chapel at Little Hucklow in 1826, but became pastor of the Unitarian Chapel at Flagg, and on Naylor's retirement was appointed to Bradwell and Hucklow. For many years he was a powerful influence in every progressive movement in the Peak, and his body lies in the tiny graveyard close to the chapel door. On the headstone is inscribed: "In memory of the Rev. Robert Shenton, of Bradwell, who died January 5th, 1889, aged 83 years. His earnestness as a preacher and devotion as a worker in every good cause won him many friends and admirers by whom this stone and the tablet in the adjoining chapel were erected as a memorial to his work. Selina, his wife, born September 18th, 1819, died on Christmas Day, 1881."

And a handsome marble scroll inside the Chapel reads: "Sacred to the memory of the Rev. Robert Shenton, of Bradwell, minister of the Old Chapel at Great Hucklow and Bradwell for upwards of 33 years, and for half a century a devoted and eloquent preacher in this district. An earnest advocate and faithful worker in any cause having for its object the welfare of the people. His labours in the interest of education were recognised by his election as the first chairman of the Bradwell School Board, which office he held till a short time before his death. This tablet, together with the stone in the adjoining graveyard, are intended as a testimony to the esteem in which he was held by Peer and Commoner alike, by whose united efforts these memorials were erected. Died January 5th, 1889, aged 83 years."

Robert Shenton retired from active ministerial work in 1871, and took as the text of his farewell sermon the words "Call to remembrance the former times," his sermon extending over an hour, being reminiscent of events during the period of his long ministry.

The other ministers of the Old Chapel have been: 1871 to 1875, R. Cowley Smith; 1876 to 1885, Henry Webb-Ellis; 1886 to 1895, R. Stuart Redfern; 1895 to 1897, W. F. Turland; 1897 to 1900, W. H. Rose; 1901 to 1903, Sydney H. Street; 1903 to 1911, Charles A. Smith.

The Chapel was endowed with certain lands by William Evans, of Smalldale, Bradwell, who died on April 13th, 1844, at the age of 72, and was buried in the chapel at the foot of the pulpit. On the wall over his grave there is a marble tablet to his memory, and at the foot of the inscription we read: "He being dead yet speaketh." In 1879 most of the old high box-like pews were removed, and modern seats substituted, but one or two were left, and remain an interesting relic of former days.

It is, perhaps, the tiniest burial ground in England, for in the whole of its two hundred years' history there have been but three interments therein.

CHAPTER IX.

METHODISM'S EARLY STRUGGLES.

John Wesley and His Pioneers.

The story of the introduction of Wesleyanism in Bradwell has already been told in Evans' "Methodism in Bradwell." It dates back to the very beginning, for in 1738 David Taylor, the earliest preacher of Methodism in Sheffield, missioned the Peak, Bradwell included.

In 1747 John Wesley himself visited Bradwell and preached in the Town Gate, close to the stocks, and in his journal for 1765 he wrote: "March 23rd, Saturday, we took horse from Sheffield in a furious wind which was ready to bear us away. About 10 I preached at Bradwell in the High Peak, where, notwithstanding the storm, abundance of people were got together. I had now an opportunity of inquiring concerning Mr. B——y. He did run well till one offence after another swallowed him up. But he scarce enjoyed himself after. First, his eldest daughter was snatched away, then his only son, then himself. And now only two or three of that large family now remain." But twenty years before Wesley came, earnest men and women were daring to carry on the work and worship God in their own fashion at the risk of their lives. The first to open their houses for the reception of the Methodists were Isabella Furness and Margaret Howe —names that yet survive—and in their homes Sarah Moore, a young woman from Sheffield, used to hold prayer meetings, and walk from Sheffield to Bradwell and back. But the first society class here was formed by William Allwood, a young butcher, of Rotherham, about 1750.

The work was carried on in those days by devoted men and women, upon whom insult and assault were heaped regardless of the consequences, and so much did Benjamin Barber suffer for his religion that he went to his grave as "the Methodist martyr." A story concerning him is well

(1) **First Primitive Methodist Chapel in Bradwell. Built 1823; now a cottage.**
(2) **Old Baptist Chapel; now the Primitive Methodist Sunday School.**
(3) **Primitive Methodist Chapel. Built 1845.**
(4) **Wesleyan Chapel. Built 1807.**

worth repeating. Mr. Joseph Clay, of Sheffield, who was interested in lead mines here, and was the principal proprietor of Water Grove Mine, which then employed between 200 and 300 men, interviewed Benjamin with a view to engaging him as his agent, but as though he had received some previous intimation, he asked "What is your religious profession?" "A Methodist, sir," was the reply. "Well, now," said Mr. Clay, "if you engage in this work I shall expect you to renounce all connection with the Methodists, and attend the services of the Church of England." "Sir," said Benjamin, "I am a poor man, and have a large family to support, but if that be one of the conditions of my engagement, I must say that from the good I have received from the Methodists, rather than renounce them I will beg my bread from door to door." Benjamin was engaged, and ever after Mr. Clay spoke of him as "my trusty servant Benjamin," and when he died he bequeathed to him his old-fashioned silver watch.

In 1760, when accompanying William Green, of Rotherham, from Castleton, where they had been endeavouring to hold a meeting, but were prevented by a mob, they were followed on the road to Bradwell and almost stoned to death, Benjamin being almost murdered, and the marks of the wounds he carried to his grave.

From a barn the Methodists removed to the upper room of a house on Smithy Hall, belonging to Wm. Cheetham, and on one of the old window-panes there still remains, cut with a diamond, the verse:

"If any ask the reason why
  We here together meet,
To such inquiries we reply,
  'To bow at Jesus' feet.'"
William Cheetham, 1768.

On another pane there is the following:

"Would you credit Jesus' cause,
Walk uprightly in His laws;
Would your soul to Jesus win,
Let your life be free from sin."
William Cheetham, June 14, 1770.

"I wish, William, your name was written in the Book of Life."

First Wesleyan Preaching Room. In William
Cheetham's House, Smithy Hill; it is now a
Bedroom marked X.

Portion of the First Wesleyan Chapel in
Treacle Street (now Fern Bank), at the
top of Smithy Hill.

The first chapel was built in 1768, in what was known as "Treacle Street," now Fern Bank. Benjamin Barber was the principal factor in the work. In 1807 the present chapel was erected at a cost of £877 3s. 5½d., on land sold by Thomas Somerset, carpenter, the first trustees being: John Middleton, miner; George Maltby, miner; Benjamin Barber, shopkeeper; Thomas Hill, miner; Philip Barber, miner; Josiah Barber, mineral agent; Joseph Barber, miner; Edward Somerset, carpenter; Nathaniel Somerset, carpenter; Thomas Cheetham, miner, all of Bradwell; and Ralph Penistone, of Baslow, farmer.

The chapel was renovated in 1891 at a cost of £1,358 3s. 1d., including a new organ, and the cemetery has been enlarged from time to time. Many of Methodism's most famous preachers have held forth in this chapel, with which all the old families in the village have been prominently connected at one time or other. Bradwell was constituted the head of an important circuit in 1812, but in 1905 was, much against its will, included in the North Derbyshire Mission.

Some Curious Items.

There are some curious and amusing entries in the well-preserved account-books of the Wesleyan body. A hundred years ago teetotallers were unknown, and ale drinking was apparently the proper thing to do. At any rate, even a chapel could not be built without it. Some of William Marsh's (the contractor's) men were thirsty souls, and the Bull's Head and White Hart were handy then as now. At Mrs. Ellen Bradwell's, the Bull's Head, they put on a shot of £7 0s. 6d. "for ale," and £2 11s. 6d. at Richard Bennett's the White Hart, and the trustees paid the bills. And seven years later even the scaffold holes could not be filled up without a wet, for we "paid Ellen Bradwell for ale that William Marsh had 7s. 6d." Twenty years later the chapel could not be painted without "ale for the workmen 5s. 9d.," and we have "ale for the workmen 4s." when the gates were erected at the entrance to the chapel yard.

Musicians were famous for having to wet their whistles, and it was feared that if the tap stopped the music would cease to have charms. Hence, when the harmonium was opened one Sunday in 1848, Clement Morton, himself a musician, and landlord of the "Rose and Crown," was paid "for refreshments to the Hayfield singers £2 1s. 4½d." It would be interesting to know how these Hayfield singers reached home.

And at festivities for children, here and elsewhere, ale was often given to children, and on Queen Victoria's Coronation Day in 1837 the scholars partook of "currant cake and ale" in the chapel. We have improved on those times.

The first Sunday School was established by Benjamn Barber about 1780, and at one time was conducted in an old silk mill, now Brook Buildings. In 1826 the school over the brook was built, now the Conservative Club; in 1844 the one at Bridge End, now the Liberal Club; and in 1878 the present school was built in Town Gate at a cost of £700.

Rise and Progress of Primitive Methodism.

As with the parent body, so with Primitive Methodism, to Bradwell belongs the distinction where it first gained foothold among the mountain villages of Derbyshire. In fact, it was one of the fruits of the Sheffield mission, begun by Jeremiah Gilbert, who was imprisoned in Bolsover Round House for preaching there in the year 1819.

Another of these pioneers was James Ingham, one of the first itinerant preachers, who afterwards left the itinerancy and settled in business at New Mills. Ingham wrote: "Six of us, including Gilbert, went from Sheffield, October 7th, 1821, to Bradwell, to hold the first camp meeting there, and I believe we had not a member in the town. Well might we say 'What are these among so many?' Many expected it would be a wet day, but God can answer prayer. It was a fine day, and the wicked were heard to say, 'See, they can change the weather.' As the result of that Michaelmas camp meeting there were quite a score of converts ready to be enrolled as members."

Thus began Primitive Methodism. Then it was that George Morton allowed the new sect to hold their services in his barn, next to his house in Netherside. That barn is now the property of the trustees.

In 1822 a chapel was opened by the famous Hugh Bourne, and in 1823 Bradwell became the head of a circuit, and had as its first minister the Rev. Jeremiah Gilbert. The old chapel was plain to the last degree; no porch, no vestibule, no pews, but loose forms without backs; no stove or heating apparatus; no boarded floor, nor even flagged, but the ground covered with what was called "small feith" or spar from the lead mines, which sparkled and glistened with little particles of lead ore; this was renewed every year. The Rev. John Verity, one of the most notable pioneers of the movement, who was appointed to this circuit in the year 1831, gave an exceedingly quaint description of this time-honoured sanctuary to those who had never seen it. He would say: "My chapel is floored with sparkling gems and diamonds; the people make no noise treading upon it, coming in or going out; if a baby cries the mother quietens it by putting it down on the floor to play with the diamonds. If I want anyone to engage in prayer two or three forms from me, I get up a handful of gems and throw them at the person's back." Yet from this humble place of worship such gifted ministers were sent forth as Joseph Hibbs, John Hallam, Joseph Middleton, George Middleton, John Morton, and others. It is now a dwelling-house on Farther Hill.

From Bradwell the seed was sown throughout the villages of the High Peak, and the circuit extended over a radius even to Marple and Disley, in Cheshire, and included what is now Bradwell, Buxton, New Mills, and Glossop circuits.

Fancy that little tabernacle, now a cottage, the principal chapel in the Peak in Derbyshire! But so it was. Many amusing stories could be told of the early Primitive Methodists, both men and women. Among their women preachers were Violet Hill and Ann Maltby, and Violet Hill (Mrs. Violet Hall) lived and died in the Chapel House after the new chapel was built.

In 1845 the new body extended their borders by erecting the present chapel at a cost of £700, and in 1878 it was enlarged at a cost of £700, other improvements, including a new organ, having been carried out since.

The Sunday School is an enlargement of the old Baptist Chapel, and the old gravestone with an undecipherable inscription, in the lower part of the graveyard, close to the school, was in the old Baptist graveyard before the Primitive Methodists acquired the premises.

The chapel contains several memorial tablets to the Eyres, Hallams, Halls, and Mortons, one of these being to George and Hannah Morton, who first opened a door for the reception of the Primitive Methodists; one to Thomas Morton Moore, a famous soldier, whose career is noticed elsewhere; one to the Rev. Jacob Morton, Wesleyan minister; one to the Rev. John Morton, Primitive Methodist minister; one to the Rev. John Hallam; to Isaac and Catherine Eyre; and to the late John Hall, of New Wall Nook.

The Baptists—" Dipping " in the Holmes.

The Baptists had a cause here in the latter part of the 18th century, and built a chapel. But the adherents were never very numerous, although there was a regular minister. Those who joined the cause were immersed in the waters of Bradwell Brook down the Holmes, and not long ago there were persons living who could well remember witnessing these "dippings," as they were termed. But the cause never prospered, and about the year 1841 services ceased and the chapel was abandoned. By this time the Primitive Methodists had established a Sunday School, and occupied the old Baptist Chapel, which they acquired, improved, and enlarged as it is seen to-day. There was a small burial ground attached to the Baptist Chapel, containing a few graves, over one of which is an old headstone still remaining. The chapel was all on the ground floor, which was composed of lime ashes, with an old stove in the centre and the pipes through the roof of the building. The ground floor, with the stove and the pulpit of the Baptists, was in its original condition down to forty-five years ago.

CHAPTER X.

EARLY CHURCHWARDENS.

How St. Barnabas' Church was Built.

There being no church here until the year 1868, the adherents of the Church of England had to attend service at the Parish Church of Hope, but there were not many after the Wesleyan Chapel was built. But prior to that time those who attended a place of worship—and it was compulsory to go to church—had to go to Hope. The the Poyntons from Bradwell and Little Hucklow; the Bockings from Hope and Bradwell; the Halls from Hope and Bradwell; and so on. Therefore, in the undermentioned list is to be found the name of the warden or wardens, bearing a Bradwell name, though some of the Greaves, Middletons, Halls, Poyntons, Bockings, Bradwalls, and Andrews lived in other places.

1686, William Bradwall; 1688, Dennis Bocking; 1689, John Bocking, Henry Ibutson, Smalldale; 1690, George Tricket, Smalldale, Henry Ibutson; 1692, John Poynton, John Hall; 1693, Edward Dernelly,

The Old Sunday School at Brookside, where the first Church Services were held.

list of churchwardens of Hope for nearly 300 years contains many old Bradwell names. There were generally three wardens, and very often one was from Bradwell, and a strange thing about it is that sometimes a Bradwell Dissenter would be filling the office. In the year 1529 Thomas Lowe, vicar of Hope, was inducted by Thomas Bradwell, chaplain of Hope.

As there are so many bearing the same surname, but resident in different places in the ancient parish of Hope, it is difficult, yea impossible, in some cases to distinguish the Bradwell wardens from others, so that accuracy in this respect is out of the question. For instance, there were the Middletons of Hope, Bradwell, and Woodlands; the Greaves from all those three places; William Poynton; 1694, John Hall, William Poynton; 1695, John Hall, Joseph Ibberson; 1697-8, John Ibbutson; 1699, Isaac Morten, Joseph Ibbutson; 1700, Thomas Middleton; 1702, John Hall; 1703-4, John Greaves, Wm. Greaves; 1705, Robert Middleton; 1707, Ralph Bocking, Nathaniel Greaves; 1708, George Burrows; 1710, Wm. Greaves; 1711, Thomas Morton; 1714, Christopher Bocking; 1715, Philemon Pickford, Smalldale; 1718, Robert Burrs; 1719, Christopher Bocking, Robert Poynton, Robert Marshall; 1720, Thomas Morton; 1723, Robert Middleton; 1724, Godfrey Hall, Bradwall, Thomas Morton; 1725, Benjamin Andrew; 1727, Ellis Needham, Robert Middleton; 1730-1, Hugh Bradwall; 1730-1, Robert French, Smalldale; 1733, Robert

Bocking; 1734, John Greaves, Bradwall; 1735-6, Isaac Morton, Bradwall; 1738-9, Charles Greaves, Thomas Bocking; 1740-1, Robert Marshall; 1743, Thomas Gleadhill; 1744, Isaac Hamilton, for Mr. Oliver, of Smalldale, William Oliver; 1745, John Elliott, Joshua Needham; 1746, Ralph Bocking, John- Yellott; 1747, Martin Middleton; 1750, Thomas Fox, Thomas Marshall; 1751, John Greaves; 1752, Joseph Ibbotson, John Greaves; 1754, Robert Needham; 1755, Samuel Oliver; 1756, Ellis Marshall; 1757, John Middleton, Thos. Fox; 1759, Ellis Marshall; 1761, Abraham Ibbotson; 1764, John Bocking, Zaccheus Middleton, Robert Middleton; 1765, Anthony Wright; 1766, Francis Ashmore; 1767, George Hall; 1768, John Wright, John Bocking; 1769, Thomas Greaves; 1770, Christopher Bocking; 1774, George Barnsley, Francis Ashmore, Thomas Bradwall; 1775, John Middleton; 1778, Thomas Gleadhill, Samuel Oliver; 1780, Robert Hill; 1781, Godfrey Fox; 1783, Robert Poynton, George Fox; 1784, Benjamin Elliott; 1785, Hugh Bradwall; 1786, Thomas Fox; 1789, Thomas Cresswell, Joshua Needham; 1792, William Ashmore; 1794, John Middleton, Thos. Greaves; 1795, Robert Hill; 1796, John Ashmore, Hugh Bradwall; 1797-8-9, Robert Middleton; 1801-2, Edmund Ashmore; 1803, John Gleadhill; 1804, Joseph Ashmore; 1806, Benjamin Pearson (Brough); 1807, Isaac Hill, Isaac Middleton, John Bradwall; 1808, Isaac Hill, Thomas Jennings; 1811, Hugh Hill.

From this date the residences of the wardens are given, and down to the year 1842 the name of the place is spelt Bradwall. Henceforward the wardens from Bradwell were: 1814, Robert Middleton; 1817, Thomas Jeffery; 1823, William Bramall; 1826, William Ashmore; 1830, Thomas Hill, George Bingham, Hazlebadge; 1833, William Bramall; 1834, Robert Middleton, Brough; 1836, Robert Middleton, Bradwall; 1839, William Ashmore; 1841, George Fox, Hazlebadge; 1842, William Kenyon; 1845-6, Elias Needham; 1849-50-51, Robert Hill; 1853, Durham Wragg, Hazlebadge; 1856, Thomas Bradwell.

For this valuable information we are indebted to Dr. Porter's "Notes on a Peakland Parish."

Building of the Church.

It was not until the year 1868 that the present church was built and dedicated to St. Barnabas. Bradwell was then in the extensive parish of Hope, and those of the inhabitants who professed to belong to the Established Church were obliged to attend service at Hope Church, although for some twenty years occasional services had been held in the town's day school, which was licensed by the Bishop of the diocese. In 1862 the Rev. Alfred Harrison was curate. At this time the Rev. Chas. John Daniel was vicar of Hope, and his curates were the Revs. Ridley Daniel Tyssen and Edwd. T. Churton, and it was through their efforts that the church was built as a chapel-of-ease to the mother church of Hope. It was a small building of local limestone, in the perpendicular style, consisting of chancel, nave, vestry, organ chamber, and a small turret containing one bell.

St. Barnabas' Church.

The contractors for the building were Messrs. Ash and Clayton, of Sheffield, whose tender for the work was £1,117, and "extras" amounted to £145 15s., making the total paid to the builders £1,262 15s. The exact sum paid to Colonel Leslie, of Hassop Hall, for the ground on which the church was built, was £76 17s. 6d., the wall round the churchyard cost £60, and other expenses connected with the building and furnishing brought up the total cost to about £1,800, which was raised by local efforts, the largest subscribers being: The Rev. C. J. Daniel, £152 10s.; Samuel Fox, Esq., £100; Robt. How-Ashton, Esq., £100; Lichfield Diocesan Society, £100; Rev. Ralph B. Somerset, £100; the Duke of Rutland, £75; the Duke of Devonshire, £50; Mr. Thos. Somerset and his sisters, £50; Miss Rawson, £50; J. R. D. Tyssen, Esq., £53 15s.; Rev. R. D. Tyssen, £37; Lichfield Dean and Chapter, £35; W. A. Tyssen-Amherst, Esq., £25; Rev. E. T. Churton, £25; T. B. Cocker, Esq., £25; John Fairburn, Esq., £25; William Pole Thornhill, Esq., £25; Rev. Chas. Bradshaw Bowles, £20; Thos. Brocklehurst, Esq., £20; Joseph Hall, Esq., £20; Wm. Jackson, Esq., M.P. for North Derbyshire, £20; Martin Middleton, Esq., £20; and many smaller sums, amounting to a total of £1,800. Many local people gave team work and labour. Samuel Fox, Esq., gave land to enlarge the churchyard, and also a site for the vicarage. The fine organ was the present of Wm. Jackson, Esq., M.P., at a cost of £200; it was built by Mr. Brindley, of Sheffield. The Rev. Chas. John Daniel presented the beautiful window in the east end, representing the Fall and Redemption of Man, and also the silver communion service. The Rev. R. B. Somerset was the donor of the communion rails, chancel screen, and pulpit, made partly from two desks given by Trinity College, Cambridge, a book-desk and light for the pulpit, and a sedilia; Rev. R. D. Tyssen, tiles for the chancel; Mr. Daniel-Tyssen, a corona; and Miss Daniel-Tyssen, a silk altar cloth. On the day of consecration the sum of £26 was collected in church. Subsequently, various improvements were effected in the grounds, the paths formed, trees planted round the churchyard, and the fine avenue leading from the gates to the church door constructed.

When the church was erected it was intended that ere long a separate parish should be formed, and with this end in view some handsome subscriptions were promised towards its endowment, including —Samuel Fox, Esq., £100; Wm. Jackson, Esq., £100; Duke of Rutland, £75; Rev. C. J. Daniel, £25: W. A. Tyssen-Amherst, Esq., £25; Rev. E. T. Churton, £20; and W. C. Moore, Esq., J.P., of Bamford, £20. For some years subscriptions continued, and in 1875, during the curacy of the Rev. Wm. James Webb, an intimation was received from the Ecclesiastical Commissioners for England that they had granted an application made to them to separate certain townships from the very extensive parish of Hope, and form them into a distinct parish. The townships referred to were Bradwell, Hazlebadge, Great Hucklow, Little Hucklow, Abney, Grindlow, and Wardlow, and from the first of May in that year those townships constituted a separate parish, with St. Barnabas' as the Parish Church. As an endowment for the new district, the Vicar of Hope (the Rev. Henry Buckston) gave up £60 per annum from the income of the mother church, and the capital sum of £1,200 was raised by the contributions of landowners and inhabitants, and other friends of the church and parish. This the Ecclesiastical Commissioners met with a grant of £1,500 from the Consolidated Fund of the Church Revenue at their disposal, and the patronage of the new parish was vested in the Dean and Chapter of Lichfield, the patrons of the parish of Hope.

The first vicar of the new parish was the Rev. Wm. Jas. Webb, who laboured here thirteen years as curate and vicar respectively, when he removed to Alrewas in 1881. In that year the vicarage was built—one of

Rev. W. J. WEBB,
First Vicar of Bradwell.

the handsomest and best-appointed parsonages in the country. In August, 1881, the Rev. Henry Thornton Dudley, M.A., of Queen's College, Oxford, was ordained to the living, and during his vicariate (in 1889) a square embattled tower in the Decorated style was added at the southwest angle of the church, at a cost of nearly £700. The tower clock has a curious history, given on another page.

The east window represents the Fall and Redemption of Man. There is a very fine window by Burlisson and Gryll to the memory of the Rev. Wm. James Webb, curate-in-charge 1868 to 1875, and vicar 1875 to 1881. An alabaster monument in the chancel commemorates Ralph Benjamin Somerset, Fellow and Dean of Trinity College, Cambridge, who died in 1891.

The Rev. George Bird has held the living since 1893.

The church schools were built in 1873, at a cost of £1,150, including a Government grant of £236 18s. 1d.

Educational History.

A perusal of the original trust deed of the ancient school of Hope makes it clear that Bradwell had an interest in that school even at the time it was founded, for in 1688 Adam Kirk and Godfrey Kirk, of Bradwell, were trustees of the school. The premises consisted of school-house and master's residence combined, and a small garden, in fact the very plot of land on which the present school at Hope is built. When a new trust was constituted, in 1742, Isaac Morton, of Bradwell, Richard Oliver, of Smalldale, and George Bagshawe, of Hazelbadge, were trustees.

First Bradwell Schools.

The first provision for elementary education was made by Elias Marshall, who in 1762 (as is noticed elsewhere) left land worth £3 per year, the rents to be paid to a schoolmaster or mistress to teach five of the poorest children in Bradwell to read. Those who availed themselves of it were described as "charity scholars." Edward Fox was a schoolmaster so long ago as 1782. In 1825 John Birley built a school-house in Hugh Lane, where the two houses now stand next to the Primitive Methodist Sunday School, and in this building John Darnley, a famous schoolmaster of that day, taught these poor children. From time to time trustees of the charity were appointed. But reading, writing, and arithmetic were then taught in the Sunday Schools. Subsequently a National School was opened in the public schoolroom over the brook (now the Conservative Club).

The National School was built in 1871 at a cost of £1,200.

School Board History.

Bradwell was one of the first places in England to take advantage of the Education Act of 1870, for at four o'clock in the afternoon of February 25th, 1871, a public meeting of the ratepayers was held in the schoolroom to consider the expediency of a School Board for Bradwell. A great deal of feeling was shown, and excitement was high. Mr. Thomas Shaw Ashton, of Wheston, Tideswell, presided. Mr. John Barber proposed "That in the opinion of this meeting it is expedient that a School Board be formed for the parish of Bradwell." Mr. John Hall seconded. Mr. Thomas Somerset proposed an amendment "That it is not expedient," and Mr. Joab Hallam seconded. Among the speakers in favour of a Board was Alderman Fairburn, of Sheffield; against it the vicar of Hope, the curate of Bradwell, and Mr. Robert Somerset. The result of the show of hands was: For the Board 72, against 52. Of course a poll was demanded on the question, and was fixed for the following Saturday.

The Saturday following, March 4th, was a memorable day. Polling went on from 10 o'clock to 5, the result being: For a Board 128, against 115, majority in favour 13.

After this steps were taken to form a School Board, and August 19th, 1871, was the polling day for the first members of the Board. Five members had to be elected, and, as at almost every election for 30 years, the struggle was to get the majority, generally three members on each side being nominated. Here is the result of the first poll:—

Elected.

Rev. Walter Graham, Primitive Methodist minister 227
John Barber, grocer, Wesleyan.. 221
Rev. Robert Shenton, Unitarian minister 213
Thomas Somerset, farmer, Eccles House, Churchman 211
Rev. Wm. James Webb, curate of Bradwell 190

Not elected.

Joshua Jeffery, farmer 173

The first five were elected, and constituted the first Board.

There were remarkable scenes at the first meeting of the Board, which was held on September 7th at the house of the Rev. Walter Graham. Mr. Shenton was elected chairman, and Mr. Webb vice-chairman.

The opening of a Board School in the Primitive Methodist Sunday School was celebrated with a tea and concert in a marquee, but a good deal of strife was engendered between those for and against a School Board.

In 1893 the premises were condemned as unsuitable, and new schools were built, and have long required extension, the Wesleyan Sunday School being used as an Infants' School in order to relieve the main building.

Subsequent triennial elections of School Board resulted as follows:—

1874 (Uncontested).

Rev. Robert Shenton, Nonconformist.
John Barber, Nonconformist.
Robert Tanfield, Nonconformist.
Dr. Joseph Henry Taylor, Churchman.
Robert Hallam, Churchman.

1877 (Uncontested).

Mr. Robert Somerset and Mr. Thomas Bradwell withdrew, leaving the following elected:
Rev. R. Shenton, Nonconformist.
John Barber, Nonconformist.
Robert Tanfield, Nonconformist.
Thomas Elliott, Churchman.
Joab Hallam, Churchman.

1880 (Uncontested).

Rev. Robert Shenton, Nonconformist.
John Barber, Nonconformist.
Robert Tanfield, Nonconformist.
Joab Hallam, Churchman.
Wm. B. Prisk, Churchman.

1883 (Contested).

Elected.

John Barber, Nonconformist ... 211
Robert Tanfield, Nonconformist 191
Rev. Robert Shenton, Noncon-
formist 188
Robert Hallam, Churchman 179
William Bramall, Churchman... 170

Not elected.

Joab Hallam, Churchman 150

1886 (Uncontested).

Rev. Robert Stuart Redfern, Unitarian
minister.
Stephen Dakin, Wesleyan.
Robert Tanfield, Primitive Methodist.
Robert Hallam, Churchman.
William Bramall, Churchman.

1889 (Contested).

Elected.

William Bramall, Churchman... 198
Zachariah Walker, Noncon-
formist 195
Robert Hallam, Churchman ... 171
Rev. R. S. Redfern, Noncon-
formist 157
Stephen Dakin, Nonconformist.. 155

Not elected.

Robert Tanfield, Nonconformist... 144

1892 (Uncontested).

Rev. R. S. Redfern, Nonconformist.
Stephen Dakin, Nonconformist.
Z. Walker, Nonconformist.
Robert Hallam, Churchman.
Wm. Bramall, Churchman.

1895 (Contested).

Elected.

Zachariah Walker, Noncon-
formist 311
Charles Castle, Nonconformist.. 295
Seth Evans, Nonconformist 274
Joseph Allen Middleton,
Churchman 239
Charles Maples, Churchman 212

Not elected.

Wm. Bramall, Churchman 183

1898 (Contested).

Seth Evans, Nonconformist 272
Z. Walker, Nonconformist 267
Chas. Castle, Nonconformist ... 261
Wm. Bramall, Churchman 254
Stenton Thos. Hallam, Church-
man 190

Not elected.

Jos. A. Middleton, Churchman 99

1901 (Uncontested).

Z. Walker, Nonconformist.
Seth Evans, Nonconformist.
Chas. Castle, Nonconformist.
Wm. Brickwood Prisk, Churchman.
Harvey Hallam, Churchman.

How the schools passed to the County
Council under the Education Act of 1902
is a matter of recent history.

CHAPTER XI.

IN THE PARISH WORKHOUSE DAYS.
HOW THE POOR EXISTED.

OVERSEERS' OLD RECORDS.

The old accounts and records of a parish
are always interesting and instructive, but
in our case we have not those of a parish
but of one township within a parish. The
accounts of the overseers of the poor, contained in an old book known as "William
Evans' Book," covering a period from 1818
to 1850, are eloquent as showing the life of
the village poor in the first half of last
century.

Before making any allusion to the contents of this book it ought to be said
that the author is in possession of the
ancient Deeds for a century and a half,
showing that a century ago, when Bradwell
kept its own poor, the workhouse was at
Edentree,—the very house that was enlarged and is now the residence of Dr.
Clegg. And real workhouses they were in
those days, for the inmates were compelled
to work, and our Bradwell workhouse was
fitted up with weavers' looms. A Deed
dated 29th October, 1812, sets forth that
John Hibberson, of Sickleholme, innholder,
a member of one of the oldest Bradwell
families, variously spelt Ibbutson, Ibbotson, Ibberson, and lastly Hibberson, sold
for £125 to Thomas Hill, shopkeeper, and
Robert Middleton, of Smalldale, miner, the
overseers, at the request and by the proper order and direction of the inhabitants
of Bradwall, the dwelling-house, cow-house,
barn, loomshop, and garden at Edentree.
But in 1819, having an eye to business, the
overseers removed the paupers and their
looms to other premises at Yard Head, now
two houses belonging to Mr. Albert Bradwell, which was the workhouse down to
the Bakewell Union being formed.

In those days the overseers expended
something like £500 a year, and collected a
rate once a quarter, and their accounts give
us a glimpse, not only of the primitive
kind of workhouse, but of the lives of the
inmates, the out-door poor, and most other
things in the parish.

For instance, in 1818 we had "oile for the
house 5 weeks at 1d., 5d."—probably to oil
the looms of the paupers, and at the same
time they were supplied with "thread,
5½d.," and when the flitting had taken place
we "paid 1s. 4d. for a pair of spindles," and
"William Kenyon for a beam 8s." Then
we have "Adam Hill for a pair of looms
£1 10s.," and being short of money we paid
"Adam Morton on account of looms 10s.,"
giving him the other half-sovereign next
year when we gave "John Smith towards
looms 18s. 6d." In 1825 we have "setting
up looms 8s. 6d.," and the following year,
determined not to allow old Webster to eat
any idle bread, they bought "a five dozen

bobbins, new pickers, cording, etc., for Webster " and paid " William Ollerenshaw 6d. for setting up Webster's looms."

In food and cooking, the inmates of this institution, and the out-door paupers as well, appear to have had a fairly good time in those days of small things. Their supplies of potatoes, butter, meat, candles, etc., were liberal, but they appear to have baked their own oatcake with the meal provided by the overseers. There was "paid *for setting up Backstone 2s. 9d."—that* "backstone" was in the house not long ago, —and there was also "paid to Jacob Eyre for two troughs 16s." Old Jacob Eyre was a baker in Nether Side, and when he got too old to carry on his business he sold his mixing troughs to the overseers for the paupers to mix their dough in.

In 1819 we "relieved old Nanny" at a cost of 11s. 9d., and soon afterwards we "paid William Revill for old Nany's shoes 2s. 3d.," and "relieved old Nany and Hannah instead of milk 12s. 8d." We also "paid for baking old Martha's bread 6d.," and later "bought flannel for old Martha." Not long after this the old lady was taken to her long home.

"Richard Kay for Townend's breeches 3s. 2½d." shows that the personal appearance of the paupers was not neglected, and 1s. 11d. was "paid for ¾ yard of fustian to mend William Hibbs' breeches." It is to be feared that William had rheumatism, for there is an entry "To William Hibbs, oil of Pigma to rub his thigh, 4½d."

The ladies had a touch of pride in them, which the overseers encouraged, for they spent 2s. 8d. on "Hannah Gee's bonnet," and sundry fineries for others. They "bought Mary Hall, Castleton, two shifts 5s. 1d.," and also a "bedgown for Mary Hall, Castleton, 2s. 6d." This lady was doubtless fond of a dance at Castleton Wakes, like most people in that famous village, and so they "relieved Mary Hall at Castleton Wakes 2s."; indeed, the entries show that Mary was often "set up" with cash to visit Castleton at a "good time." And the inmates had generally a spree at these "good times," especially at Bradwell Wakes, on the second Sunday in July, for there are numerous entries. Here is one, in the handwriting of William Evans, overseer, "1831. July 9, To cash to the House for the Wakes 7s. 6d."

Unfortunately, the records disclosed many lapses from the strict path of morality, for a great deal of money was spent in tracing runaway fathers of illegitimate children. The custom seemed to be to outrun the constable, who had to follow them all over the country with a warrant in his possession. The expense was enormous. And when magisterial business had to be transacted journeys had to be made to Chesterfield, Bakewell, Hathersage, Hayfield, Chapel-en-le-Frith, Tideswell, Glossop, Low Leighton, or anywhere else where a magistrate lived.

The sick poor were well looked after, judging from the quantity of intoxicants that found its way into the "House," for there are hundreds of such items. On one occasion there had been a new arrival at the workhouse, increasing the population by one, when there seems to have been a very nice feast over the job at the ratepayers' expense, for they paid for "goods to the House for the merry meal 3s.," and "Ale for Charlotte Palfrey 4s." It is the first time we have come across a merry meal in a workhouse on such an occasion, and paid for out of the rates too! In 1824 we "relieved Isaac Furness when going to the doctor 1s.," and when a man was in Chapel Gaol we "gave his wife Sukey 4s. 6d." We can imagine the wry faces that would be pulled after half-a-crown had been "paid for saults and pills for Mary Wragg's child," and five shillings was given "to Robert Hawksworth's wife having a bad leg."

Behind these entries there may be many a tragedy. For instance, in 1831, "To Alice Smith, for wine, being poorly, 2s." Poor Alice evidently got worse, for she lingered on more than a year, when we read "To Alice Smith for a peck of malt, being poorly, 2s. 5d." The end was fast approaching, for the next entry mentions old Doctor Lowe, "To James Lowe attending Alice Smith, 5s.," followed by "Alice Smith, extra, being poorly, 2s.," the story closing with the items, "Alice Smith's coffin 18s., fees 8s., shroud 1s. 3d."

The wayfarer was not turned empty away —the overseer had at least a copper for him. He gave a shilling "to relieve a woman in distress from America," and another shilling "to a man in distress through loss at sea," and he paid "to a poor woman in distress to pay her lodgings 3d."

And the overseer interested himself in getting employment for those who would otherwise be on his hands, and an entry tells us that we paid "expenses to Bamford getting Deborah Walker a place 1s." He got a good many others a "place" so as to keep them off the rates, and there is an item, "To Elizabeth and Jane Marshall to prevent them being excluded from the club at Bakewell 5s. 6d." One man, although wanting bread, had great expectations, for the overseers gave "Robert Hobson for bread, and promised to return it on the receipt of his fortune, 5s. 6d." Amongst the hundreds of curious entries are: "To two chamber potts to House 6d.," and "Idleback 1d."—an almost obsolete name for potmould.

How poor lads were rigged up and placed out as parish apprentices is shown by numerous payments. In 1818 we have a payment "for Isaac Eyre's hat," and five years later there was "paid with Isaac Eyre to his master £2 2s." "paid for his new cloaths 14s. 6d." "for his new hat 2s. 6d.," "expenses at binding him 6s. 6d.," "expenses going to Whetstone about Isaac

Eyre 1s." One poor lad who wanted to make his way in the world is mentioned where there was "given to John Middleton going to seek a situation 6s." He was successful at Bollington, twenty miles distant, and the next item we come across reads: "To Joseph Wright taking John Middleton to Bollington 13s." That lad became a prosperous tradesman at Bollington. Why a door-tenter was necessary at the workhouse is a puzzle, but there was paid "to William Smith for door-tenting two years 5s. 3d."

There are numerous payments of good stiff sums for law costs, mainly cases of settlement that had been taken to Quarter Sessions. In 1818 there was "Pade Mr. Cheek and Counselors £8 17s." This was old Lawyer Cheek, of Wheston, near Tideswell, who was often "pade" to unravel legal problems. There is "Expenses to Pontefract Sessions £22 16s. 8d.," and a payment of £40 14s. "Parker and Brown's law bill."

It would be interesting to know where were the rights of turbary, and what led to half a guinea being paid for "Parker and Brown's opinion on turf," and 12s. 6d. to Benjamin Barber for drawing up the above case."

It would appear that teetotalism was then unknown, for everything had to be washed down with liquor. All the meetings were held and the business transacted in public-houses—good old inns of the olden times. The Bull's Head was kept by Ellen Bradwell; the Green Dragon by Joseph Bocking; the Rose Tree by William Bradwell; the Rose and Crown by Robert Morton; the Newburgh Arms by William Kenyon; the White Hart by Elias Needham; the Miners' Arms by Robert Howe; and the Lord Nelson at Brough by Joseph Sidebottom. These appear to have reaped a rich harvest, for nothing could be done without something being "spent," and the amounts per meeting varied from five to ten shillings; indeed, there are hundreds of these items.

About a dozen of the solons of the village attended when there was "spent at the accompts 5s.," and often more. Even Outram's Dole of 15s. could not be paid without those who doled it out spending 5s. at the Bull's Head.

The Headborough was an important functionary, who was responsible for the township list of Militia men, and there appears to have been a good deal "spent" when he was appointed. In 1818 there was "paid to William Revill for serving Headborough £1," and in the following year "William Fox for serving Headborough £2 4s. 8d." Revill was a shoemaker and kept a beerhouse in Nether Side, where the bank now stands, and Wm. Fox was a shuttle maker.

Considerable sums were paid to "Militia men, 19s. 4d."; and "Given Militia men 3s." A meeting respecting the militia resulted in 6s. 6d. being "spent," and it is followed by some curious entries. Here they are: "expenses of three

Militia men over the subscriptions, £6 2s. 6d.;" "Paid for 737 parts of two Militia men, 19s. 4½d.;" and "Given Militia men, 3s. The second item is a mathematical problem that will bear solution. Of course we "spent at Headborough meeting 5s." The next year we "expended at two Militia meetings 7s. 7d.," and "paid for Militia men £5 5s. 4d." In 1824 we "spent at choosing a new Headborough 3s. 6d." and at "marking a Militia list 5s," while "George Elliott headborough's bill" was £1 9s. 3d., and "Thomas Bocking do." £1 6s. 7d. Next year we have "To a Militia man £3 12s. 4½d." and so on ad lib, and in 1829 we have "To soldiers red coats 2s. 6d."

We are also given an insight of the old Church rates, a rate levied on the parishioners for the support of the Parish Church. In this township it was unpopular, because most of the people were Dissenters. The amount appears to have varied, for while the "Church score" in 1819 was six guineas without any information as to how the amount was arrived at, we have next year "Church rate 7 penny lay £6," while in 1823 "Church score" had gone up to £9. Of course, something had to be "spent" at the inn where these men were paid as well as where the overseers were appointed, indeed there appears to have been a jovial time when William Evans and William Ashmore were appointed overseers, for 15s. 6d. was "spent," and later, "meeting at William Bradwell's, nominating overseer, 15s." In 1823 there apears to have been a good deal spent in ale and tobacco over the tithes for we have "Tobacco and pipes at Tythe meeting. 6d." "spent at Joseph Sidebottom's on Tythe business 1s.," "spent at Elias Needham's on Tythe business 5s," and "spent at Robert Morton's on Tythe business 8s. 8d."

There appears to have been a "Town's Box" in those days. We wish it was in existence now, and all its former contents in evidence. It would tell a strange tale. Whether or not its contents had been tampered with is not said, but in 1824 we "paid for a key for the Town's Box 7d." After this there appears to have been a systematic inspection of the box, for in the early part of 1826 we "spent at a meeting at Robert Morton's 5s.," and the very next day "a meeting at Ellen Bradwell's 3s. 6d."

Another important functionary, the constable, had plenty to do, and a rate was levied to recompense him, for in 1821 we read "Constable rate 3 penny lay £2 14s.," and in the previous year the "constable's score" was £1 10s. There was "paid for ale on the appointment of constable at Robert Morton's 5s," and Henry Hill was paid £11 for serving the office. Who the poor creature was, who was hustled off to the asylum is not stated, but there was "paid to Constable and John Bradwell going to Bedlam, together with Glossop constable expenses 13s." The constable's accounts would be still more interesting reading.

The mole-catcher was quite an institution in the place. In 1819 we " paid mole-catcher half a year's wage £4," and the payment is continued from year to year. And the same year we " paid for a lock for the pinfold 8d.," and " paid John Cooper for pinning 10s," but both mole-catcher and pinner are functionaries of the past, and the pinfold in Hungry Lane was thrown into the road widening a few years ago.

How or by what means King George was ' proclaimed " we are not told, but in the accounts of 1820 we have "expenses at proclaiming King George the Fourth 10s."

There was no "penny post" in those days, but the overseers had occasional letters for which they had to pay. Here are a few of the items: " Paid for a letter for Micah Wright 2s. 5d." " a letter from Manchester 9d," "letter to Oldham 10d." And they were occasionally worried with communications from London, thus " letter from Parliament 2d." " paid for a letter from the House of Commons 3d." " a letter from London respecting a petitioner 2d.," " making a return to the House of Commons and expenses 5s."

We have an entry "To a letter from London to take the population 1s. 1d." This relates to the census of 1831, when the population of Bradwell was found to be 1153. Another entry reads: " To expenses at justice meeting with population 3s. 6d." We don't suppose that William Evans, the overseer, took "the population" to the justice meeting, or he would have his hands full. The stormy period of the Reform Bill was just over, and so under date July 16th, 1832, we read "To the Reform Act from London 2d." Two years afterwards we have "To instructions respecting voting from London 2d." and "To a second instruction respecting voting from London 2d." In 1837 there is the entry "To a parcil from Bakewell respecting the Polling Places 3d." A complete change came over the scene when Poor Law Unions were formed. and so we came across the entry in 1838, "To an order from London to join the Union 2d." And this joining the union caused ructions. The Workhouse was closed, and the few paupers removed to Bakewell. But that was not all. The accounts of the overseers had to come under the lynx-eyed Government auditor, and at the end of the accounts for 1841 we have the ominous entry: "The accounts of Thomas Middleton and Henry Hill of items which the auditor will not allow." And these items totalled £50 5s. 10d. But our overseers cared not for auditors, for they kept strictly to the old path. They "paid for ale at a meeting 5s," "paid for ale and tobacco at a meeting with John Hall 5s. 1½d." and "to ale, gin. and tobacco at meeting William Butcher 6s. 6d." In fact, they had a separate list of "the items which the auditors will not allow," for they never "allowed" him to see them, but paid them out of the rates all the same.

Our book ends with 1852 when George Fox and Robert Evans were the overseers, and from that date the accounts are not such as to call for special mention.

A deed dated 17th June, 1831, in the author's possession, is interesting as showing how and when the old Workhouse at historical Edentree passed into other hands and became private property. The parties to the deed are Thomas Hill, shopkeeper, Isaac Somerset and William Evans, overseers of the poor, and the several persons—principal inhabitants of the township of Bradwell. Those " principal persons " are Thomas Hill, Isaac Somerset, William Evans, Robert Middleton, Josiah Barber, Abraham Dakin, George Bradwell, Thomas Middleton, Thomas Jeffrey, Thomas Andrew, Thomas Somerset, Abraham Ashmore, Joseph Wright, William Burrows, and Robert Morton.

The deed goes on to recite that at a vestry meeting of the inhabitants held in the Sunday School house in Bradwell, on the 15th of April last, convened by public notice for the purpose, it was unanimously agreed by all the said inhabitants then present who were the major part in value of the inhabitants of the township, that the property should be forthwith sold by auction to the best bidder, the purchase money to be paid to Isaac Somerset and William Evans, and applied by them as the inhabitants should direct.

Accordingly the overseers offered for sale the two dwelling-houses (forming one house called Edentree House), barn, cowhouse, loomshed and garden, also a croft adjoining the said garden, and an allotment late part of the waste which was allotted to the devises of George Ibberson, by an Act of Parliament enclosing the Commons in Bradwell, the properties being in the occupation of William Burrows, Benjamin Hill and Thomas Elliott. The sale took place on May 15th, 1831, when Mr. John Maltby was declared the purchaser for £110.

CHAPTER XII.

INDUSTRIES OF THE PAST.

Lead Mining Vicissitudes.

The oldest industry in this locality is that of lead mining, and it is known that some of the mines here were worked by the Romans, whose pigs of lead have been found. Pieces of ore have been found during the explorations of the military camp at Brough, doubtless from the Bradwell mines. It is asserted by ancient authors that the lead, tin and copper mines of Great Britain were known to the Belgians, Romans, Saxons, Danes. and Normans, who invaded the Kings of this Isle to rob them of their mineral possessions.

GROUP OF OLD LEAD MINERS.

Reading left to right—

Top Row—Wm. Bagshaw Ashmore, Robert Furness, jun., Isaac Elliott, George Ashmore, Charles Andrew, Thomas Morton, Elias Jeffrey.

Middle Row—Thomas Hallam, Isaac Evans, Isaac Hibbs, John Jackson, Joseph Jackson, John Morton, John Jennings, James Evans, Caleb Morton.

Bottom Row—Robert Bocking, Benjamin Morton, Robert Ashmore, John Howe (barmaster), Benjamin Barber, Robert How Ashton, Robert Furness, sen., Robert Evans, and William Jeffrey.

At Rake Head Mine, 45 years ago.

That the inhabitants of this isle were anciently very careful in defending and securing their mines is evident from the speech of King Canutus to his army when drawing them up against the Romans. He called upon his soldiers to defend his rich mines, which would be to show themselves Englishmen, truly valiant, tenacious of their rights, and inspired with a due sense of the price of their country and its productions.

A few mines were left by the Romans at the conquest of this isle, under the command of Julius Cæsar, whose descendants continued their work in the lead mines of the High Peak. The Kings of England were always jealous of the mines and minerals, several of whom, after the conquest, would not allow their mines to be worked. In 1246, Henry the Third executed a writ of inquiry at Ashbourne, when it was given for the King that the mines in the High Peak were the royal prerogative of the Crown, and not the property of those who had by long custom worked them, but he permitted the miners to proceed till further order, paying to him the thirteenth dish, cope and lot.

A volume could be written on the history of Peakland lead mining. At an inquisition taken at Ashbourne in the year 1288, one of the jury was " William, son of the smith of Bradwell." Their findings are highly interesting. A miner could, and still can, dig where he likes in search of lead ore (gardens, orchards, burial grounds, and highways excepted), and having found a vein he can call in the Barmaster and have staked out to him a meer of ground, sufficient to work and dress and prepare his ore and generally carry on his workings. And he can go to the nearest water and conduct it to his mine for use in dressing the ore, and can also make a road across anyone's land to the nearest highway for the purpose of conveying his ore from the mine. And the miners still govern themselves through their ancient Barmote Court, though many of their ancient laws have been very much modified. Formerly when convicted of stealing the ore of another miner he was fined the first and second times, but for the third offence he was taken to the top of the shaft where are the " stowses," a contrivance for winding the buckets of ore up the shaft, and a knife sent through the palm of his right hand up to the haft in the stowse, where he was left either to tear himself loose or die on the spot. And the miner could have as much timber as he chose for working his mine without paying for it.

Coroners had no jurisdiction whatever over the miner, and fatal accidents in the mine were inquired into by the Barmaster only, and a jury of miners themselves.

The Bradwell mines are in the King's Field, and formerly belonged mostly to the working miners and held in shares frequently very small, as 48ths, 96ths, and even 384ths and 768ths. The very smallest mines often had many partners concerned in them.

For hundreds of years lead mining was the principal employment of the inhabitants. Both men and boys worked therein, while women were employed on the surface dressing the ore. The whole district is completely undermined, and scores of shafts have been covered over, and their exact locale not now known. Veins of ore run east to west for miles and cross veins in all directions, as well as " pipe " mines. There are several main " rakes," such as Moss Rake, Hills Rake, Shuttle Rake, and Dirtlow, and among the mines that have been extensively worked for centuries on Moss Rake are Yeld, Mule Spinner, Butts, Outland Head, Windy, Bank Top, Hartle Dale, Sykes, Bennetts, Nether Cross, Upper Cross, Raddlepits, Rake Head, Hills Grove, Broctor, Providence, and New York. There were also Peveril, Dirtlow, Bird, Hazard, Holland Twine, Nunley, Smalldale Head, Picture End, Tanner's Venture, Virgin, Wet Rake, Moor Furlong, Cronstadt, Maiden Rake, Nall Hole, Chance, Gateside, Neverfear, Pack of Meal, Hungry Knoll, Dore, Bradwell Edge, Water Shaft, Palfrey's, Cobbler's, Frog Hole, Burrows, Eyre's, Ripper, God Speed, and many others.

Miners wages were always exceedingly low, and 15s. a week was the top price to the one who was foreman. Here is the exact copy of " A Reckoning at Naw Hole, ending May 15th, 1806." This was at " Nall Hole," at the top of Hill's Rake, in Hartle Dale.

" Jacob Maltby wages £3 5s. 0d., Robert Maltby £3 5s. 0d., Edwd. Bennett £3 10s. 0d., Godfrey Walker £3 0s. 0d., John Cheetham £1 12s. 8d., Pegy Maltby £1 2s. 0d., Betty Maltby £1 3s. 0d., Sarah Maltby £1 2s. 0d., Mary Palfrey £1 3s. 0d., Ann Walker £1 3s. 0d., drawing to Jacob Maltby 11½, drites £1 3s. 0d., driving to do. 5s. 9d., To Robert Maltby ax and spade shafts 5s. 6d., John Ellis' bill 4s. 2d., Thomas Somerset Bill 12s. 6d., for ale 8s. 9d., total £23 6s. 0d."

" Ore, 8 load, at £4 4s. 0d., comes to £33 12s. 0d. Calamy £4 2s. 0d., total £37 14s. 0d., profit £14 8s. 0d."

This was a five week's " reckoning," and from the accounts before us, extending over a period of three years at this small mine, it is plain that the men's wages varied from 10s. to 15s. per week, and the women 1s. per day.

But however low the wages, or small the quantity of ore raised, there was no diminution in the quantity of " ale " at the reckoning. The old lead miner is known to history as having loved good ale as well as good music, for

" On takin'-days when wit and ale were
    free,
He join'd the light duet and merry glee,
Sang such a powerful bass, the story goes,
As shook the optics on his ample nose."

And Philip Kinder in the preface to his intended History of Derbyshire, written about the middle of the seventeenth century, tells us that "They love their cards. The miners at Christmas tyme will carry ten or twenty pounds about them, game freely, return home again, all the year after good husbands."

Right away down for years, at every "reckoning" the item for ale is in evidence, varying anywhere from 4s. to 25s., and at one reckoning extending over a period of four months, the sum paid to "Richard Bennett for ale" was £5 4s. 0d. The host at the "White Hart" evidently had good times, judging from the patronage extended to him from Nall Hole, where not more than eight persons were employed, some of whom were women. Two of these men, both named George Maltby were killed at this mine. And at many of the larger mines where large numbers were employed, the workmen—and women too—were expected to buy a quantity of malt every pay day to brew their own beer at home.

We came across an item in 1780, "given men when rearing coes 2s." and "spent at Windmill 1s." There was formerly a public house at Windmill. The "coe" was a small building over the climbing shaft by which the miners descended the mine, and in which they divested themselves of their clothing for the ordinary attire of the miner. On every mine there was another and larger "coe" in which the ore was deposited when dressed, and on the 13th of May the miners used to dress their "coes" with oak branches, garlands, etc. The day was always kept as a general holiday, and a dinner of beef, pudding, and ale provided in the open air, music and singing at the inns concluding the carousals of the day.

Miners' Liberties and Customs in Rhyme.

In the year 1746 there was found in the office of the Duchy of Lancaster the following relating to "the Liberties and Customs of the Lead Mines within the Wapentake of Wirksworth, in the County of Derby, part thereof appearing by extracts from the bundles of the Exchequer, and inquisitions taken in the 16th year of the reign of King Edward the First, and in other kings' reigns, and continued ever since." "Composed in meter by Edward Manlove, Esq., heretofore steward of the Barghmoot Court, for the lead ines within the Wapentake. London. Printed Anno Dom. 1653." It should be remembered that this is exactly applicable to the "King's Field," of which the Bradwell district forms a part:—

By custom old in Wirksworth wapentake,
If any of this nation find a rake,
Or sign, leading to the same, may set,
In any ground, and there lead oar may get;
They may make crosses, holes, and set their stowes,
Sink shafts, build lodges, cottages, or coes;
But churches, houses, gardens, all are free
From this strange custom of the minery.

A cross and hole a good possession is
But for three days, and then the custom's this:
To set down stowes, timbered in all men's sight,
Then such possession stands for three week's right,
If that the stowes, bossinned, and well wrought
With yokings, sole-trees, else they stand for nought;
Or if a spindle wanting to be nick,
'Tis not possession, no not for a week,
But may be lost, and by another taken.
As any grove that's left, quit or forsaken;
For the Barghmaster (by the custom) ought
To walk the field to see that works be wrought,
And on the spindle ought to let a nick,
If that the grove unworked be three week,
According to the custom of the mines,
Then the Barghmaster may the stowes remove
And he that set them loseth the same grove;
Unless the work by water hindered be,
From losing any meer of ground or grove,
For then such stowes none ought to remove,
And the Barghmaster ought to make arrest,
Upon complaint, if mines be in contest,
Receiving four pound for his lawfull fee,
Or else by wind, the miner then is free
That the next court the wrong redressed may be.
The vulgar term is, setting for a mine,
For th' grace of God, and what I there can find,
And then at him some other miners take,
And gain possession in the selfsame rake;
Another miner for a cross-vein sets.
Some take at him, and then possession gets,
Some take for one thing, some for other free,
As new thing, old thing, cross-vein, tee, or pee;
But yet a difference may be taken clear,
Betwixt a founder and a taker meer,
Because the finder that do find a rake
May have two meers met, and set out by stake,
Which is in length twice eighty-seven feet.
And so is to be measured and laid out.
But first the finder his two meers must free
With oar there found for the Barghmaster's fee.
Which is one dish for one meer of the ground;
The other's free, because the miner found;
But by encroachment they do two demand
And wrong the miner which they might withstand;
Then one-half mere at either end is due,
And to the lord or farmers doth accrue:
And if two founders in one rake be set,
Perchance the farmers may a prime-gapp get.
To nick the miners' spindles that offend;
And when the spindle nicked is three times,
And every three weeks, until nine weeks' end,
Then must the miners chase the stole to 'h' stake,
From mere to mere, and one at other take:
Each taker gains a mere, no more he can
Have that finds oar in working an old man
And he (by custom) that his mine doth free.
A good estate thereby doth gain in fee
And if he die and leave behind a wife
The custom doth endow her for her life;
But if the grove be lost for want of stowes,
Or forfeited, her dower she doth lose.
By word of mouth eke any miner may
Such fee and freehold freely give away.
Egress and regress to the King's highway
The miners have, and lot and cope they may.

The thirteenth dish of oar within their mine,
To th' lord for lot they pay at measuring
time,
Sixpence a load for cope the lord demands.
And that is paid to the Barghmaster's hands.
Against good times the lord ought to provide
A lawful measure, equal for both sides,
Both for the buyer's and the seller's use,
And forfeits forty pence if he refuse;
And he that sells by any other dish,
His oar so sold thereby forfeited is;
Small parcels yet poor men may sell for need,
If they cannot procure the dish with speed;
Provided always that to church and lord
They pay all duties custom doth afford,
For which the vicar daily ought to pray
For all the miners that such duties pay,
And reason good, they venture lives full dear
In dangers great, the vicar's tythe comes
clear;
If miners lose their lives, or limbs, or
strength,
He loseth not, but looketh for a tenth;
But yet methinks if he a tenth part claim,
It ought to be but a tenth of clear gain,
For miners spend much money, pains and
time,
In sinking shafts before lead oar they find,
And one in ten scarce finds, and then to pay
One out of ten, poor miners would dismay;
But use them well, they are laborious men,
And work for you, you ought to pray for
them.
And suit for oar must be in Barghmoot
Court,
For justice thither miners must resort;
If they such suits in other courts commence,
They lose their due oar debt for such
offence,
And must pay costs, because they did
proceed
Against the custom; miners all take heed.
No man may sell his grove that's in contest,
Till suit be ended after the arrest;
The seller's grove is lost by such offence,
The buyer fined for such maintenance.
And two great courts of Barghmoot ought
to be,
In every year, upon the minery;
To punish miners that transgress the law,
To curb offenders and to keep in awe
Such as be cavers, or do rob men's coes,
Such as be pilferers, or do steal mens' stowes,
To order grovers, make them pay their part,
Join with their fellows, or their grove desert,
To fine such miners as men's groves abuse,
And such as orders to observe refuse;
Or work their meers beyond their length and
stake,
Or otherwise abuse the mine and rake,
Or set their stowes upon their neighbour's
ground,
Against the custom, or exceed their bound:
Or purchasers, that miners from their way
To their wash-troughs do either stop or stay;
Or dig or delve in any man's bing-place,
Or do his stowes throw off, break or reface:
To fine offenders that do break the peace,
Or shed men's blood, or any tumults raise,
Or weapons bear upon the mine or rake,
Or that possessions forcibly do take,
Or that disturb the court, the court may fine
For their contempt (by the custom of the
mine),
And likewise such as dispossessed be,
And yet set stowes against authority,
And open leave their shafts, or groves, or
holes,
By which men lose their cattle, sheep, or
foals;
And to lay pains, that grievance be
redressed,

To ease the burdens of poor men oppressed,
To swear Barghmasters, that they faithfully
Perform their duties on the minery;
And make arrest, and eke, impartially,
Impannell jurors, causes for to try,
And see that right be done from time to
time,
Both to the lord, and farmers, on the mine;
To swear a jury for a half year's time,
(By custom called) the body of the mine,
Who miners are, and custom understand,
And by the custom they have some
command:
They may view groves when miners do
complain:
Relieve the wronged, wrong-doers restrain,
They may view trespass done in any grove,
Value the trespasser, the trespassers remove
They may lay pains that workmanship be
made:
And fines impose if they be not obey'd.
They may cause opens, drifts, or sumps, to
see,
If anyone by other wronged be.
When strife doth rise in groves, the miners
all
These four and twenty miners use to call,
To make inquiry and to view the rake,
To plum and dial (if beyond the stake)
(A mere bewrought and miners wrongéd be),
For by that art they made discovery.
The steward ought a three weeks court
withal,
To keep at Wirksworth in the Barghmoot
Hall,
For hearing causes (after the arrests)
And doing right to them that be opprest.
And if the Barghmaster make an arrest,
The steward may (at the plaintiff's request)
Appoint a court for tryal on the rake,
Within ten days, that th' jury view may
take,
And for attendance there, the steward be
By mineral custom, hath a noble fee.
Four shillings to the jury must be paid,
Who for that cause were summoned and
array'd.
And if the verdict be for the plaintiff found,
The Barghmaster delivers him the ground;
And if the adverse party him resist,
The four and twenty ought him to assist,
Then may he work (by custom) without let,
Till the defendant do a verdict get.
Then the Barghmaster ought to do him right,
Him to restore unto his ancient plight;
But if three verdicts for the plaintiff's found,
By custom the defendants all are bound;
So if three verdicts with defendants go,
The plaintiffs are (by custom) bound also.
And neither side may make a new arrest,
For the same title that was in contest;
And yet the Duchy Court (if just cause be)
May yield relief against these verdicts three:
Or by injunction parties all injoin
From getting oar in such a meer or mine,
Unt 'l the cause be heard, and here appear
A title just for them that worked there,
Or may appoint a steward that may try
The cause again upon the minery,
Or may sequester any such lead-mine
Untill the title shall be tryd again.
And if the plaintiff chance non-suit to be,
He pays a noble for a penalty;
For which (by custom) Barghmasters dis-
train,
The party non-suited must pay the pain.
No miner's timber, pick, or lawfull stowes,
May be removed from their ground or coes;
If by mischance a miner damped be,
Or on the mine be slain by chance-medley,
The Barghmaster or else his deputie,
Must view the corpse before it buried be,

And take the inquest by Jury who shall try
By what mischance the miner there did die;
No coroner or escheator ought may do,
Nor of dead bodies may not take their view,
For stealing oar twice from the minery,
The thief that's taken fined twice shall be,
But the third time that he commits such
  theft,
Shall have a knife stuck through his hand to
  th' haft,
Into the stow, and there till death shall
  stand,
Or loose himself by cutting loose his hand;
And shall forswear the franchise of the mine,
And always lose his freedom from that time.
No miner ought of an old man to set
To seek a lead mine, or lead oar to get,
Untill the Barghmaster a view hath taken,
And find such work an old work quite
  forsaken;
With him two of the body of the mine
To take such view (by custom) ought to join;
Which being done the miner may go on
To sink and free his mere (the lord hath
  none)
If oar be found, the fruit of his desire,
And woughs he strete the miner then may
  fire,
Yet not at all times of his own accord,
But at such times as custom doth afford,
I' th' afternoon, and after four o'clock,
He may make fire on the ragged rock;
But first he must give notice, lest the smoke
(In other groves) his fellow miners choke;
And after notice if they careless be
And lose their lives, the firers shall go free.
If miners' groves arrested be, yet they
Go on and work, the arrest must make no
  stay,
But for oar got before the tryal be,
The Barghmaster must take security,
And at next court all parties do appear,
And the arrest must be returned there,
And then and there the cause must tryed be
Before the steward of the minery.
Most of the customs of the lead mines here
I have describ'd, as they are used there;
But many words of art you still may seek,
The miners' term are like to heathen Greek,
Both strange and uncouth, if you some would
  see,
Read these rough verses here compos'd by me.
Bunnings, polings, stemples, forks, and
  slyder.
Stoprice, yokings, soletrees, roath, and rider,
Water-holes, wind-holes, veins, coe-shafts,
  and woughs,
Main-rakes, cross-rakes, brown-henns,
  buddles, and soughs,
Breakoffs, and buckers, randum of the rake
Freeing, and chasing of the stole to th' stake.
Starting of oar, smelting, and driving drifts,
Primgaps, roof-works, flat-works, pipe-works,
  and shifts,
Cauke, spar, lid-stones, twitches, daulings,
  and pees,
Fell, bous, and knock-bark, forstid-oar and
  tees,
Bing-place, Barmoot Court, Barghmaster,
  and stowes,
Crosses, holes, hange-benches, turntree, and
  coes,
Founder-meers, taker-meers, lot, cope, and
  sump,
Stickings, and strings of oar, wash-oar, and
  pump,
Corfes, clivies, deads, meres, groves, rake-soil,
  the guage,
Bing-oar, a spindle, a lamp-turn, a fauge,
Fleaks, knockings, coestis, trunks, and sparks
  of oar,
Sole of the rake, smitham, and many more.

This have I written for the miner's sake,
That miners are in Wirksworth wappentake;
Perchance if these few lines accepted be,
An exposition may be made by me,
Of mineral terms, to most men now obstruse,
Which by expounding may be of more use;
But for the present I commit to view
This little book, the mineral law to shew;
Which ancient custom hath confirmed to
  them
That miners are, and poor laborious men,
And much desire this custom to present
Unto the worthies of the Parliament,
And humbly pray, that they for justice sake,
Will them confirm in Wirksworth wappen-
  take.
Good reader spare me if I thee offend
With this strange custom, which I have here
  penn'd;
But miner read me, take me for thy friend,
Stand to thy custom, thus my poems end.

A Precarious Occupation.

In 1830, before the passing of the Reform
Bill, there must have been a great deal of
poverty owing to the depression in lead-
mining, when the "Sun," an influential
paper published in London, wrote thus:
" A numerous and respectable meeting of
the inhabitants of the village of Bradwell,
held on Wednesday the 29th ult., for the
purpose of considering the best means of
administering relief to the suffering families in the neighbourhood, especially those
who are in indigent circumstances, in consequence of the low rate of wages afforded
to those employed in the above trades, who,
it is well known, cannot by the most difficult exertion earn more than three to four
shillings per week. It is impossible to
conceive the vast depth of misery which
exists. It appeared from the statements of
some of the speakers that many of these
poor sufferers had their children in bed
when visited, whose bedclothes had not a
vestige of either linen or flannel about
them, but was composed of wrappers and
old clothes; others had not a little of fire.
The respectable inhabitants of the village
and neighbourhood subscribed nearly £50,
which sums they are actively distributing
in coals, meats, and blankets. Several
resolutions were unanimously adopted, ap-
pointing a committee, and earnestly recom-
mending a subscription from all who could
afford it." The working miners gradually
abandoned the small workings, for they had
no capital to work in a scientific way and
put down machinery to cope with the
water, and the larger mines followed suit
when the low price of lead made them no
longer profitable.

But doubtless there is yet much more
ore in the bowels of the earth than has ever
been got out, and a rich harvest awaits
those capitalists who acquire the miles of
mines and work them on up-to-date
methods.

Calamine.

Calamine was formerly found in large
quantities in most of the Bradwell mines,
and was separated from the lead in the ordinary process of dressing the ore. It is an

ore of zinc, and was much used in the manufacture of brass, and was formerly raised in considerable quantities from the Nall Hole Mine.

Sulphur and Petroleum.

Sulphur has been found in layers, and in very great purity in the Virgin Mine, also on Tideswell Moor, and at the Odin Mine, Castleton. It is generally combined with lead, barytus, and fluor spar. Sulphur was formerly met with in the cellural parts of baroselenite, and also in galena. It was found in a layer four inches thick in the mines at Hazlebadge, Bradwell, and in a layer of one inch thick in the toadstone at Tideswell Moor. It was in a state of such purity in these places that it would flame with a candle. "Petroleum, or rock oil, was found in veins of the black marble at Ashford, and when the sun shone upon the stone it gently exuded. Stones containing a considerable quantity of rock oil were formerly met with near Stoney Middleton, and were so common that the miners used to burn the oil they produced in lamps."

Barytus.

From the lead mines barytus was raised in very large quantities, especially in the New York vein and in the Moor Furlong mines. Millions of tons of this mineral have been got. It is known as cauk, and was converted into a material which is used for many of the purposes for which white lead was formerly applied.

Fluor Spar.

This mineral has become exceedingly valuable during recent years, and as many of the Bradwell mines abound with it—yea, there are thousands of tons ready got in the mines, and left there by the miners of former days as refuse—these mines have been acquired by capitalists, who have sent large quantities of the mineral abroad. But it should be explained that in the mineral laws of the Peak only the lead ore belongs to the miner, every other mineral, cauk, spar, feigh, etc., being the property of the landowner.

Lead Smelting.

When the ore is dressed and sold it is conveyed to the smelting furnaces. The cupola furnace was introduced into Derbyshire nearly 200 years ago, and several of them were erected at Bradwell. One of these was at the bottom of the Dale, and was worked by Thomas Burgoyne, of Edensor, seventy years ago, and afterwards down to its closing by John Fairburn, of Sheffield. It was known as the "Slag Works," from the slag made by smelting. The only vestige of these once extensive works is the base of the once tall chimney, and the dilapidated old flues along which the poisonous fumes passed and deposited most of their poison before reaching the chimney.

There were other cupolas for the smelting of lead on Bradwell Hills, one where Overdale houses now stand, and the other, "th' owd cupola," on the site now occupied by Mr. Z. Walker's houses. Nearly a century ago these were worked by James Furness and Company, and Jeremy Royse, of Castleton. A fourth cupola was in the meadow below Edentree. It belonged to Messrs. John, Thomas, and Edward Middleton, three brothers, who were mineowners as well. The cupola has long been used as farm buildings.

Many elderly people remember that awful calamity on the night of the 19th of April, 1854, when there was a fearful catastrophe at the Slag Works. Two workmen, William Mitchell and Joseph Hallam, were suffocated by the poisonous fumes, and other two, highly respected young men of the village, John Edwy Darnley and Jonah Elliott, met with a similar fate by venturing too near the spot in their eagerness to lend a helping hand in the work of rescue

White Lead Making.

The importance of Bradwell as a centre of the lead industry may be gathered also by the fact that on this very spot the article is not only raised from the mines, but smelted into lead, and actually manufactured into the genuine article, white lead. The late Mr. Robert How Ashton, of Castleton, erected the works at Brough, or rather enlarged a disused cotton mill, about 1860, and there commenced the manufacture of white, grey, and red lead. Subsequently the works were extended by his son, Mr. R. H. Ashton, J.P., who built smelting mills and a refinery, and these industries are still carried on successfully by Colonel Joseph Hall Moore, J.P.

CHAPTER XIII.

Some Tragedies of the Lead Mines.

"By Death, who suddenly o'erwhelmed them there,
Where they themselves had digged a Sepulcher."

"Before our feet, a Corps digged up we see,
Which minds us what we are, or ought to be."

To compile anything like a complete list of tragedies of the lead mines in this part of the Peak district is an impossible task. Thousands of men and boys must have lost their lives in pursuit of this dangerous occupation. Formerly the Coroner had no jurisdiction over the fatalities in lead mines, the Barmaster being the coroner for such inquiries down to about sixty years ago. Every effort has been made to trace the old books of the Barmaster for this district without success. The appended list has been compiled from various sources, but it represents only a comparative few that must have occurred during the period covered. It will be seen that the cases are taken from mines not only in Bradwell, but in Castleton, Eyam, Hucklow, and other places in the locality.

1637—April 27th, William Grooves, Eyam, killed in a mine at Eyam.

1658—January 24th, John Syddall, Eyam, killed in a mine at Eyam.

1690—May 11th, John Daniel and Robert Berry, killed in a mine at Eyam.

1697—January 6th, Francis Gregory, killed in Eyam mine.

1699—June 30th, Edward Torre, Eyam, killed in mine.

1708—November 27th, Arthur Skidmore, killed in mine at Eyam.

1721—May 12th, George Knowles, Eyam, killed in Haycliff mine.

1732—June 23rd, Richard Turner, Foolow, killed at Stoke Sough.

1734—April 20th, Robert Andrew, killed at Middleton Pasture Mine.

1734—November 18th, Joseph Marsden and John Taylor, killed at Stoke Sough.

1734—September 20th, Richard Holmes, the Bridge, killed at Stoke Sough.

1734—February 28th, Benjamin Pidcock, killed in a mine at Eyam.

1736—Ottiwell Bramall, Castleton, killed in the mine.

1736—John Barber, junior, Castleton, killed in the mine.

1741—February 13th, John Barber, Richard Winterbotham, and Henry Merrill, killed in Haycliff Mine, Eyam.

1742—John Bennett, Castleton, killed in the mine.

1744—John Dakin, killed in a mine at Castleton.

1744—March 4th, Edward Cooper, Foolow, killed in a mine.

1746—November 5th, Wm. Townsend, Bretton, killed in Haycliff mine.

1746—Robert Allen, Castleton, killed in a mine.

1747—Godfrey Morton, killed in the mine.

1751—June 16th, Francis Mower, killed in Haycliff Mine, Eyam.

1763—October 15th, William Fox, killed in Show Engine, Eyam.

1766—Philip Hinch, killed in Shaw Engine Mine.

1773—December 19th, James Drabble, killed at Watergrove.

1777—February 14th, Wm. Hancock, killed in Watergrove Mine.

1778—December 21st, William Syddall, Eyam, drowned in Stoke Sough Mine.

1782—William Bradshaw, Castleton, drowned in a mine.

1782—Joseph Frost, Castleton, killed in the mine.

1784—John Nall, Castleton, died in the mine.

1786—William Cheetham, Bradwell, killed in a Moss Rake mine.

1790—James How, Castleton, killed in the mine.

1791—May 10th, Edward Dooley, killed in Haycliff Mine, Eyam.

1795, January 19th, Robert Unwin, Eyam, killed in Haycliff Mine.

1800 (about), Michael Walker, —. Bramwell, and —. Simpson, of Hucklow, killed in Twelve Meers Mine; J. Bennett, killed in New Engine; —. Fearest, killed at Stoke Sough; and —. Staley, killed in Twelve Meers.

1804—Samuel Heyward, killed at Water Grove, Eyam.

1805—George Benson, Eyam, killed in Pasture Grove, Eyam.

1805—Thomas Middleton, killed in Morewood Engine, Eyam.

1805—Robert Middleton, killed in Slater's Engine, Eyam.

1808—George Broadbent, Castleton, killed in Odin Mine.

1810—James Clayton, killed in a mine on Oxlow.

1811—Isaac Royse, Castleton, killed by lightning in a coe at the top of Linacre Mine.

1812—February 3rd, Humphrey Rowland, Eyam, killed in Black Hole Mine.

1827—George Maltby (64), killed in Nall Hole Mine, Bradwell.

1830—Francis Taylor, Tom J. Water, —. Longstone, and Isaac Bagshaw, Sheldon, suffocated with sulphur in Maypits Mine, Sheldon.

1830 (about)—Robert Elliott, killed in Southfield Mine, Bradwell.

1833—April 27th, Thomas Wildgoose (11) killed at a mine in Bradwell.

1833—July 11th, Joseph Middleton (28), killed in a mine at Bradwell.

1836 (about)—Benjamin Bennett, killed at Bennett's Mine, Bradwell.

1838—John Evans, Bradwell, killed in Hazard Mine.

1840 (about)—Benjamin Barber, Bradwell, killed in Town End Mine, Great Hucklow.

1840 (about)—Robert Maltby, killed at Syke's Mine, Bradwell.

1840 (about)—John Cheetham, killed at Red Rake Mine, Bradwell.

1841—Edwin Barber (23), killed in Bank Top Mine, Bradwell.

1841—September 2nd, George Maltby (45), killed in Nall Mine, Hartle Dale, Bradwell.

1842—Jacob Furness (10), killed by falling down a mine shaft in Wortley, Bradwell, whilst birdnesting.

1844—Samuel Wright (29), killed by a stone at Outland Head Mine, Bradwell.

1845—Henry Jackson (18), killed in Nether Liberty Mine, Great Hucklow.

1845 (about)—Thomas Middleton, killed in Raddlepits Mine, Bradwell.

1845 (about), Samuel Bradwell, of Bradwell, killed by falling down shaft at Water Grove.

1854—February 16th—Isaac Morton (21), killed by falling down shaft of Ripper Mine, Bradwell.

1854—April 19th, William Mitchell, Joseph Hallam, John Edwy Darnley (30), and Jonah Elliott (27), suffocated by sulphurous fumes at Slag Works, Dale End, Bradwell. This catastrophe caused great consternation in the place more than half a century ago. The pump engine not acting properly, William Mitchell, the manager, had occasion to let out air by opening a valve fixed on a stage that covered a well six feet six inches deep and five feet diameter. He went down by means of a ladder, but as he did not return Joseph Hallam went to his assistance, and he, too, remained in the pit. Men ran for assistance, and the first to arrive at the spot were John Edwy Darnley, a schoolmaster, who lived with his widowed mother at Dale End, and Jonah Elliott (also the son of a widow), who had only just returned from Australia. These two young men, whose names have been handed down as heroes, were returning from a prayer meeting at the Primitive Methodist Chapel. Elliott went down the pit regardless of danger, but on getting one of the men part way up the ladder he, too, was overpowered by the fumes, and let him go, while Darnley, who tried to save his friend, shared a similar fate, and all four men were suffocated in the pit. Mitchell left a widow and two children, Hallam a widow and four children, and the other two were unmarried.

1855—William Bagshaw, Hucklow, killed by falling down a mine.

1855—Benjamin Barber (39), Bradwell, killed in a mine.

1857—November 20th, Abraham Middleton (36), killed in Scrin Rake Mine, Bradwell.

1857 (about)—John Evans (8), when at play fell down shaft at Shuttle Rake Mine, Bradwell.

1857 (about)—Richard Andrew, killed at Bird Mine, Bradwell

1858—May 3rd, Abram Marshall (16), crushed to death by a grinder at a mine at Hazlebadge

1858—March 2nd, James Gilbert, Tideswell, killed at Dusty Pit Mine, Eyam.

1858—John Alsop, Wardlow, killed in Crosslow Head Mine.

1859—April 18th, John Barker, Foolow, killed in Back Dale Mine.

1859—Wm. Bradshaw, killed in Pippin Mine, Eyam.

1861—September 8th, Aaron Hallam (26), of Bradwell, and Martin Chapman, sen., of Little Hucklow, fell to the bottom of shaft whilst being lowered down at Mill Dam Mine, Great Hucklow.

1862—George Mitchell, killed in Calver Sough Mine.

1863—May 29th, Samuel Andrew (19), killed at Hill Top Mine.

1864—September 6th, Benjamin Barber (19), killed by a fall of gravel at Gateside Mine, Great Hucklow.

1864—John Dale, Tideswell, killed in Dusty Pits Mine.

1764—September 10th, William Wragg (15), killed at Outland Head Mine, Bradwell. He was drawn up the engine shaft by the thumb. When near the top his thumb came off, and he fell to the bottom.

1866.—October 3rd, Isaac Andrew, Bradwell, killed by a stone at Dirtlow Mine.

1867.—Benjamin Bagshaw, Bradwell (35), killed in Seedlow Mine.

1867.—William Oldfield, Hucklow, killed in Mill Dam Mine.

1868.—June 9th. Matthew Hodgkinson, shot in a mine at Magclough, Eyam.

1869.—Jan. 26th, Francis Hodgkinson (43), killed by a fall at Cliff-stile Mine, Eyam.

1870.—Thomas Elliott, Bradwell, killed in Seedlow Mine, Bradwell.

1870.—March 24th. Isaac Middleton (49), Smalldale, killed in "Co-op" Mine, Moss Rake, Bradwell.

1871.—February 24th. Isaac Middleton (43), Smalldale, killed in Shuttle Rake Mine, Bradwell.

1872.—April 5th, Robert Elliott and George Watson, killed by a shot in Glebe Mine, Eyam.

1874.—August 21st, William Unwin, killed in a mine at Eyam.

1877.—October 8th, George Ashmore (48), killed in Wortley Mine shaft, Bradwell, by bar of iron falling down shaft.

1882.—September 11th, Aaron Maltby (22), Bradwell, killed by fall of roof in Silence Mine, Hucklow.

1889.—July 20th, Joseph Middleton (51), hung himself in Outland Head Mine, Bradwell.

Rescued from a Living Tomb.

There have been many hairbreadth escapes from death in the lead mines, and some have been rescued from a living grave. One or two such cases may be noticed.

In the winter of 1815, John Frost, a young local preacher in the Wesleyan body, who was engaged in one of the mines at Hucklow, had a miraculous escape from a most perilous situation, in which he was involved by the falling in of the earth where he was at work. A scribe of that day remarks that "his voice was heard from beneath the ground in which he was entombed, and it was ascertained that his head and body remained unhurt, the principal weight having fallen upon and bruised his thighs and legs. Great care was required to accomplish his release, and some of the most experienced miners were employed. A mass of earth was strangely and almost miraculously suspended over his head, where it hung like an avalanche, ready at the slightest touch to crush him to pieces with its fall. The miners, aware that his situation was one of infinite peril, durst not attempt the attainment of their object by the most direct and expeditious means; slower operations were, in their opinion, essential, even though they dreaded the consequences that might attend their protracted efforts. Had that impetuosity of feeling, which, however honourable to our nature, sometimes defeats its most benevolent purposes, been alone consulted on this occasion, the poor man must inevitably have perished. They therefore proceeded with great caution and the most unwearied perseverance from Monday, the day when the accident took place, until the evening of the following Thursday, at which time they had the satisfaction of witnessing the complete success of their exertions, and the restoration of a fellow creature to his family and the world. The man was extricated from his dreadful situation with only a few slight bruises and a broken leg, after a temporary burial of upwards of seventy-five hours. A drop of water that fell near his head, which he contrived to catch in the bottom of his hand, allayed his thirst that otherwise would, probably, have become excessive; this fortunate occurrence, no doubt, contributed to the preservation of his existence. He was a Wesleyan Methodist, and his strong religious feeling supplied him with fortitude. Neither pain nor apprehension destroyed his composure, and he employed many of the hours of his premature interment in singing those psalms and hymns he was previously acquainted with. Under any circumstances this man would have been a hero." So runs the account of the premature burial of John Frost, who lived to be an old man, remained a local preacher to the end of his days, and is still remembered by many.

The hero of another memorable incident is still living. In 1879 Dennis Bagshaw, of Hucklow, was working with others in Black Engine Mine, on Eyam Edge, when the roof fell in. Bagshaw's workmates were on the engine shaft side, and could get out, but he was on the other side of the subsidence, and so was imprisoned in the workings from Monday morning until the following Sunday at noon. Miners from Bradwell, Tideswell, Hucklow, Eyam, and other places bravely worked in relays day and night, not lagging a single moment. At one time the work of rescue became dangerous owing to foul air, and the candles of the workmen would not burn, but ventilation in the mine was restored by the opening of a "gate." Some of the workmen were on duty continuously all the time, never changing their clothes, and having their food brought to the mine, and after nearly a week they opened the tomb of Dennis Bagshaw, completely exhausted, but living, having kept himself alive by sipping water that had dripped from the roof, having caught the drops in a cup which he made of clay. Dennis Bagshaw removed to Hayfield some time afterwards, and still lives there.

The Magpie Mine Tragedy.

About the year 1830 two lead mines were being worked at Sheldon, the "Magpie" and the "Maypits." For some time the owners of the two mines were "cutting things very fine" in their workings, and considerable animosity existed between them as to their limits. The Maypits lay to the south of the Magpie, and their borings were continued until the workings met or crossed, and at this stage a fearful tragedy was said to have been perpetrated by the Magpie party.

It was alleged that on the Magpie side—one of the Maypits men having "turned coat" and given them all the information they desired—straw, saturated with coal tar or impregnated with sulphur, was taken down the mine and placed at their boundary, then lighted, and the fumes driven into the Maypits workings during the time the miners were busy there. As may be supposed, whether the effects were intended to cause death or not, they did so. Three of the workmen, Francis Taylor and Tom J. Wager, of Longstone, and Isaac Bagshawe, of Sheldon, were overcome by the fumes and succumbed, about twenty others being rendered insensible and taken up for dead, but eventually were restored. Several of the Magpie men were arrested and tried at Derby for murder, but the whole were acquitted, the evidence being purely circumstantial, for, of course, the Magpie party declined to give any information that would tend to incriminate their associates.

Weaving.

Weaving of silk and cotton by the handloom process was extensively carried on more than a century ago. The block of buildings at the bottom of Water Lane now known as Brook Buildings, was formerly a silk mill worked by a Mr. Street, and a considerable number of hands were employed there. There were other small weaving establishments, and many of the cottages had their pairs of looms from 150 down to 80 years ago. Indeed, there was also a manufactory of weavers' shuttles, the Fox family carrying on this business. But the last of the weavers has long ago passed away.

Cotton Spinning.

For quite 200 years cotton spinning was carried on at various small mills in the locality. The most ancient of these, now a ruin, is the old "Bump Mill," by the brookside just below Edentree, which derived its name from the "bump," or coarse kind of cotton, which was manufactured there. This mill was working in the latter part of the 18th century, as appears from an Indenture of Assignment (in the possession of the author), in which James Hyde, cotton spinner, of Bradwall, on June 25th, 1798, assigned to Benjamin Barber, shopkeeper, and Wm. Palfreyman, shopkeeper, as trustees for the benefit of his creditors, all his "household goods and furniture, stock-in-trade, working tools, machines and implements of his trade or calling, goods, wares, merchandise, book debts," etc. The creditors were Messrs. Hugh and Isaac Hill, Benjamin Barber, Wm. Palfreyman, James Ramsden, and Catherine Dakin, and the witnesses to the deed were Thomas Morton, Joseph Barber, and Kitty Bocking. The mill then appears to have got into the hands of Hugh Hill, but it has been disused since the Hills gave up the business about 1830.

The next oldest cotton mill was the one which now forms part of the lead works at Brough. This was extensive. It was worked by Messrs. Pearson a century ago, and the same firm had two other mills, one at the bottom of Stretfield, now converted into farm buildings and a house for the farm bailiff, and the other what is known as the "New Mill," in Stretfield. The latter was in later years worked by the late Mr. Thomas Somerset.

The Hat Trade.

Another industry, now extinct, was the manufacture of felt hats, which was carried on for quite a hundred years. There were some half-dozen of these hatting shops on the Hills, and others in Smalldale.

As showing the importance of this industry nearly a century ago, it may be mentioned that in the year 1820 the following had manufactories of hats here: William Evans, James Evans, Robert Jackson, Charles Middleton, Joseph Middleton, Robert Middleton, George Middleton, and Obadiah Stafford. Twenty years later those carrying on the business were Job Middleton, Wm. Middleton, Robert Middleton, and Thomas Howe, but as these manufacturers retired or died, the trade gradually declined, the old hat shops were deserted, and all have long ago been demolished, and houses erected on the ground,

JOB MIDDLETON,
The last of many generations of Hatters.
Player of the "Serpent." Died 1899.

with one exception, that of the "shop" of the Evans family, which still stands at the bottom of Smalldale, a detached building of three storeys, now used as a warehouse.

Opticians.

Another industry of which the village could boast for many years was that of optician. The business was established about 1850 by the late Isaac Barber, and here, at the top of Smithy Hill, was the manufactory of telescopes, opera glasses, etc., where a number of young men served their apprenticeship. About 1862 another establishment was started by Evans Brothers (Stephen, Isaac, and Joshua), in Smalldale, in the building formerly the hat manufactory, and later still the late John Dakin carried on the business in the old Sunday School, now the Conservative Club. But this trade is now extinct.

Lime Burning.

A considerable trade in lime burning was carried on here more than a century ago. There were small lime kilns along one side of Bradwell Dale, and many in Smalldale. Some place names, as "Kiln Lane," denote the extensive trade formerly carried on in lime burning, and there are many disused quarries where the stone for burning was got. Here is a description of a night scene in Smalldale close on a century back. Rhodes, in his "Peak Scenery" (1818), and his friend Chantry, the famous sculptor, found themselves when darkness set in on the road overlooking Smalldale, and he writes thus:

"The burning of lime is here a considerable trade, and the kilns used for the purpose are situate at the bottom of the dell, one side of which was formed by the rocks where we stood; of the other, aided by a transient light emitted from the fires of the lime kilns, we caught occasionally an uncertain glimpse; all beneath was a gloomy vacuity, which the eye could not penetrate. The whole dale, indeed, was one immense cauldron steaming with smoke, that at intervals was partly illuminated by momentary gleams and flashes from the fires below —then curling into mid-air, it rolled over our heads in murky volumes, forming a canopy as dark as Erebus. The obscurity that pervaded this nocturnal scene, together with the short and feeble emanations of light shot from the kilns in the deep dale beneath, only made darkness more palpable, and powerfully assisted the impressions it produced. We stood to contemplate the picture before us until some heavy drops of rain and the hoarse murmurs of distant thunder warned us to depart."

Such was a night scene among the Bradwell lime kilns a hundred years ago.

CHAPTER XIV.

Some Ancient Customs and Superstitions.

Funeral Customs.

In common with other Peakland villages, Bradwell had its own funeral customs. People in very poor circumstances had what was known as "pay buryings," which meant that those who attended the funeral would be expected to pay something—generally a shilling or sixpence—towards defraying the expenses of the funeral. When the person went round to "bid to th' burying" he was generally asked whether it was to be a "pay burying." Many of the old inhabitants can well remember the custom, which has become obsolete within the last forty years.

"Burying-cakes"—a large round spice cake of excellent quality—used to be given, one to each person at the funeral, so large that it was tied in a handkerchief and carried home. That custom has given way to the biscuit and wine.

A century ago, when flour bread was the luxury of the well-to-do, the children of the poor tasted it only at funerals. In those days old Jacob Eyre, the baker in Nether Side, whose descendants in Bradwell are numerous, used to stand at the door of the deceased's home with a basketful of small pieces of white bread about two inches square. There would be quite a crowd of village children round the door to get a piece of the bread.

Formerly all the singers and music people in the place were invited to the funeral of an old resident, and the oldest of them used to chant a solemn dirge all the way to the cemetery, the rest of the company joining in the responses. For many years old Daniel Bocking, a well-known resident, was the leader on these solemn occasions. The last time this was done it was so impressive that those who were present will never forget it. It was at the funeral, in 1900, of Mr. Job Middleton, aged 85, a notable native, a leading Wesleyan, who sixty years before was a well-known performer at Sunday-school anniversaries in many of the surrounding villages, with a curious instrument called "The Serpent."

One ancient funeral custom still survives. In the Bradwell Oddfellows' Lodge there is what is known as "The Twelve." A dozen members are chosen every year to attend the funerals of members during the year. Attired in black sashes and white gloves, they walk in front of the coffin, and drop sprigs of thyme upon the coffin of their dead brother before they leave the graveside.

"Cucking" at Easter.

An Easter custom in which scores now living have taken part was that of "cucking." On Easter Monday morning girls who refused to kiss young men had to be cucked, or tossed up, and on Easter Tuesday the girls returned the compliment. But the practice was not only vulgar, but sometimes positively indecent, and very properly died a natural death.

Another Easter Monday, but confined to the children, was "Shaking," or "Shakking." Even this has almost "gone out." "Shakking" is a mixture of peppermints, Spanish juice, and other sweets placed in a bottle, which is filled with water from a well and then shaked up, and sipped by the children, the youngest of whom had the bottle fastened round their necks by a piece of string. There was a superstitious belief that unless the children put pins into a well on Palm Sunday they would break their bottles at Easter, and that the lady of the well would not let them have any clean water. There were many of these wells where children used to deposit their pins—behind Micklow, in a field called "Daniel's Garden," on the slope of Bradwell Edge; in Charlotte Lane; in New Road, leading up to the Bradwell Edge Road to Abney; and many others where children might be seen merrily trooping to deposit their pins. The writer remembers, when a child, with other children, depositing his pin in a well in New Road, and

finding whole handfuls of pins in the sand at the bottom of the well, the deposits of the village children for many generations. Nearly all these wells are now disused, filled up, and no longer exist.

Christmas Eve Mischief.

Many are the stories that could be related anent the old custom of doing mischief on Christmas Eve. It was formerly quite a common thing for gates to be lifted off their hinges, and with carts, barrows, etc., found in the brook next morning. On one occasion a wheel was taken off a cart at Hill Head, started off down Town Gate, and gaining in velocity all the way down the hill, it crashed into a grocer's shop at the bottom.

One Christmas Eve a number of young men were bringing a cart down Smalldale, and taking it to the brook, when they were met by a farmer named Wright, who was eager to join in the mischief. He did so, and assisted them with the cart until, when about to pitch it into the brook, he found out that it was his own cart. "How'd on, chaps, it's mine!" he shouted, but the cart went into the water all the same.

But the custom was attended with loss of cattle and sheep through gates being removed, and damage to property, that after the advent of the police it gradually fell off, and is now observed only to a very small extent as compared with former days.

A much pleasanter Christmas Eve custom was the giving of a candle, called a "Yule candle," by the shopkeepers to their customers, and a "Yule log" by the carpenters to the children who fetched it. And with the candle burning on the table, and the log on the fire on the cold Christmas Eve, the family would sit round the table joining in the big mug of "posset," made of hot ale and milk, spiced with sugar and nutmeg. But the Yule log and the candle are no more, though some of the older inhabitants cling to the posset.

An Old Wedding Custom.

Down to within a few years ago it was the custom to exact toll from wedding parties before they would allow them to get married. The method was to stretch a rope across the road to prevent them passing to church or chapel, and not to allow the bride and bridegroom to pass until the latter had paid toll. Often the church or chapel gates were fastened while the ceremony was going on, and only unfastened when the toll was paid. The money was generally spent at the nearest public-house.

The "Lumb Boggart."

"Woman and fish, so strangely blent in one, So fables tell, and so old legends run. Now on the wave greeting the newborn day; Now on the velvet bank in sportive play; And when prevailed the part of woman fair, Into long flowing locks it curled its hair,

Breathes the swift zephyrs as they gently rise,
And its fair bosom heaves with human sighs:
But when the fish prevails beneath the tides,
Like lightning it a scaly monster glides;
And in its wat'ry cavern must remain
Till Easter Sunday morning comes again."

Redfern, Hayfield.

Like all other mountain villages, Bradwell has its superstitions, and they would not be complete without the ghost story. Many a time have we crouched and run past "The Lumb," on a dark night, and oftener still has the hair on many heads stood straight when passing "Lumbly Pool," between Brough and Bamford.

It used to be said that about a century and a half ago the body of a young girl, who was supposed to have been murdered was found buried under the staircase of a house at Hill Head. The ghost of the girl appeared every night until everybody in the neighbourhood were terrified and thrown into a cold sweat. Unable to bear it any longer the people got a well known individual who belonged to the Baptists, then called "the new-fangled body," to undertake the task of "laying" the ghost. As this individual professed to be able to rule the planets, of course no one doubted his power of getting rid of the ghost.

The time came, and the haunted house was filled with affrighted spectators when the exorcist appeared among them with his paraphernalia, and when he prayed until streams of sweat poured from his face as he knelt within a ring he had chalked on the chamber floor, the lookers-on kneeling around, and later afterwards declared that they "felt the floor move for yards up and down in quick succession." Then the magician arose and exclaimed, "Arise! arise! I charge and command thee," when the spirit appeared, and the man ordered it to depart and assume the body of a fish, and to locate itself in the Lumb Mouth. He also ordered that every Christmas eve the ghost should assume the form of a white ousel, and fly to Lumbly Pool.

Such is the story of the "Lumb Boggart," an absurd tale which everybody believed even down to half a century ago.

The Lady on Horseback.

It would never do for the romantic Bradwell Dale, the dell of the fairies, with such an ancient hall as that of the Vernons at Hazlebadge to be without its ghost story, hence we are told that, "On any wild night, when the winds howl furiously and the rain falls in torrents, there can be seen in the gorge between Bradwell and Hazlebadge the spirit of a lady on horseback, the steed rushing madly in the direction of the old Hall. They say it is the ghost of Margaret Vernon, the last of that line of the Vernons who were living at Hazlebadge for three centuries. She had given her heart, with its fulness of affection, into the keeping of one who had plighted his troth with another, and when she discovered his treachery she had braced up her nerves to witness his union in Hope Church. But at the finish of the ceremony she had ridden to her home as if pursued by fiends, with eyeballs starting from their sockets, and her brain seized with a fever from which she would never have recovered only from the tender nursing of those around her. Her spirit, they say, on a spectre steed, still rushes madly between Hope and Hazlebadge at midnight."

Well Dressing and Garland Day.

Bradwell had formerly its Garland Day and Well Dressing, as also had Hope. The garland was similar to that at Castleton, a man riding round the village with a huge garland of flowers on his head, the band heading a procession, and dancing taking place in the Town Gate. On the same day was the well dressing, several wells, notably the one with a pump affixed, in Water Lane, opposite the Shoulder of Mutton, being beautifully decorated with flowers. But the custom has been discontinued nearly half a century.

Bull Baiting.

"The wisdom of our ancestors
(A well known fact I'm stating),
Thought Bulls and Bears, as well as Hooks
Were suitable for baiting.
But now this most degenerate age
Destroys half our resources—
We've nothing but our hooks to bait,
Unless we bait our horses."

Ward.

Bull and bear baiting were very popular in Derbyshire at one time, and Bradwell Wakes never passed without one or the other of them, often both. The villagers, or those who delighted in such a brutal sport, gathered in some open space, either the Town Gate or the Town Bottom, where the bull was tied to a post securely fixed in a stone let into the ground. At a given signal dogs were let loose on the bull, and betting was made on the dogs, the one that could pin the bull by the nose being declared the winner. The dogs were trained to avoid the bull's rushes, but now and then he would toss the animal into the air.

There have been some strange scenes at Town Bottom during these baitings. Sometimes the bull would break loose, when the spectators would take to their heels helter skelter for their life to elude him. But one of the most exciting scenes was witnessed at one of these bull baitings, about the year 1820. There was the bull, the dogs, and the crown, but no post. Among the spectators was old Frank Bagshaw, of Hazlebadge, who stepped into the breach, and runing into the ring cried "Tey him to mev; tey him to mev." They tied the bull by the tail to poor Bagshaw, and when the dogs were set at the brute it darted off, dragging Bagshaw at its tail up Bradwell Brook—a deplorable spectacle. Fortunately this cruel amusement has long been a thing of the past.

CHAPTER XV.

" Yes, I will leave my father's halls,
To roam along with thee;
Adieu, adieu, my native walls!
To other scenes I flee."

Families of the Past.

Although many of the oldest families remain, having tenaciously clung to the homes of their forefathers, a few have completely disappeared, among them being those mentioned below :

In a previous chapter those voted from Bradwell at the election of 1734 were mentioned. But we have been favoured with an extract from the Poll Book of the Election at Derby on the 11th, 12th, and 13th December, 1701, when the candidates were the Right Hon. William, Marquis of Hartington, Right Hon. Lord John Roos, John Curzon, Esq., and Thomas Coke, Esq. The following electors from " Bradwall " voted :

At the Crown Barr, Thursday, 11th December, George Trickett voted for Hartington and Roos.

At the Nisi Prius Barr, same day, Robert Balguy, Edmund Greaves, and Ellis Middleton voted for Curzon and Coke.

At the Town Hall, 12 December, there voted from " Bradwall " the following : Thomas Hallam, Thomas Toft, and Ellis Slack voted for Hartington and Roos; Godfrey Webster, Godfrey Kirk, and Joseph Ward for Curzon and Coke; and Ellis Middleton for Roos and Coke.

The total number of voters in the county who polled at this election was 3057, and the candidates polled as follows : Coke 1659, Curzon 1581 elected, Hartington 1562, Roos 1289.

Cresswell.

A history of this once notable family would be highly interesting. Their seat was at " The Old Hall," at Smalldale Head, a fine old house that ought not to be allowed to suffer any further disfigurement. This spacious hall, now in two tenements, has over its main entrance " I. H. 1670," so that it is clear the Cresswells did not build it. But it was not long their seat for they did not live here a century. The lands above were allotted to them when the Commons were enclosed, hence their name " Cresswell Part." The splendid fences round the gardens, and some of the fine old yew trees still remain. It is said that the carriage drive to the Hall was from Granby, along what is now known as " Boggart Lane," and forward through the lands (since enclosed) to the Hall. There are still distinct traces of the drive. The Rev.

Jacob Cresswell was vicar of Hope 200 years ago, and Thomas Cresswell, of the old Hall was a churchwarden in 1789. It is said the last of the Cresswell's to reside at the Hall, a famous sportsman, was killed whilst hunting.

The Cresswells were an ancient Derbyshire family from Malcalf, Chapel-en-le-Frith, and Ralph Cresswell bought lands in Edale in 1630. Thomas Cresswell, of Blakelow, Edale, afterwards of Smalldale Hall, yeoman, was baptised on the 27th of March, 1726, and died on the 12th August, 1808, and was buried at Hope. He married Betty, daughter and heriess of Mr. Oliver, and niece of Daniel Roe, of the Hall, Smalldale, at Hope Church, on the 12th July, 1749, and she died on May 17th, 1801. From this short pedigree it will be seen that the heiress of these brought the estate to the Cresswells.

Trickett.

The Tricketts were a family of wealth and influence here and in other parts of the Peak for many generations, but they have long ago completely disappeared, and no one knows where their Bradwell residence was. But they had land and residence in other places. One of their old homes was in Smalldale. In 1599 Mark Trickett had a tax levied upon his land for imperial purpose, and in 1658 Henry Trickett resided at the old home and occupied the lands of his ancestors. A member of the next generation, George Trickett, was a churchwarden of Hope, in 1690. A George Trickett was the owner of the Smalldale estate in 1701 and 1734, and went to Derby to record his vote. The Trickett lands have long passed into other hands.

Greaves.

The Greaves family, long ago extant so far as Bradwell is concerned, has left its name as a place name in the village. They were a family of influence, position, and substance, and although no trace of their old homestead remains, we have the well known " Greaves Croft," a portion of their estate through which a public footpath runs. Edmund Greaves was here in 1701 and voted at Derby in that year. John Greaves was the owner of the family estate at the beginning of the 18th century, for he voted at Derby in 1734, and in the same year was a churchwarden for Hope. The importance of this family may be gathered from the fact that their vaults are inside Hope Church, and beneath their tombstones in the central aisle lie many generations of the family.

Padley.

The ancient family of Padley held lands here for several centuries, but they have long ago disappeared. In 1448 Thomas Padley and Rose, his wife, sold some of their property, but several members of the family were here more than 200 years later, for in 1658 there was Adam Padley, two Thomas Padleys, and the widow of a Thomas Padley, all holding lands in Bradwell.

Wagstaff.

One branch of this old Glossop family appears to have long been settled at Bradwell, and were considerable landowners here. Their estate was at "Wortley Fold," near the Bridge, at the bottom of Church Street. That John Wagstaff was one of the leading lights centuries back may be imagined from the fact that he was one

Worsley.

Certainly far more than two hundred years the family of Worsley were settled here, and for more than a century it was a family of considerable property and some influence. When this ancient family first settled here is not known, but George Worsley was a landowner, farming his own lands in the year 1658, when his "Easter due" to the vicar of Hope was one of the largest in the parish. And nearly a century later—in 1734—Richard Worsley was owner of the lands. The family appear to

THE OLD HALL, SMALLDALE,
For long the residence of the family of Oliver.

who, in 1685, dared to proceed against the great Eyre, of Highlow, which resulted in his having to give up certain lands belonging to the Bradwell Commons, which he had enclosed. The last of the family of which we have any record, is another John Wagstaff, in 1774, then late of Glossop, farmer, who sold "a messuage in Bradwell, a parcel of land thereunto belonging, one other messuage and one croft called Whortley Yard, in Bradwall, another messuage there, and a little building in Bradwall aforesaid, and a barn called the Cock Barn, and the several hereditaments subject to a life estate therein of Oliver Wagstaff."

have fallen on evil days, for the last of the Worsleys is remembered to have been in humble circumstances.

Oliver.

For many years the family of Oliver resided at the Old Hall, in Smalldale. They were people of substance, and strong Churchmen, but the members of the family were not numerous. In 1744 "Mr. Oliver, of Smalldale," and William Oliver too, were churchwardens of Hope, an office which in those days was held only by prominent people. More than thirty years later Samuel Oliver was one of the wardens, but these are the only records we have of the family, other than that the heiress took the estate to the Creswells.

Millward.

A family of ancient lineage and substance was that of Millward. Nearly seven hundred years ago, to be exact, in the year 1284, Richard Millward de Bradwall, with other notabilities of those times, were proceeded against for breaking the forest laws. That they held lands here for several centuries is proved by the fact that in 1599 John Millward and Robert Millward were defendants in an action brought against them by Rowland and Jarvis Eyre, some of the properties, etc., in dispute being the demesne of Bradwall, fishing of the river, and lott and cope of the lead mines. They were still here in 1658, when Richard Millward paid Easter dues to the parson of Hope, but the name is afterwards lost. It would be interesting to know whether the family had any connections with the famous Millwards of Snitterton Hall. We suspect they were, as their shield contains the heraldic quarterings of the families of Savage of Hope, Balguy of Hope, and Daniel of Tideswell.

Pearson.

The Pearsons were an old family. In the eighteenth century they were in business as cotton spinners with the Arkwright family, at Cromford, when the Preston banker, afterwards Sir Richard Arkwright, was laying the foundation of the family's fortunes. From Cromford they removed to Brough, where they erected three cotton mills, one of which was afterwards converted into white lead works, another transformed into farm buildings and a house for the farm bailiff, at the bottom of Stretfield Road, and the third was the large mill between Bradwell and Brough. These three mills were kept running by the family for over half a century, during which time they were the largest employers of labour in the district. They built and resided at Brough House, and were owners of considerable property in the neighbourhood. But they must not be confounded with the still older family of Pearson, many of whom still remain.

In the 12th year of the reign of Elizabeth (1570), there was a great case in which the plaintiffs were Robert Pereson and Anthony Marshall, tenants of the Town of Bradwell, and the defendants were John Marshall and William Smythe, claiming by conveyance from Thurstran Townsende as seized in fee. The premises and matters in dispute were "divers specified lands, parcel of the waste of the Manor of Castleton, particularly Smaldale and Edwentrie, and Lands in Bradwall Field."

Pickford.

The old family of Pickford has long ago been forgotten by those who remain on the soil. They were landowners and residents here centuries ago, and became famous folks in the world. Few are there who know that their old home was here. They were a family of substance and importance, and Philemon Pickford was a churchwarden of Hope, in 1715. He voted as a freeholder of Bradwell at the Parliamentary election of 1734, and died in 1749. Thomas Pickford, probably his son, was a churchwarden in 1753.

Other Families that have Disappeared.

Other old families of note that have long ago removed are those of Hamilton, Charlesworth, and others mentioned in various parts of this work.

The Dudden or Goodwin Family.
An Interesting Romance.

One of the most ancient families is that of Goodwin. It may not be generally known to this generation that Goodwin (locally pronounced "Guddin") is merely a corruption of the name "Dudden" or "Dudding." The Duddens will be seen throughout this work in various capacities, down to about the middle of the eighteenth century, when the name is spelt "Goodwin." They were prominent people here at least three hundred years ago. In the year 1658, George Doodin, Thomas Doodin, and the widow of John Doodin, all paid Easter dues to the vicar of Hope, and in 1638 among the inhabitants of Bradwell between 16 and 60 years of age were John Dudden, George Dudden, and Thomas Dudden. Thomas Dudden was the owner of a freehold estate in Bradwell in 1734, and voted at Derby at the election of members of Parliament for the county. And so late as 1782 Samuel Duding was one of those liable to be called upon to serve in the Militia. A member of this family was connected with what may be described as one of the most interesting romances of modern times, and revealed a claim to the earldom and estate forty years ago.

This, indeed, is a highly interesting romance, contained in the documents put forward at that time. In these it was stated that:

The Honourable Charlotte Radcliffe, eldest daughter of Charlotte Maria, Countess of Newburgh, and Charles Radclyffe, Earl of Derwentwater, was born in France in 1729. In the year 1743, when a girl of fourteen, she was brought to Scotland by Sir Archibald Primrose, a Jacobite confederate of her father in the cause of the Prince Charles Edward, and placed with Mrs. Murray, of Perth, a relation of James Murray, the Prince's secretary, with whom she resided till 1747, suffering in consequence of her father's attainder and ignominious death.

It is at this time that the Bradwell lad comes on the scene, for on the second of April, 1747, the Hon. Charlotte Radcliffe, when 18 years of age, was married in Scotland, it is said at the house of Mrs. Murray, to George Goodwin (or Dudding), who descended from an old Derbyshire family, and was a native of Bradwell, in the parish of Hope. This marriage at Perth was solemnised in accordance with Scotch law.

Here the trouble began. George Goodwin was a Protestant, and his wife a Catholic, but they were devoted to each other, and so they journeyed over to England, landed at Bradwell, and on the 25th of the same month, it is said, that the marriage was again solemnised according to the rites of the Church of England, at Hope Church, by the Rev. Thomas Wormald, who was vicar of Hope at that time.

The course of true love did not run smooth, and so the aristocratic young bride, having married a Protestant, became alienated from her family, and was anathematised. The couple made their home at Bradwell, where the husband's ancestors had lived for generations, and there in a cottage in Hugh Lane, dwelt those who had contracted a wedding under such romantic circumstances.

But tragedy followed comedy. On the 14th of February, 1749, they had born to them a son—her only child. This son was named George, after the father. But Goodwin lived only eight years after his child was born, for he died in the year 1757. As often follows such marriages, differences arose as to the religious training of the child, and at the father's death the child was adopted by its uncle, who resided in Bradwell, the mother returning to Lisle in France, where she re-entered the Roman Catholic Church, and lived at Lisle, "suffering great mental and pecuniary distress," until 1790 when she removed to London, where she died on March 11th, 1800. She lived under her maiden name.

But what about the child—the Hon. George Goodwin? As time goes on the story grows in interest. His uncle Birley was his Protestant guardian. The father had desired that his son should be brought up in the Protestant faith, and therefore the mother, under the influence of the guardian, had not been allowed to interfere with the religious training of her son, who was received into and brought up in his uncle's family. When a young man he went Barnsley way, and at the age of 27 married Margaret Senior, of Dodworth, but he had to fight the battle of life "in obscurity and poverty," and when three score years and ten. George Goodwin and his wife entered the Shrewsbury Almshouses at Sheffield, where he died in 1835 at the age of eighty six.

Thereon hangs a tale that has often been told, in which the registers of Hope Church are concerned, for it being alleged that certain entries therein were tampered with a century ago. The Bishop of Lichfield held a Court of Inquiry into the matter in the year 1870. Evidence was heard at great length, and here is the affidavit of the Parish Clerk of that day, or rather that portion of it relating to the romantic wedding, omitting all reference to the registers:

The Parish Clerk's Recollections.

1. I, Nathan Woodroofe Ashton, of Hope, in the County of Derby, deceased, make oath and say that I am the sexton of the parish of Hope aforesaid; and that I am the grandson of Nathan Woodroofe, the parish clerk of the said parish of Hope, deceased; and that I was brought up with my said grandfather and lived in his house until I was about seven years of age, when I went to live with my said father, and lived with him until he died in 1837, when I again went and lived with my grandfather, the said Nathan Woodroofe, again, I being then nearly 13 years old, and I lived with him till October, 1844, I being then over twenty years old.

2. And I further say that I first heard, in February, 1838, about the marriage of George Goodwin, of Bradwell, and Lady Charlotte Radclyffe (the daughter of the Earl of Derwentwater) when my grandfather, the said Nathan Woodroofe, and William Evans, of Smalldale, deceased, were talking about it at my said grandfather's public-house, and were wondering if the Goodwin family would ever get anything from the Radclyffe family; and that whilst my grandfather and William Evans were talking about the said marriage and the families, Thomas Elliott, of Eden Tree, deceased, came into my said grandfather's house to order a grave to be made for his father, and the same subject was talked over again, and thereupon the said Thomas Elliott told my said grandfather that the said George Goodwin and Charlotte (formerly Radclyffe) his wife, lived at Bradwell in a house in Hugh Lane; and I declare that I know that such talk as aforesaid took place in the month of February, 1838, because it was at the end of a long and very severe frost, and just after my said grandfather and I had to dig a grave in the cross-roads for Thomas Bagshawe, of Hazlebadge, who had hung himself, and we found great difficulty in digging the grave on account of the frost having struck upwards of a foot into the ground; and I further say that my said grandfather frequently afterwards during his life told me of the said marriage of the said George Goodwin and Charlotte Radclyffe, the daughter of the Earl of Derwentwater.

3. And I further say that up to some years after eighteen hundred there is only one book for the entry of the register of baptisms, deaths, and marriages for the said parish of Hope. And I further say that my said grandfather, Nathan Woodroofe, was parish clerk from about the year 1798 until the time of his death in 1855, and that the said Nathan Woodroofe

had access to the registers from the time he commenced clerking, which was in March, 1798 (when his father, who was parish clerk up to the time of his death, died), until the death of the Rev. John Ibbotson, the vicar, which took place in December, 1828, as is shown by the entries of baptisms, deaths, and marriages, in the said registers made in my grandfather's handwriting; and that after that time the said Nathan Woodroofe, my said grandfather, had the sole charge of the said registers until May, 1843, when they were taken possession of by the Rev. W. C. B. Cave, the then new vicar; and I say that the said registers were generally kept in an old oak chest in the church, but if any person wanted to see them the said Nathan Woodroofe would often fetch them to his own house and get what was required from the said book of registers there while sitting over their glasses, the parish clerk's house being a public-house. And I further say that I have seen the said book of parish registers lying on the table in the parlour of my said grandfather's public-house for weeks and months together, in fact, until it was taken back into the church, so that any person who went into the room might have access to them. And I say that I often stayed away from Church on Sunday afternoons to look at the said book of registers, to find out how old different people were whom I knew.

* * * * *

4. And I further say that from what I have heard from my said grandfather and others talking about the said George Goodwin and Charlotte his wife (formerly Lady Charlotte Radclyffe, the daughter of the Earl of Derwentwater), I firmly believe that they, the said George and Charlotte Goodwin, were man and wife.

5. And I say that I have always heard, and I believe, that George Goodwin, the son of the said George and Lady Charlotte Goodwin, lived with his relatives at Bradwell village, in the parish of Hope, in the County of Derby aforesaid, from the time of his father's death till he was old enough to go to work for himself, when he went to and settled at Sheffield.

Such is a romance of the Duddens.

CHAPTER XVI.

Bradwell's Benefactors.

The parish has not many charities, but those bequests it does enjoy have been left by natives of the place, other than the charity of Gisborne, which was common to a hundred Derbyshire parishes.

Outram's Charity.

The Outram family were settled in Bradwell several hundred years ago, and their burials are recorded in Hope Church registers. It is recorded on a board in Hope Church that "Mr. Artram" left to the poor of Bradwall 12s. to be paid every St. Thomas' Day. The family had extensive possessions at Grindleford, where they were settled for centuries, and still remain. It would seem as if the money came from that district, for in the account book of the overseers of the Lordship of Stoke, near Grindleford, for the years 1794 and 95, we have the item—"Paid to the poor of Bradda 7s. 6d." The charity is still distributed.

THOMAS MIDDLETON. Nearly two centuries have gone by since Thomas Middleton died in 1729. He owned a field called the Bank Close, in the meadow on the road to Hope, and left a rent charge of five shillings a year to be paid out of it for ever to the poor of his native place. And it is paid yet.

An Old Weaver's Bequest.

THOMAS MIDDLETON. He was one of the old weavers when most of the cottages contained hand looms, and he was son of the above, and came into possession of his father's land. When he died in 1786 he followed in the footsteps of his father, and doubled the rent charge on Bank Close, and the 10s. is paid to the poor to this day.

Thomas Hallam's Charity.

THOMAS HALLAM, by will 1729, gave to the poor of Bradwell half an acre of land in a place called the Moor Hall, for ever, the rents thereof to be distributed to poor widows and fatherless children on St. Thomas' Day. George Barnsley, who for many years occupied this land at the rent of 12s. 6d., sold it about the year 1806 as his own property, subject to the above rent for the poor. About 1811 an allotment of seven perches on Bradwell Edge was awarded in respect of it, the whole of which was formerly let for £2 17s. per annum. A Commission of Inquiry reported that he had no title to the premises, and that the charity was entitled to the land, with the allotment set out in respect of it. The owner, at the time of the inquiry about 1830, paid 12s. 6d. to the overseer, who distributed it on St. Thomas' Day.

A Friend to Poor Children.

ELIAS MARSHALL, a churchwarden of Hope in 1759. This worthy, who died in 1765, gave a piece of land beneath the Long Meadow causeway, containing half an acre: another parcel of enclosed land in the town furlong, with a barnstead at the east end, upon trust, out of the rents, to cause five of the poorest children in Bradwell to read. The property now consists of a close called the Molly Pingle, in Town Lane, containing 2r. 34p., and an allotment set out at the enclosure of 1r. 22p. in the Butts. Another small allotment, too trifling to enclose, was sold for £5. The land lets for £3 per annum, and since the abolition of school fees the trustees of the charity have divided the money between the Council School and the Church School for the purchase of prizes for the scholars.

Mary Hall's Charity.

MARY HALL, by will 1762, bequeathed to poor widows and fatherless children of Bradwell 15s. yearly, to be paid on St. Thomas' Day by her executor, George Barnsley, chargeable on a piece of land called "The Moor Law." By an agreement with the overseers dated 16th December, 1799, the said George Barnsley gave to the poor of Bradwell two cottage houses on Bradwell Hills, each of them let at the rent of 18s. a year, on the payment of £5 to the said George Barnsley, and 15s. yearly on St. Thomas' Day. When the Charity Commissioners held an inquiry about 1830, the overseers of the township were in possession of the cottages, and the yearly sum of 15s. was paid out of the poor rates and distributed according to the donor's intention.

It would appear that George Barnsley was grandson of the lady who left this charity—at least such may be surmised from the inscription on an ancient but very handsome tombstone near the Bradwell entrance to Hope churchyard, as follows:

"Godfrey Hall, died September the 26th, 1755, aged 78. Also Mary, his wife, died May the 11th, 1762, aged 77."

> " Their lives exemplar were,
> In death to heaven resigned.
> May all survivors keep with care
> Eternity in mind."

"George Barnsley, of Hasslebadge, died the 3rd day of February, 1825, aged 82 years."

"Also Mary, his wife, died the 25th of November, 1810, aged 67 years."

We have the will of Mrs. Mary Hall. It reads:—

"In the Name of God. Amen.

" I Mary Hall of Bradwall, in the Parish of Hope, in the County of Darby, Widow and Executrix of Godfrey Hall, late of Bradwall, aforesaid, being Sick and Weak in Body, but of Sound Mind and Memory (Blessed be God for his Mercies), do hereby make, and Ordain this my Last Will and Testament, in Manner and form following: (That is to say) first and principally I commend my Soul into the Hands of Almighty God who gave it, and my Body to the earth to be decently Interred, at the discretion of my Executor herein after Named. And as touching my worldly Estate, I give and dispose thereof as followeth. Imprimis I will that all my just Depts, funeral expenses and Probat of this my last Will and Testament be Paid out of my Personal Estate; then I give, devise, and bequeath all my Real and Personal Estate whatsoever, to my Grandson George Barnsley, he paying such legacies as shall be herein after mentioned: viz., first I give and bequeath to my Granddaughter Mary the Wife of William Steeple of Aldwark and her Heirs the Sum of Seventy Pounds of Good and lawful Money of great Britain to paid in twelve Months after my decease: Item, I give and bequeath to my Granddaughter Catherine Barnsley and her Heirs the Sum of Seventy Pound of Good and lawful Money, of Great Britain to Paid likewise in twelve Months. Item, I give and bequeath to Elizabeth Barnsley the Sum of Seventy Pounds of Good and lawfull Money of great Britain, to paid to her when She attains to the Age of twenty one Years, or to her Heirs or Assigns:

Item, I give and bequeath to Joshua the Son of John Barnsley late of Aldwark Grange, the Sum of forty Pounds, of good and lawfull Money of great Britain to be paid to him when he comes to the age of twenty one Years, if he so long live. Item, I give and bequeath to my Godson Martin Middleton the sum of five Pound, of good and lawful Money of great Britain, to be Paid in twelve Months after my decease.

Item, I give and bequeath to the Poor Widows or Fatherless Children of the Town of Bradwall the Sum of fifteen Shillings Yearly, to be paid out of the Rents and Profits of a certain Piece of land Moorlow Torr, and distributed by the overseer and Principal Inhabitants on St. Thomas Day for ever.

Item, I will that whatever Charge or Loss shall attend getting or receiving a certain Sum of Money due to me upon Bond from John Barnsley his Executors, Admrs. or Assigns: the aforesaid George Catherine and Elizabeth Barnsley shall Bear or pay out of their fore mentioned Legacies each an equal share: Lastly I do hereby Nominate and apoint George Barnsley Sole Executor of this my Last Will and Testament, and I do hereby revoke all former Will and Wills made by me at any time heretofore: In Witness whereof I have hereunto set my Hand and Seal this fifth Day of May, in the Year of our Lord one Thousand Seven Hundred and Sixty Two.

MARY HALL, her X mark.

Signed, Sealed, Published, and Declared by the within Named Mary Hall as and for her Last Will and Testament. in the presence of us who have hereunto Subscribed our names as witness to the Same,

THOMAS FANSHAW,
ROBT. HILL,
MARGRET MIDDLETON."

The charity is paid to the poor out of Moorlow Torr.

Built a School House for Poor Children.

JOHN BIRLEY was an old worthy of the early days of the last century, and a member of an old Presbyterian family. He was a Baptist, and owned the land on which the chapel was built. It was he who built the first day school. It stood on the lower side of the Baptist Chapel, and here the "free scholars" were taught by a schoolmistress who received the rent from Marshall's Charity land. But after the Baptists left and John Birley died the school fell into decay, and it was pulled down about 1864.

Endowed and Buried in the Old Chapel.

William Evans' name will be handed down to posterity as having endowed the old chapel of the Apostle of the Peak. A man of considerable means, derived from the business of hat making, he resided in

Samuel Fox.
Bradwell Lad's Distinguished Career.
A World-Wide Celebrity.

One of Bradwell's most distinguished sons was Samuel Fox, the founder of the extensive works at Stocksbridge, in Yorkshire, who died in February, 1887. This lad, born of humble parents, attained not merely local, but a world-wide reputation. He was the son of William Fox, a weaver's shuttle maker, who carried on his humble avocation and lived in a cottage in Water Lane. He was born in June, 1815, and served part

Cottage in Water Lane (now Church Street) where Samuel Fox was born.
This is one of the most interesting cottages in Derbyshire.

Smalldale, and at his death in 1844, at the age of 72, he left certain lands the rents of which were to be paid to the preacher at the Old Chapel. He is buried inside the chapel at the foot of the pulpit, and at the funeral there was a remarkable incident. There was a crowd round the open grave while the funeral service was going on, and a lady was accidentally pushed into the grave from which she was with difficulty extricated. The accident caused quite a sensation among the crowd. On his monument inside the chapel is the passage "He being dead yet speaketh."

of his apprenticeship to the wire trade at Hathersage and the remainder near Sheffield. Being an exceedingly sharp lad, he allowed no opportunity for advancement to escape him, and on attaining manhood commenced business on his own account in an old mill in a secluded valley with but few houses in the neighbourhood. For some years his operations were on a limited scale, but his energy and perseverance soon told, and one development succeeded another with such rapidity that his workmen were soon to be numbered by hundreds, and afterwards by thousands. This big concern was converted into a limited company, with Samuel Fox as chairman and managing director, and the name of this Bradwell lad is known the world over as the inventor of Fox's Paragon Umbrellas."

A humorous scribe once wrote: "I should say that Mr. Fox had the Peak to thank for. some of his commercial success. He was born in the Peak. There the rain-clouds are always gathering. What more natural than that Mr. Fox should turn his attention to umbrellas? He was not one of the umbrella-making chiefs of Thibet,

THE LATE SAMUEL FOX.
Inventor of the Umbrella Frame, a native of Bradwell and benefactor of the place.

but he was the umbrella-making chief of the world—he was the world's friend, for his paragon frames have and do still shield people of all nations from the wet. They have served other useful purposes too—they have stopped mad bulls, beat dogs, and thrashed erring husbands; and an old Quakeress had such faith in them that, when one of her servants was emigrating, she gave the girl one of Fox's paragon frame umbrellas and a pair of thick boots, saying 'Now, Martha, if thou must emi-grate thou had better take these. Cling to thy umbrella. It will be a comfort to thee when it's wet, and when it's dry thou may want it to drive off some man.' "

With the anxiety attendant on the management of one of the biggest manufac-turing concerns in England, Mr. Fox al-ways took a kindly interest in his native place, and assisted many of the natives to good positions in life. A more hardworking couple than Mr. and Mrs. Fox in their early days it would be impossible to find.

He was a frequent visitor to his native place, took interest in most things con-nected with it, and for many years he regularly sent large sums of money which were expended at midwinter in household requisites for the poor. These charities were sent anonymously, and it was only a few years before his death the actual donor, though long suspected, became known to the people. In many ways he exhibited his attachment to the village un-der the shadow of the hills where he first saw the light, and at last bequeathed £1,000, the interest to be given to the poor of Bradwell for ever.

There are many memorials of several generations of the family in their old burial place at Hope, one of which this famous man erected to the memory of his parents. He also erected a memorial to his sister, Mrs. Adam Hill, in the Bradwell Wesleyan Cemetery. His only son, William Henry Fox, Esq., J.P., D.L., of Bradwell Grove, Oxfordshire, was High Sheriff of that county in 1883-4.

Benefactor and Benefactress.

Horatio Bradwell was a worthy son of the oldest family. He was one of three brothers —John, Edwin, and Horatio, sons of George Bradwell—who were all in business as grocers in Sheffield at one time. He took considerable interest in the lead mines of his native place, and invested a great deal of money in undertakings without much recompense. Mr. Bradwell died on the 5th of July, 1887, and his will proved that he never forgot the place of his nativity. He gave his wife a life interest in his property, and at her death bequeathed certain charitable legacies. He bequeathed £500 to the National Lifeboat Institution, as a donation towards the cost of building a lifeboat, with its necessary house, boat fittings, carriage, and rocket apparatus, to be named "Ann Fox," and fixed on the coast between Lynn in Norfolk, and Berwick-on-Tweed. A legacy of £150 he gave to each of the following institutions: Sheffield Public Hospital, Sheffield General Infirmary, Jessop Hospital for Women, and the Totley Orphanage, with these con-ditions to the gifts—That each of these in-stitutions should give to a committee repre-senting the village of Bradwell, and con-sisting of the vicar for the time being, the Wesleyan minister and the Primitive Methodist minister for the time being, and of four parishioners to be appointed at the annual vestry meeting to be held at Brad-well, a certain number of tickets of ad-mission to each of the before-mentioned in-stitutions, corresponding to the annual value of the sum of £150, such tickets to be distributed by the committee as they may think fit; and if any of those institutions refuse to accept the legacy under the conditions named, such legacy was to fall in the residue of the estate. Among other legacies were £50 to the Redhill Sunday School, Sheffield, £200 to the Wesleyan Foreign Missionary Society, and £50 to the Wesleyan Worn-out Ministers' Fund.

Ann Bradwell, widow of the above gentleman, who survived him many years, also

place are to be found in every quarter of the globe. It is impossible in this twentieth century to locate the ancient home or homes of the family, but in all probability they formerly were seated at a mansion or large hall just at the entrance to the town of Brough, where a large block of buildings now used as farm buildings, still occupy the site. And the road here is to this day known as "Hall Gate," and the fields about as "Hall Gate Fields," and the large plot of table land immediately adjoining the

REV. JOSEPH HIBBS.   REV. GEO. BIRLEY.

remembered her native place. She bequeathed £600 on mortgage to found "The Anne Fox Memorial Sick Poor Nursing Society for Bradwell." She also bequeathed the following sums: Sheffield Royal Hospital £250, Sheffield Royal Infirmary £250, Children's Hospital £250, and Jessop's Hospital for Women £250.

CHAPTER XVII.

ANCIENT FAMILIES AND NOTABLE PEOPLE.

It goes without saying that the family of Bradwell is the most ancient on the soil. They took their name from the place itself, and they are as numerous as ever to day, while the sons and daughters of the old

buildings is called "Beggar Pleck," or Place, a spot where the wayfaring poor waited for charity at the gates of the Hall. Rowland Eyre was assessed for "Nether Hall" in 1709. Nether Side is the name of the road leading from the old Hall. There have been many distinguished sons and daughters of the old families, concerning whom a volume might be written, but brief notices of some, in alphabetical order, must suffice, in addition to the references throughout this work.

DISTINGUISHED SONS AND DAUGHTERS
As Clergymen and Ministers.

Bradwell has contributed to the ranks of the Clergy and Ministers of various denominations. The following may be mentioned:

The Rev. Thomas Middleton, clergyman, was witness to a deed in 1766.

JOSEPH HIBBS.

The Rev. Joseph Hibbs, who was born here on February 8th, 1801, joined the Primitive Methodists when they first commenced services in a barn in 1821. When he was only 22 years of age he was employed as a hired local preacher in his native circuit, entered the ministry in 1829, and in 1867 was superannuated after an active ministry of 38 years. The greater part of his ministerial life was spent in South Wales, and he was often spoken of as "The Bishop of South Wales." For 14 years he was a supernumerary minister, and died in December, 1881, at the age of eighty.

JOHN HALLAM.

Rev. John Hallam, Primitive Methodist minister. From a lead miner he entered the ministry, being one of the pioneer preachers, and associated with the famous Hugh Bourne. He was engaged a great deal at the Connexional Book Room in London, and was called upon to preach in all parts of the country in the early days of the movement. He was a victim to overwork and came to his native place to die at the early age of 44. His death took place on September 18th, 1845, and he was buried inside the walls of the chapel, which was then in course of erection, underneath where the pulpit was to be placed.

GEORGE BIRLEY.

The Rev. George Birley. He entered the Wesleyan Ministry in 1812, became one of the best known ministers in the Connexion, and died about 1870.

JACOB MORTON.

Rev. Jacob Morton, a well known Wesleyan Minister, and was a Fellow of the Royal Astronomical Society. He was distinguished by Christian sympathy and sincerity, possessed of a vigorous mind, familiar with a wide range of theological and general study, and was an earnest and successful preacher. He entered the ministry in 1840, and died at Exeter in 1873.

JOHN MORTON.

Rev. John Morton, another brother, entered the Primitive Methodist ministry, and had a distinguished career. He was an author of several popular works. He died at West Bromwich in 1862.

RALPH BENJAMIN SOMERSET.

The eldest son of Benjamin Somerset. He was born in 1834. He became Fellow of

Trinity College, Cambridge, took his B.A. Degree in 1857, was wrangler, and 2nd Class Classical Tripos, took his M.A. degree in 1860, became Dean of his College, and first censor of non collegiate students in that University from 1869 to 1881. He died in 1891.

ADAM MORTON.

Rev. Adam Morton (living), a well known Primitive Methodist minister, a popular preacher, well known throughout the Connexion. Son of the late Thomas Morton, lead miner.

REV. GEORGE MIDDLETON.

REV. JOSEPH MIDDLETON.

On the north wall of the Chancel there is a splendid tablet to the memory of this gentleman, surmounted with a bust, in bas-relief, of the deceased. In deep black letters there is the inscription :—" In memory of the Reverend Ralph Benjamin Somerset, M.A., son of Benjamin and Fanny Somerset, of this place; Fellow and Dean of Trinity College Cambridge; First Censor of Non-Collegiate students in that University; honoured and beloved. The righteous shall be had in everlasting remembrance. Born February 20, 1834; died March 23, 1891."

GEORGE MIDDLETON.

Rev. George Middleton, one of the most distinguished of Bradwell lads, as a boy worked in the lead mines, but when a young man he became a local preacher among the Primitive Methodists, entered the itinerancy and became a regular minister. He became one of the most famous men in the denomination, gave up circuit work and was appointed Governor of Bourne College, Birmingham, which post he held down to his death in 1908, at the age of 77.

ROBERT MIDDLETON.

Rev. Robert Middleton was a nephew of the Revs. George and Joseph Middleton.

He was for half a century a Primitive Methodist minister, but when a young man was a lead miner. He died in 1901, and lies in the Primitive Methodist burial ground.

EDWARD TOWNSON CHURTON
(living).

From being curate at Bradwell when preaching service was held in the old schoolroom, before the church was built, had a distinguished career in the church. In the year 1896 the Right Rev. Edward Townson Churton became Bishop of Nassau. He is a prolific writer on ecclesiastical subjects, and the author of a number of works, including "First Island Missionary of the Bahamas," "The Missionary's Foundation of Christian Doctrine," "Retreat Addresses," "The Sanctuary of Missions," "Foreign Missions," and "The Use of Penitence." He married a daughter of the Rev. C. J. Daniel, Vicar of Hope, and the lady died when on the voyage out to Nassau.

JOHN C. BOCKING.

Rev. John Child Bocking (living), Vicar of Gnosall, Staffordshire, to which living he was preferred in 1906. He was educated at St. Peter's College, Cambridge, took his B.A. degree in 1889, and was ordained deacon the following year. He is a surrogate of Lichfield diocese, and formerly held curacies at Tipton and Fenton.

POETS AND MINSTRELS.
JOHN E. BRADWELL.

John Edwy Bradwell. The son of a miner, and himself a miner in his early days. He has long been a prominent personage in the friendly society world, and is editor of the magazine of the Sheffield Equalised Independent Druids. He is the writer of a number of poems of considerable merit, including "A Coronation Ode," which was dedicated to King Edward and Queen Alexandra. A copy of the Ode was sent to Queen Alexandra, which she graciously accepted, and sent a letter of thanks to the author.

ADAM HILL COOPER.
A Witty Rhymster of Half a Century Ago.
Interesting Local Ditties.

One who was famous as a poet in the middle of the last century was Adam Hill Cooper, who was a son of Samuel Cooper. This gentleman had five sons, all of whom bore scriptural names—Adam, Job, Benjamin, Elias, and Jabez. Adam was a born rhymster. He was manager of Mr. Ashton's white lead works, at Brough, and died in 1879. His ditties would fill a volume, but they were never issued to the world in that form. They were, mainly, humorous rhymes on local men and things, just a few of which will be interesting to the present generation. But he produced pieces other than humorous. One of his first productions about 1860, was dedicated to his infant son, who, however, died young. Here it is:

Dear little stranger thou art come,
Not knowing where, nor yet to whom;
But still thou art a welcome guest,
With such a prize I feel I'm blest—
　　My little son.

Thy home is not a stately hall,
With servants to attend each call;
'Mid parks and shrubberies sublime,
But yet it stands unstained with crime—
　　My little son.

Our best endeavour we will try
Thy little comforts to supply;
When we divide our humble fare
It's sweets and bitters thou must share—
　　My little son.

I love to see those coral lips
As from its father's cup it sips;
Thou little sprightly busy bee,
Pray, who could harm a lamb like thee?—
　　My little son.

May thou be spared and learn to grow
In knowledge, and true wisdom know;
And never cause they parents shame,
But be an honour to their name—
　　My little son.

Those dimpled cheeks and sparkling eyes
They make a father realise
Pleasures that never can be got
In mansion nor in humble cot—
　　My little son.

That manly arm, that chubby fist,
That doubled chin, that wrinkled wrist,
Those mottled limbs that glow with health,
Are treasured more than earthly wealth—
　　My little son.

Those little pegs are peeping out,
That little tongue, it rolls about,
It cannot yet articulate,
Though it must guide thy future state—
　　My little son.

About the same time Mr. Cooper's pen produced the following on

MAN.

Man! what art thou? I meekly ask,
Reveal thyself to me;
Hard labour seems an endless task
Allotted unto thee.

I'm bone and sinew, born of earth,
Composed of living clay;
With breath infused, there starts my birth,
At least the scriptures say.

I'm very old and cannot give
To you my exact age;
The eve I began to live
Stands a disputed page.

The changes that you daily see,
Display my busy hand;
I must continue faithfully,
I'm not allowed to stand.

Each morning brings a special task
That tries both wit and skill,
Which to avoid I must not ask,
But willingly fulfil.

Stern competition creeps behind,
And keeps me on the move,
And gently whispers to the mind
"Continually improve."

What difficulties I have wrought
With wire, and steam, and rails,
The new inventions I have wrought,
Throughout the world prevails.

The scythe, the sickle, and the flail.
I've left them by the way;
They find their power of slight avail
While steam and engine play.

Proud Theodore did little know,
When he refused my claims,
That to his country I should go
And snap his monstrous chains.

The heights of Magdala to me,
My freedom to defend,
Was thought too big a job to be
Successful in the end.

The heathen now may plainly see
Through our Creator's plan;
It's hard to say what cannot be
Performed by thinking man.

THE LATE ADAM HILL COOPER.

But those of greatest local interest were
his humorous ditties. These were legion,
and in them he hit off local characters admirably, regardless of offence either to
friend or foe. Here is his poetical description showing how the people of the Peak
celebrated the wedding of the Prince of
Wales (afterwards King Edward VII.), in
1863 :—

The folks in large towns have long cut it
fine,
Telling all country villages that they'd take
the shine,
But the men in the Peak have true English
blood,

And thought opposition would perhaps do
good.
So the clergy, the gentry, and farmers
combined
Their gold in abundance some pleasure to
find;
Old veterans were there with their tottering
hand,
Seated side by side with the lords of the
land,
Tho' appearance denoted their race almost
run
They drank health to our Queen and her
newly-married son.
Young maidens were dancing in ribbon so
gay
And all seemed to enjoy the memorable
day.
Hathersage people, regardless of cost,
Determined their loyalty should not be lost;
Miss Bamford, their neighbour, seemed
rather dejected,
For more wanted dinners than what she
expected.
Hope is a village without any trade,
Though tea and spice buns for the children
were made.
The Castleton people were happily blest,
For they could not get through without a
night's rest.
At Bramall's, in Smalldale, we now take a
glance,
Where youth is engaged in a country dance,
One hundred and twenty were seated at tea,
And all seemed as happy as happy can be.
O'er Granby to Bradwell we now must
adjourn,
And see the great bonfire brilliantly burn,
Sack racing, and jumping, and all sorts of
fun,
Besides Mr. Elliott with his Armstrong gun;
The Wesleyans and Primitives by this had
shook hands,
Were parading the town with both Bradwell
bands,
Thus showing the world that in friendship
they meet
After giving their scholars an excellent
treat,
The conclusion presented a beautiful scene,
For teachers and scholars sang " God Save
the Queen."

THE FREE RANGERS.

One Sunday night in 1868 three young men
from Bamford visited the Rose and Crown
Inn, a public house—now cottages—at the
top of Smithy Hill, Bradwell. After
patronising the landlord, Anthony Middleton, they left at closing time, groped by the
wall in the dark, until reaching the corner
of the building at the top of the Gutter, the
first of the trio, John Robinson, for many
years the mechanic at Bamford Mills, fell
over a low wall into a heap of manure below. The incident was admirably hit off by
Cooper in these lines :—

On a late Sunday night,
Just after daylight,
There came into Bradwell three strangers;
To mention a name
I should be much to blame,
So I think I will call them free-rangers.

Some beer did they want,
So they went up to " Tant,"
At a house called the Rose and the Crown;
To have just a sup
They went right enough up,
The misfortune was as they came down.

They reel'd to and fro,
As they did not well know
The guides of the place in the dark;
It was too rough a street
For to stand on their feet.
And to fall would be more than a lark.

They groped for the wall,
For fear they might fall,
And one of them started to grumble;
For want of the moon
He turned rather too soon,
And into a dirt hole did tumble.

What a pity he fell
For he caused such a smell,
As he rolled himself o'er on his back;
And his face and his shirt
Were both covered with dirt,
In what a sad plight was poor Jack.

I am told in the end
That he met with a friend,
Who assisted him with an immersion;
He emphatically says
He will see longer days
Before he's another excursion.

At this time Bradwell Church was being
built, and one of the contractors, a Sheffield gentleman, wished to visit the gritstone quarries at Eyam, but not knowing
the way he took Charles Gledhill, one of
the workmen, with him as his guide. Their
experiences were hit off in this ditty :—

A JOURNEY TO EYAM AND BACK.

On Saturday last,
A tradesman was fast
To find his way over to Eyam;
O'er hedges and stiles,
About seven miles,
Required considerable steam.

One Charles he employed
To act as his guide.
The rest of his name I'll keep back;
It's the very same man,
Find him out if you can,
Who laughed at the fall of poor Jack.

After two hours chase
They got to the place
Where at first they intended to go;
They measured some stone,
Then turned towards home
And agreed they should dine at Foolow.

They did not go far
After passing the bar,
Before they turned in to their right,
At a house kept by Jerry
They made themselves merry
With something that baffled their sight.

Now, whiskey's a thing
That should make a chap sing,
But Charles would do nought but take snuff;
Sometimes he would talk,
But he would not walk,
So the tradesman became rather gruff.

"I engaged you to-day
To show me the way,
If we're lost it may cost me my life;"
"Don't be in a sweat,
There is time enough yet,
We must shake hands with Jer. and his
    wife."

I am sorry to say
They turned the wrong way,
So the tradesman politely enquires;
What gave him a shock,
It was past ten o'clock
When they landed at Wardlow Mines.

With uplifted hands
He implicitly stands,
And wished he'd never been born;
They both out of breath,
Almost frightened to death
Got to Bradwell at two the next morn.

"THE GOOSE FROM CALLOW,"

told its own tale. It was about half a
century ago. The goose was procured from
Callow Farm, near Hathersage, and cooked
at the Green Dragon Inn, at that time
kept by Michael and Ann Hall. The license
has long since lapsed. Here is the lively
ditty :—

Dear reader, it is by request
That I enclose this simple jest;
To tell the truth I'll do my best,
    About a goose at Callow.

One person said he dare be bound
This goose would weigh full fifteen pound;
He'd warrant it both fat and sound,
    Because it came from Callow.

This person could not make a sale,
For very few believed his tale;
His mates, to have a drop of ale,
    Raffled the goose from Callow.

When we the public-house did reach,
It cost all five shillings each,
And many a very wicked speech,
    Did this goose that came from Callow.

To make all previous matters right,
We had it cooked for Monday night;
This caused a very funny sight
    While plucking the goose from Callow.

There was Mike, and Ann, and Harry, too;
Joe "Bradda" pulled his fingers through;
Like snowflakes down and feathers flew
    As they plucked this goose from Callow.

Six pounds was just the weight of it!
Six hours it hung upon the spit;
But all the coal from Staveley pit
    Would not cook this goose from Callow.

Both cook and stoker in despair,
Exhausted sat upon a chair;
It proved a serious affair
    To cook a goose from Callow.

At last the cloth and plates came in,
We got the signal to begin,
And Mike cried out, "Now lads, walk in,
    And eat this goose from Callow."

We all tried hard to pick his bones,
But might as well have tried at stones;
So off we toddled to our homes,
    And left the goose from Callow.

In the sixties the Bradwell Moss Rake
Mining Company was formed on the co-
operative principle, to drive a level and
open out the mines, but after some years
of unprofitable working the project was
abandoned. But here is

"AN ODE,"

written by Cooper in encouragement:

Ye sons of toil, allow a friend
    To make an observation,
And my opinion I will spend
    About Co-operation.

To benefit the working-class
    The project was begun,
But many years of toil must pass
    Before the work is done.

What gives an impulse to a cause?
  Intelligent directors,
Not men that's looking for applause;
  Such are not your protectors.

'Twas time the miners made a move,
  Turned over some new leaf;
Co-operation it may prove
  A permanent relief.

To get an honest livelihood,
  No doubt was their ambition,
But this could never be achieved
  Without an alteration.

Month after month they used their tools
  At jobs that never paid;
For want of some established rules
  It's been a wretched trade.

But men of patience hey must find,
  And perseverance too,
To guide the prejudiced and blind
  And lead the project through.

The men who care for others well
  Must stimulate the scheme,
Who for their fellow men can feel.
  Without regard to fame.

The men who have their cash to wear,
  And never seem to doubt it.
But cheerfully support their share
  And think no more about it.

The moment you the treasure find,
  Your shares begin to rise;
Don't follow every change of wind,
  Stick firmly to your prize.

Encouragement may seem but small
  And things appear perplexed,
But never let a single call
  On your part be neglected.

Your ancestors have often said
  That there was lead in store;
If there could be a level made
  That you'd get lots of ore.

Then work like men as you've begun,
  May no one e'er repent,
And let what ever may be done,
  Be done with good intent.

Cooper was no respector of persons. He had a dig at everybody he thought deserved it. Here is one :—

TO HIS INDIGENT COBBLER.

I sent you my order to Sparrow pit,
Expecting good boots and a capital fit;
You said you would send them in course of
  a week,
A pair well adapted for Derbyshire Peak
After such a firm promise I'm filled with
  surprise
To think you should send me such thunder-
  ing lies,
I need not remind you—you know it quite
  well
That liars must all have their portion in
  hell.
I cannot imagine you waiting of leather
And other odd matters to put them
  together,
Such as wax, or hemp, or any such stuff,
And the order I'm sure you've had that
  long enough,
Do you mean to make them? I fancy you
  don't,
Then —— it write back and tell me you
  won't.

Cooper's butcher shared the same fate as his cobbler, for here is his

SHANK STEAKS.

I wish the country all to know,
In Bradwell we are not so slow;
A cow was killed for Hucklow wakes,
The shanks were pared and sold for steaks.
There's no deception in this case,
The trick was done before my face.
Now, had he cut them off the round,
And charged a market price per pound,
I'd then adopt the proper plan.
And pay the butcher like a man.
But steaks from shanks are " all my eye;"
No cook on earth can make them fry,
They are both tasteless, dry, and tough,
For such there's no demand at Brough.

Cooper was at a loss to know how a total abstainer could be such an inveterate smoker, and after a wordy warfare with some of these, this is how he lectured and exposed them in rhyme :—

TO AN ABSTAINER FROM DRINK, BUT AN INVETERATE SMOKER.

Lights of the world without a doubt
They never ought to be put out,
And certainly I look upon
A temperance advocate as one,
Why not annihilate the pipe
If for improvements they are ripe,
And benefit their fellow men
By all the legal means they can?
But don't presume to be a light
Except your lamp be burning bright,
Free from tobacco smoke and snuff,
And all such superfluous stuff,
For if by taking snuff or smoking,
The atmosphere is almost choking,
Such lights as those pray never handle,
They are not worth a farthing candle.
Give up the pipe, and not till then
Can they set up as model men.

The following is the last piece composed by this local celebrity, on the occasion of the occasion of the renovation of the Primitive Methodist Chapel, in 1878 :—

THE BRADWELL CONVERT.

Ye followers of the firm old faith,
Come, hear what *Billy Longden saith
About the chapel in Hugh Lane,
Which lately hath been born again.
The inner part hath been renewed,
Re-organised and nicely pewed,
With alterations here and there,
And one additional gallery stair.
The heart hath undergone a change,
So wonderful and passing strange;
The system of the inner man
Is formed upon the gospel plan.
The outer man, the entire frame,
(Except the vestry) is the same,
And to complete the whole attire
There stands a chimney for a spire.
Now, chapels, they like man's estate,
Grow old and sadly out of date,
And this was charged with many crimes,
And ill adapted to the times.
Anterior to this changing state,
The structure was degenerate
In all its aspects, out and in.
Conceived in error, formed in sin

*William Longden, familiarly known as Billy Longden, was the chapel keeper.

The under bearings ill arranged,
The upper gearings quite deranged,
The organ too, did rant and roar
In a corner on the floor.
The music of the sacred lyre
Was sadly mangled by the choir,
The ventilation and the light
Were never altogether right,
The air was dense, the place was dull,
And, should the chapel chance be full,
How frequently it's been my lot
To gasp for breath when reeking hot.
The windows, I'm ashamed to own,
Were seldom opened up or down;
And further more confess I must,
The seats were covered o'er with dust.
At times there was a brimstone smell,
From whence it came I dare not tell,
But then, you see, as I've asserted,
The chapel then was not converted,
And all their evils were, of course,
The outcome of an evil source.
Long it withstood the Gospel blast,
But *Mr. Smith arrived at last,
Who, by his faith and great exertion
Became the means of its conversion.
From hidden treasures manifold
He gathered silver, pence, and gold;
The wind was raised, the fabric stormed,
And now the Chapel is transformed
Into a noble, bright example
Of a real converted temple.
Renewed within, improved without,
A true conversion none need doubt,
Long may its past and present state
To sinful man illustrate
That self improvement is not vain—
That men must all be born again,
If they would see or realise
God's kingdom here or in the skies.

*The Rev. William Smith, Primitive
Methodist minister.

SAMUEL COOPER.

He was father of the above, and like his
son, he aspired to poetic fame. Such a hatred
had he of smoking, and so pained was he
to see the habit growing among both young
and old that he composed and published a
poem, his object being to induce the
habitual smoker to throw away his pipe,
and "to prevent the inititiated from learning
a habit which will make unlawful demands
upon his purse, injure his health, and give
him much vexation." As the author himself frankly admitted, "in point of poetical
beauty there is nothing to admire, and
therefore poetry in the verses which follow,
must not be sought for," but if his end was
accomplished he should "reap more heart-
felt satisfaction than if my brow were to
be wreathed with poetical laurels gathered
from the top of Parnassus' mountain." It
is a remarkable piece of composition, put
together when its author was nearly seventy
years old. He died in 1872, aged 73, and is
buried in the Primitive Cemetery.

REV. GEORGE BIRD.

The Rev. George Bird, the Vicar of Bradwell, has from a youth been a lover of verse,
and gifted with the spirit of poetry. His
masterpiece is, perhaps, "Ronald's Farewell," issued to the world in 1892.

HORACE E. MIDDLETON.

Horace E. Middleton, a distinguished and
talented musican, appointed in 1908
Musical Director of the Kings' Theatre,
Hammersmith, London.

THOMAS FANSHAW MIDDLETON.

First Bishop of Calcutta, a Middleton of Bradwell.

Thomas Fanshaw Middleton, the first
Bishop of Calcutta, was the only son of the
Rev. Thomas Middleton, one of the oldest
of the family of Bradwell Middletons, who
was born in a cottage in Nether Side, now
used as a lock-up shop, and still the property of the Middleton family. Thomas
Middleton became rector of Kedleston,
near Derby, and he was allied by marriage
with the family of Fanshaw of Brough.
It was whilst he was rector of Kedleston
that his son Thomas Fanshawe Middleton
was born on January 26th, 1769. He entered Christ's Hospital on 21st April, 1779,
and he became a "Grecian." Among his
schoolfellows were S. T. Coleridge and
Charles Lamb, who describes him as "a
scholar and a gentleman in his teens,"
whose manner at school was "firm, but
mild and unassuming." Middleton was
always grateful to Christ's Hospital, and
shortly before his death gave a donation
of £400, and was elected a governor of the
institution. Entering Pembroke College,
Cambridge, he graduated B.A., January,

1792, as fourth in the list of senior optimes. He became M.A. in 1795, and D.D. 1808. In March, 1792, he was ordained deacon by Dr. Pretyman, Bishop of Lincoln, and became curate of Gainsborough, Lincolnshire, where he edited, and in great part wrote, a weekly periodical called "The Country Spectator." This periodical—an echo of Addison and Steele—attracted the attention of Dr. John Pretyman, archdeacon of Lincoln, and brother of Bishop Pretyman, and he made Middleton tutor to his sons, first at Lincoln, then at Norwich. In 1795 Middleton was presented by Dr. Pretyman to the rectory of Tansor, Northamptonshire, and in 1802 to the consolidated rectory of Little and Castle Bytham, Lincolnshire. At this time he began his well-known work on the Greek article, being incited by a controversy of this subject in which Granville Sharp, Wordsworth, Master of Trinity, and Calvin Winstanley engaged. The volume appeared in 1808 as "The Doctrine of the Greek Article applied to the Criticism and the Illustration of the New Testament." It was praised in the "Quarterly Review" as a learned and useful work, and went through five editions. In 1809 Middleton obtained a Prebendal stall at Lincoln, and in 1811 exchanged Tansor and Bytham for the vicarage of St. Pancras, London, and the rectory of Pultenham, Hertfordshire. In 1812 he became archdeacon of Huntingdon. On his removal to London in 1811 he undertook the editorship of the "British Critic," and took an active part in the proceedings of the Society for Promoting Christian Knowledge. He endeavoured, unsuccessfully, to raise funds for a new church in St. Pancras' parish.

The Act of 1813, which renewed the charter of the East India Company, erected their territories into one vast diocese with a bishop (of Calcutta) and three archdeacons. The number of Anglican clergy in India was very small. The bishopric, the salary of which was £5,000, was offered to Middleton. He was consecrated at Lambeth Palace on May 8th, 1814, and reached Calcutta on November 28th, 1814. Difficulties had been prophesied with the natives on religious grounds, but the Bishop's arrival and subsequent visitations created no alarm or disturbance He found the Bible Society established at Calcutta, but declined an invitation to join it. He had a difficulty with the Presbyterian ministers, who were maintained by the court of directors of the East India Company. In 1815 he organised the Free School and the Orphan School at Calcutta, and in May of the same year formed a diocesan committee of the Society for Promoting Christian Knowledge, a society which, when he left England, had placed £1,000 at his disposal in furtherance of its views. On December 18th, 1815, he left Calcutta to make his primary visitation, attended by a party of about 450 people. The whole journey was one of about 5,000 miles. He had an inter-

view with the Nabob of the Carnatic at Madras, traversed Southern India, visited Bombay, Goa, Ceylon, and the Syrian Christians at Cochin. During this visitation, which ended in 1816, the Bishop made no heathen converts. His view, frequently expressed, was that the "fabric of idolatry" in India would never be shaken merely by the preaching of missionaries. He trusted rather to the general diffusion of knowledge and the arts to pave the way for Christianity. The first duty of the Anglican Church was to bring the European inhabitants under its influence, and to set up a high standard of moral and religious life. About September, 1820, the Bishop's house was struck by lightning while the family were at dinner, but no one was injured.

On December 15th, 1820, Middleton laid the foundation stone of Bishop's Mission College, on a site within three miles of Calcutta. The establishment of this college was the Bishop's favourite scheme. The institution was to consist of a principal and professors, and of students who were afterwards to be provided for as missionaries and schoolmasters in India. In 1821 he again visited Cochin to ascertain the condition of the Syrian Church there, and in December held his third visitation at Calcutta. He died on July 8th, 1822, of a fever, in the 54th year of his age and the ninth of his episcopate. He was buried in Calcutta Cathedral.

The Society for the Propagation of the Gospel, to which he left £500 and five hundred volumes from his library, joined the Society for Promoting Christian Knowledge, in subscribing for a monument to him in the nave of St. Paul's Cathedral. This memorial—a marble group, by J. G. Lough—represents Bishop Middleton blessing two Indian children kneeling before him. In accordance with Middleton's will, all his writings in manuscript were destroyed, including a memoir on the Syrian Church. While in India he collected Syrian manuscripts and learnt Hindustani, but gave up the study of Greek. His "Sermons and Charges" were published with a memoir, in 1824, by Archdeacon Bonney. Middleton was a Fellow of the Royal Society and a Vice-President of the Asiatic Society.

Middleton's life was written in 1831 by his friend the Rev. C. W. Le Bas, and it contains a portrait of the Bishop in his robes. He was a man of handsome and vigorous appearance, his voice was clear and sonorous, and his preaching impressive. In Kay's "Christianity in India" he is called "a cold and stately formalist," who had "an over-weening sense of the dignity of the episcopal office," though she admits that the Bishop was not actuated by personal vanity, and that the externals of religion had been too much neglected in India before his arrival. Other friends of Middleton found him stiff and proud in his manner, though, as

Charles Lamb expressed it, the newly and imperfectly defined position of the first Anglican Bishop of India, perhaps, justified his high carriage. As an organiser he was cautious, able, and active, and his successor, Bishop Heber, was not a little indebted to him.

Middleton married, in 1797, Elizabeth, eldest daughter of John Maddison, of Alvingham, Lincolnshire. His wife survived him, but there were no children of the marriage.

CHAPTER XVIII.

FAMOUS SOLDIERS.

THOMAS MORTON.

Thomas Morton (who took the name of Thomas Morton Moore), who was a son of George Morton, was a distinguished son of his native place. Although only 44 when he died at Parkhurst Barracks, Isle of Wight, in March, 1860, he had probably seen as much active service as any man of that age. He was a Quartermaster of the 5th Depot. Batt., and served in India with the 31st Regiment throughout the Afghan and Sutlej campaign, and with the 68th Regiment during the whole of the Crimean War, in which he was wounded. In the course of his career he was present in thirty-six engagements, and for his services he received four medals and six clasps. He was honoured by the Turkish Order of the Medjidie being conferred upon him. His widow erected a handsome memorial of him in the Primitive Methodist Chapel.

CHARLES CASTLE, J.P.

CHARLES CASTLE.

Although not a native of Bradwell, he resided here many years, loved the place and its people, took interest in all its affairs, and was for many years chairman of the School Board. He was a fine fellow, a member of the Sheffield Corporation, and a magistrate. In 1856, when only 18, he enlisted in the 7th Hussars, and by the end of November in the following year he was out in India. The Indian Mutiny was going on, and Charles Castle was in the thick of the fighting. He was present at the repulse of the enemy's attack on the Alumbagh, and through the siege and operations against Lucknow. He was with Hodson, the dashing Colonel of "Hodson's Horse," when he fell. He was continually engaged throughout the years 1858 and 1859, and for his bravery received promotion. When in hot pursuit of the enemy, a shell burst over him and brought the horse down dead hit in seven places, and the horse fell heavily on him, and crushing him into the land.

Mr. Castle passed through the campaign with only one wound, although of 78 men who belonged to his troop when they rode to Lucknow, only 13 were left at the end of the operations. After the war was over, Mr. Castle, who had become Acting Troop Sergeant-Major, and Assistant Instructor in Musketry, accompanied Lord and Lady Canning and Sir Colin Campbell on their tour through the Punjab and North-West Provinces as sergeant in the escort. He had always belonged to the "select side" of his regiment, and had in this country again and again ridden in the escort of Queen Victoria. He purchased his discharge in 1862, and joined his brother-in-law, Mr. Batty Langley (afterwards M.P.) in business in Sheffield. He died in 1904, and his funeral, one of the largest ever seen in Sheffield, was attended by 45 Indian Mutiny veterans.

HARRY FISKE (Living).

Eldest son of Mr. S. Fiske. Studied for the army under the late Mark H. Wild, of Sheffield. Determined to be a soldier he enlisted in the 2nd Devon Regiment with a view of obtaining a commission through the ranks. He was, as a sergeant, in all the fights on the banks of the Tugela, in the South African War, and assisted in the relief of Ladysmith, when he was invalided home.

WILFRED FISKE.

Another son of Mr. S. Fiskè. He went through the South African campaign with distinction, remained in that country. He was killed when walking over a railway crossing in 1904.

LUTHER BRADWELL (Living).

Served in the South African War.

OTHER CHRONOLOGY.
BARNSLEY.

For 400 years the Barnsley family resided at Nether Water Farm, an old house nestling in a hollow just above Hazlebadge Hall, from whence different branches of the family have gone out and settled at Peak Forest, Aldwark Grange, and other places. One of the Peak Forest family was blessed with six children—four sons and two daughters—all of whom early in life agreed that they would never marry, that they would leave their estate to the survivors, and that they would all find a resting place in the same vault at Peak Forest Church. Five of them were faithful to their vow, and rest in the vault, but the erring one, who tasted matrimonial bliss, to some extent "made up" for his brothers and sisters, for he had no fewer than three wives, and, well, the Peak Forest vault does not contain his ashes.

Miss Mary Barnsley, the last of the five who remained unmarried, and died a few years ago, left £500 to Peak Forest Church and School in augmentation of the stipend of the vicar; £250 to increase the salary of the day schoolmaster connected with the church, and £250 for maintaining and improving the choir; and in order that her bequests might not be lost sight of and that the parishioners might ever be reminded of them, she directed her executors to have such bequests recorded by a suitable inscription on a brass plate affixed against the wall inside the church.

John Barnsley, the Peak centenarian, was born in 1689, and died in 1787.

WILLIAM BOCKING,

who died in 1869, aged 87, was a Wesleyan Sunday School teacher over 60 years.

BENJAMIN BARBER.

One of the pioneers of Methodism, a lead mine manager, known as "the Methodist Martyr," owing to the persecutions he suffered in the early ages of Methodism. He was the principal stay of Methodism here from 1760 to 1800, and about 1780 established the first Sunday School. He was buried at Hope Church.

CAPTAIN BENJAMIN BARBER.

He was son of the above, and was a local preacher and a captain in the Militia, the first company formed in 1803. This remarkable individual was part owner of many lead mines in the district 100 years ago. He built and resided in the house known as the Old Post Office, at the bottom of Smithy Hill.

JOHN BARBER.

Another member of the same family, who died in 1910. He worthily upheld the traditions of his greatgrandfather, the Methodist martyr, for he was a talented and hardworking local preacher 51 years, and filled every office open to a layman. He was one of the first members of the School Board, and held his seat many years.

THE RIGHT HONOURABLE SIR JOHN WINFIELD BONSER.

This gentleman confers honour upon Bradwell, where he lived for several years when a boy. He was the only son of the Rev. John Bonser, B.A., who was stationed as the Wesleyan minister at Bradwell from 1851 to 1854, and resided in the house immediately below and opposite the chapel. Born in 1847 he was educated at Ashby-de-la-Zouch, Loughborough, and Heath Grammar Schools; Tancred student in Common Law at Lincoln's Inn, 1869; and Senior Classics, 1870. In 1883 he was appointed Attorney-General of the Straits Settlements, and retained that position for ten years, when he was appointed Chief Justice of the same, and retired in 1902. In the previous year he had been appointed Privy Counsellor, and in 1902 he was appointed a member of the Judicial Committee of Privy Council.

FAMILY OF BRADWELL.

Walter de Braddewall sat on a jury at the Assizes of the Forest, in the year 1216.

Gregory de Bradwall, bail for the Prior of Lenton, for an offence against the forest laws in 1237.

Galf de Bradwall, an offender against the forest laws in 1272.

Elias de Bradwall, often bail for offenders against the forest laws about 1280.

William Fabre de Bradwall, Gregory de Bradwall, Matthew de Bradwall, and Nicholas, son of William de Bradwall, were among the first to enclose land in Bradwall, in the year 1237.

Galf de Bradwall, in 1283, was called to account for having raised three houses in the forest without warrant; and Clement De-la Ford (Ford Hall) became bail for him.

Nicholas, the Clerk of Bradwall, in 1283.

William, son of the Smith of Bradwall, sat on an Inquisition re lead mining at Ashbourne, 1288.

Thomas Bradwall, Chaplain of Hope, in 1529.

JOHN BRADWELL.

Although landlord of the Bull's Head, where his parents lived before him, he was a popular local preacher in the Wesleyan body, and a friend of William Wood, the historian, of Eyam. Here is what a newspaper said about him after his death in 1853:—"The deceased for upwards of forty years had generously officiated as village scribe; as counsellor and confidential adviser to the whole village and its immediate locality. To the counsel and judgment of the deceased were referred all matters of dispute occurring around him, and it is some praise to his deeply revered memory to add that but rarely indeed did he fail to bring matters to a satisfactory and peaceful termination. In the political world he was an ardent and acute observer; as a literary character he was at least locally conspicuous; as a wit and racy humorist he had, in his own locale, few equals; as a general reader his great variety of book knowledge amply testified; and as a kind and open-hearted neighbour and friend his loss will be long experienced and deeply lamented. To the provincial press the deceased was an occasional contributor, while his correspondence with many eminent characters of the present day is all sufficient testimony of the appreciation of high mental qualities. As a husband and parent he was truly exemplary; as an advocate of Liberal principles he was courageous and unflinching; and as a Christian he bore up under a long and severe affliction, and finally passed from this stage of life in a happy state of blissful peace and sweet serenity. His end was peace."

HENRY BRADWELL,

who died at Bradwell, for the greater part of his life held an important post with the famous firm of Fox, at their Stocksbridge works. During his connection with the business he worked out several ideas he evolved for improving various machines used in the factories. He invented machines with certain labour-saving devices of an entirely new and intricate character, and which, when tested, proved to be of immense value to the industry.

Bradwell Ebenezer (living). — Been a local preacher in the Wesleyan body 51 years, and held various offices in Wesleyanism.

DARNLEY.

A very old family, who still retain one of their old homesteads at Dale End, and properties in other parts of the village. They have always been a family of education and refinement, and repute. Edward Derneley was a churchwarden of Hope, in 1693, but no other member of the family ever held that office, as they were prominently connected with Nonconformity, but their old burial place is still at Hope Church. John Darnley was a famous schoolmaster nearly a century ago.

Dakin Stephen (living).—Been a Wesleyan local preacher, and a most active Nonconformist 51 years.

MRS. VIOLET HALL.

Evans William.—In a large way of business as hat manufacturer nearly a century ago. Endowed the Chapel of the Apostle of the Peak, and is buried under the pulpit.

Evans Seth (living).—Author of the "History of Wesleyanism in Bradwell," "Bradwell Ancient and Modern," etc.

Furness Isabella.—In 1740 one of the first to open her house for Methodist prayer meetings when the very earliest Methodist pioneer ventured to Bradwell.

Goodwin George, son of George Goodwin and the Hon. Charlotte Radclyffe, born at Bradwell in 1749, died at Sheffield, in poverty, in 1835.

Hall Mary.—Benefactress. Died 1762.

Hall Violet.—Forty years a Primitive Methodist local preacher. Died 1881.

Hallam Absolom (living). — Colour-sergeant 21 years in Sherwood Foresters. Medals: Punjaub Frontier (India), 1897-8; long service and good conduct, 1906.

Howe Margaret.—One of the first Methodists who opened her house for prayer meetings about 1740.

FAMILY OF MARSHALL.

Next to the Bradwells, the Marshalls are the oldest family in the locality, and they can boast an unbroken descent of at least 600 years. They were among the first Foresters; they rebelled against the bad old forest laws, cleared the first patches of land, built some of the first houses; for several centuries ranked amongst the principal families of the Peak; and they were often involved in litigation with people of greater power than themselves, who were attempting to take the common lands to which the people were entitled. The principal seat of this distinguished family was at "The Butts," between the Bagshawe Cavern and Outland Head. Here they had a large hall, not a vestige of which now remains, but there are traces on every hand of the former splendour of the home of the family. The houses close by are known as "Hall Barn," indeed the lands were in the hands of Elias Marshall when he died in 1768, and left an enclosure, the rent of which was to pay for the education of poor children. The family were very numerous, and had several residences. One of these was at the foot of Smithy Hill. It was in their occupation 200 years ago, but was soon afterwards converted into farm buildings, and about ten years ago these were demolished and a new house, "North View," built on the site. To mention the various members of this distinguished family through six hundred years would be impossible, but in the fifteenth or sixteenth centuries they ranked among the principal families of the Peak, and their daughters married into other famous families of the Peak. Their armoury is among that of the High Peak gentry, and their crest was a man in armour proper holding in his hand a truncheon.

Elias Marshall de Butts, in the Forest Pleas for land in 1399.

Elias Marshall and Dennis Marshall, at a great Court Leet of Henry Vernon, Esq., at Hazlebadge, in 1480.

Nicholas Marshall, at a great Court at Hazlebadge, 1488.

Walter Marshall and Hugh Marshall proceeded (with others) against Thomas Eyre for illegal possession of demesne lands in bradwall, 1594.

Willelmus Marshall and Milo Marshall, among the vills and freeholders of Bradwall in 1633.

Elias Marshall, a large landowner at Derbyshire election of 1734.

Adam, Edward, Godfrey, Humphrey, Lawrence, Martin, Robert, Thomas, and Miles Marshall, all landowners in 1658.

Robert Marshall, churchwarden of Hope, in 1749.

Thomas Marshall, churchwarden of Hope in 1750.

MIDDLETON.

The Middleton family ranks among the very oldest in the district. For 600 years they have been located here, and are here still, in various branches. To give anything like a history of this family is an impossible task. John Myddleton and Robert Myddleton were farming lands in Bradwell, as shown in the Forest Pleas, in the year 1399, and they have been on the soil ever since, taking active part in the affairs of their native place. There is not a single Court Leet record right through all these centuries without the names of some of this yeoman stock. Two Martin Middletons, two Richard Middletons, and a Thomas Middleton were freeholders in 1734. Thomas Middleton, benefactor, died 1729.

Robert Middleton, Town Gate, died 1854, aged 94.

Martin Middleton, native of Bradwell, was a member of the Manchester Corporation 1849 to 1858.

John Middleton, member of Manchester Corporation 1848 to 1851.

Bob Middleton, the last of the hat manufacturers, died 1899, aged 84

MORTON.

A famous family whose sons have gone out into all parts of the world, many of whom have distinguished themselves, especially in the Army, and the Nonconformist ministry. They were for centuries connected with lead-mining, and they were prominent people here in the year 1472, and have taken active part in the life of their native place through all these centuries, and their names are frequently met with throughout this work. They have been freeholders for centuries.

George Morton was the first to open his building for the reception of the Primitive Methodists, in 1821. He died in 1852.

Morton, Rev. Jacob.—Famous Wesleyan minister. Died 1870

Morton, Rev. John.—Primitive Methodist minister. Died 1862.

OLIVER MORTON.

Morton Oliver, who died in 1910, a miner, joined the Liverpool police force when a young man, volunteered for service abroad, and for the long period of 18 years occupied the position of Chief Inspector of the Penang and Singapore (Straits Settlements) Police, retiring to his native place in 1901. He lies in the family grave in the Wesleyan Cemetery, where there is a handsome monument to his memory.

Morton Thomas.—A famous soldier. Died at Parkhurst Barracks.

SOMERSET.

A family of repute and substance who were among the leading Wesleyans more than a century ago. They were in business as joiners, wheelwrights, fellmongers, and general shopkeepers, and while some of their sons have gone out and become distinguished divines, others have remained prominent laymen at home, and the present generation of the family are prominently connected with Wesleyanism.

Somerset Benjamin.—He was a Wesleyan local preacher forty years, and a prominent layman all that time.

Somerset Jabez Birley.—A prominent Wesleyan leader and official. Died in 1864.

ROBERT SOMERSET.

Somerset Robert.—He was a Wesleyan local preacher, class leader, and trustee more than forty years, and died in 1897.

THOMAS SOMERSET.

Somerset Thomas.—20 years guardian of the poor for Bradwell.

A GROUP OF WESLEYAN CLASS LEADERS,
As assembled in the old School, now the Liberal Club, in 1861.

Adam Hill, John Middleton, Thomas Middleton,
Benjamin Somerset, Rev. Richard Smailes, William Bennett, Jabez Birley Somerset.

Somerset, Rev. Ralph Benjamin.—Dean of Trinity College, Cambridge. Died 1891.

OBADIAH STAFFORD.

Stafford Obadiah. — Wesleyan Sunday School teacher over 60 years. Died 1884.

Strelley Robert.—Hazlebadge, M.P. for Derbyshire in 1407.

Strelley John. — Hazlebadge. M.P. for Derbyshire 1420.

DR. J. H. TAYLOR.

Taylor, Dr. Joseph Henry.—One of the best-known medical practitioners in the Peak. Practised in the district more than half a century. Died in 1897.

Taylor, Dr. Thomas (living).—Born at Bradwell. Son of Dr. Joseph Henry Taylor. Resides at Bournemouth.

Tanfield Robert (living).—One of the best-known Primitive Methodists in the Connexion. Been a local preacher and active official 60 years. An overseer of the poor for 40 years.

Vernon, Sir Richard.—Resided at Hazlebadge Hall in the fifteenth century.

Walker, Zachariah (living).—Been assistant overseer for Bradwell, and secretary of the Welcome Traveller of the Peak Lodge of Oddfellows nearly 40 years. The family have for centuries been interested in lead mining.

CHAPTER XIX.

SOME REMARKABLE CHARACTERS.

Left His Bride to Follow the Hounds.

A century ago there lived on Hunter's Green, an old worthy named Adam Morton, who was so much devoted to hunting that at one time he kept a small pack himself. A good story is told of this individual, who on the most momentous occasion of his life, preferred the hounds to his bride. He had such a love and passion for hunting that it showed itself at the altar. He was in the Hope Church just about to be married. Just as the ceremony was commencing he heard the hounds pass through, when out of the church he bounded in quest of the pack, regardless of the feelings even of his bride, and the marriage had to be solemnized on a subsequent day.

AN ECCENTRIC WORTHY.

A curious make-up of eccentricity, a strange picture, but an honest worthy, was Richard Jeffery.

"Dick," as he was generally called, was the character of the village. He had always a cheery word both for young and old, and by his eccentric manner of dress and general character was quite a noted individual. especially with visitors. His clever reciting of " Death and the Lady " was a treat. On one occasion he turned up at the Sheffield pantomime, which he enjoyed amazingly. With mouth agape, eyes filled with wonder. and constantly lifting up his hands in amazement, he kept exclaiming " Gold upon gold; there can be nothing grander in Heaven than this; if Queen Victoria was only here it would be complete." Alluding to the stage girls, he shouted out that he "should just like to take half a dozen of them to Bradda, just to let them see." He was a tall, big-boned man, with a ruddy complexion, high cheek bones, and a prominent nose, and, despite his penurious habits was the picture of health. His general appearance was most grotesque. A hat of enormous proportions, tied on his head with twine, was painted red and blue. His shoulders were covered with rough sacking, and a piece of the same material served as an apron. His trousers were so patched that in their mosaic appearance they resembled Sir John Cutler's silken hose that had been darned by his maid with diverse materials so frequently that none of the original fabric remained. At one time he played the drum in the Bradwell band, and he would sometimes illustrate his proficiency on that instrument by imitating vocally a cornet solo, with drum accompaniment executed with his fist on a door. But he was most effective as an elocutionist. On inspired occasions he would recite a dithery dialogue of some twenty or thirty dismal verses in length entitled "Death and the Lady," in which the struggle of a wealthy woman to ward off the fatal summonses with coaxes and bribes was graphically and gruesomely set forth. He was carried to his last resting place in the churchyard on Good Friday in 1885, in the presence of hundreds of spectators.

DONE AS MANY AS HAD EVER DONE HIM.

One of the characters in the middle of the last century was George Goodwin—"Owd Goodin" as he was known to every child in the place. He lived in the whitewashed cottage at the top of Farther Hill, almost opposite Dialstone Villas, and was a small farmer. Many there are who can well remember the old man fetch water from the brook with a yoke and chains and two big milking cans. Stories concerning him would fill a pamphlet.

He never attended a place of worship, and studiously avoided religious people. When he lay on his death bed in 1868, the Rev. Thomas Meredith, who was the Primitive Methodist minister at that time, visited him, and when he inquired about his state the old man retorted "Have you seen my fat pig? It's good meat; best in the country." The rev. gentleman told him that he wished to talk to him about his soul, but still the old man persisted in talking about his fat pigs. Mr. Meredith spoke to him about the story of the Cross, of the sufferings, death and resurrection of Christ, and when he spoke of Christ leaving the tomb the old man exclaimed "He was never likely to stop there if he could get out." This circumstance is related in "The Book of Marvels."

It is related of the same eccentric character that when a local preacher asked him if his mind was easy, he replied "Ah, I think it is." "Why?" "What makes it easy?" he was asked. "Well," was his reply, "I think I've done as many as have ivver done me."

STRANGE CHARACTER'S MONEY BUYS CHURCH CLOCK.

Benjamin Giles, known throughout the Peak as "Old Benny," for the greater part of his lifetime travelled the country as a hawker of small articles which he dragged about up hill and down dale on a handcart. The old gentleman's life was a mystery, but it was said that when a young man he was a London merchant, and lost every penny by misfortune, and the rest of his life was spent in the manner indicated. His home—if home it could be called—was in a small chamber behind some lead smelting works on Bradwell Hills, where "Overdale Houses" now stand, and when on his rounds he never lodged at houses, but was allowed to sleep in outhouses at lead smelting works belonging to Mr. E. M. Wass, a wealthy mine owner near Matlock. He lived to be more than eighty years of age, and when he died in 1883 he left a large sum of money—£150 or £200—to Mr. Wass, who returned it to Bradwell in the shape of a public clock, which he placed in the church tower at a cost of £150, and erected a monument over the grave of this strange character, which is noticed elsewhere.

MONEY ALL OVER THE HOUSE.

The curious habits of a well-known character, Mr. Joseph Wright, a farmer, of Smalldale, were revealed when his furniture came to be sold after his death in the year 1893. He was a highly respected man, a member of a very old family who had been on the spot at least 300 years. His wife having long predeceased him, he lived alone many years. During the sale of furniture the auctioneer observed that there was a secret drawer in an old box he was offering, and a secret drawer there proved to be. It was opened before the box was sold, and yielded a rich reward, for it was found to contain a bank note, a bag of gold, and a large quantity of silver coins. There were small sums of money all over the house, including fifty shillings in copper coins in a jug.

PUTTING THE "AXINS" IN.

A good story used to be told of a Bradwellite who was on the point of entering into conjugal relations. He went to the clerk of the parish church at Hope and ordered the banns to be published anent his forthcoming espousal, but he strictly charged the clerk to tell nobody about it so as to keep it as secret as possible. The clerk acting strictly on his injunctions, never told the Vicar, and the consequence was that on the following Sunday the banns were not published in the church. On the Sunday he was very eager to hear who had been "called out" in church, and on ascertaining that his own name had not been called he was very wroth. Rushing off to the clerk in a great rage he demanded to know why he had not been "spurred," when the clerk naively replied, "Why you charged me not to tell anybody, and consequently I did not tell the Vicar." This was an interpretation of the secrecy which the worthy fellow had never contemplated and he thereupon ordered the clerk to let the proceedings take the usual course. The banns were published on the following Sunday.

LITTLE MARTIN MIDDLETON, THE DUKE'S FAVOURITE.

A comical character was Martin Middleton, known as "Little Martin." But he was such a trusted and faithful retainer of several successive Dukes of Rutland of that period that one of them had his portrait painted life size, and it hung in Haddon Hall until a few years back. And over his grave in Hope Churchyard there is a midget of a headstone, no doubt corresponding with the stature of the character it commemorates, and it informs the passers by that "Here lyeth the body of Little Martin Middleton, of Hasslebatch, who died 1815, aged 90."

REUBEN HALLAM, AUTHOR AND PUBLICAN.

Reuben Hallam, although not a native of Bradwell, lived here for several years in the early seventies, when he kept the "Shoulder of Mutton." A clever and widely read man, full of knowledge of men and things, and possessed of considerable talent, his life was one of strange vicissitudes and unusual experiences. He was born in Sheffield in 1819, and died there in 1909, aged 90. He was a roving spirit, and wrote a serial story "Wadsley Jack, the humours and adventures of a travelling cutler." "Lilia Nightingale," and "T'ups and Dahns o' Sheffield life," were among his productions. It was really an account of his own experiences in early life. For some years he learnt carving, afterwards forged knife blades; he was a talented violinist, for some time performed in a travelling theatre, became proprietor of a boxing saloon and a professor of pugilism, and was at one time double bass singer, scenic artist and assistant manager at the Theatre Royal, Sheffield. He was for many years choirmaster at St. John's Church, Sheffield, and published "An introduction to the Art of Singing," and in his early days he was a famous cricketer. He was, indeed a most entertaining person, and many a time has he related his reminiscences in the "Shoulder of Mutton."

CHAPTER XX.

SOME REMARKABLE ENTRIES.

Curious Epitaphs and Gretna Green Weddings.

The Hope Church Registers, which date from the year 1599, have been well kept, and are in a good state of preservation. But the clergymen have contented themselves with the bare entry of the burial of the deceased without any remarks, except in a few instances, and where men have been "killed in the mine." But hundreds of these latter could doubtless have been shown.

Under date, March 10th, 1688, we read: "William, son of Robert Marshall de Bradwall, buried. Memorandum, no affidavit brought within 8 days and same certified to ye overseers of ye poor for Bradwall."

The very next entry is the burial on March 15th, of "Alicia, fil Thomas Padley de Bradwall," and there is a similar memorandum to the above.

"1778, July 31. Buried the body of a man found upon the moors in the Woodlands, and place of abode unknown."

But this was not the only body buried in the Churchyard that had been found upon the moors. In the Philosophical Transactions:—

"The moors of Hope parish afford an extraordinary instance of the preservation of human bodies interred in them. One Barber, a grazier, and his maid servant, going to Ireland in the year 1764, were lost in the snow, and remained covered with it from January to May, when they were so offensive that the Coroner ordered them to be buried on the spot. About twenty-nine years afterwards, some countrymen, probably having observed the extraordinary properties of this soil in preserving dead bodies, had the curiosity to open the ground, and found them in no way altered, the colour of the skin being fair and natural, and their flesh as soft as that of persons newly dead. They were exposed for a sight during the course of twenty years following, though they were much changed in that time by being so often uncovered. In 1716, Mr. Henry Brown, M.B., of Chesterfield, saw the man perfect, his beard strong and about a quarter of an inch long; the hair of his head short; his skin hard, and of a tanned leather colour, pretty much the same as the liquor and earth they lay in. He had on a broad cloth coat, of which the doctor in vain tried to tear off the skirt. The woman was more decayed, having been taken out of the ground and rudely handled; her flesh, partially decayed, her hair long and spongy like that of a living person. Mr. Barber, of Rotherham, the man's grandson, had both bodies buried in Hope Church, and upon looking into the graves some time afterwards it was found they were entirely consumed. Mr. Wormald, the minister of Hope, was present at their removal. He observed that they lay about a yard deep in moist soil or moss, but no water stood in the place. He saw their stockings drawn off, and the man's legs, which had not been uncovered before, were quite fair. The flesh, when pressed by his finger, pitted a little, and the joints played freely, and without the least stiffness. The other parts were much decayed. What was left of their clothes, not cut off for curiosity, was firm and good, and the woman had a piece of new serge, which seemed never the worse."

Body snatching would appear to have been a considerable trade a century ago, and there are still people living who can relate strange tales about the "Resurrection Carts" coming from Manchester and Sheffield, gliding silently in the middle of the night, and returning with bodies out of the churchyard. There are two entries to this effect in the register, and singularly enough, both relate to Bradwell people. Here they are:—

"1831. October 26, aged 28, William Bradwell, Smalldale. The body stolen same night."

"1834. October 2nd, aged 21, Benjamin Wragg, Bradwall. This body stolen."

Evidently those who trafficked in this ghoulish business carried on their nefarious job when the dark nights of October came.

"1636. Began the great death of many children and others by a contagious disease called the children pock and purple pock."

This relates to the small-pox that was formerly very prevalent in this country. It carried on its ravages for at least two hundred years, and killed many. There is the entry, "1834, Dec. 16th. Hannah Cheetham, Bradwall, small-pox."

"1819. Buried Widow Hannah Rose, Woodland, aged 100."

"1835. Nancy Furness, 26, child birth, married only 6 weeks."

"1836. Robert Bird, 80, Bradwall, sojourner."

There are many of these "sojourners" in the register, probably wayfarers.

"1837. Ellis Poynton, suddenly at market."

"1837, July 3rd. Rachel Cheetham, perished on the way.

This was the first burial in the parish to be registered under the new Act by which the returns were to be sent to the Registrar General.

"1837. James Oldfield, Little Hucklow. Killed by a cart."

"1838, February 2nd. Thomas Bagshaw, Hazlebadge, found hanged."

"1851, June 29th. A youth unknown found in the River Ashop. About 17 years old."

Baptisms.—"1835, April 8. Nancy, daughter of John and Nancy Furness, Bradwall. Mother buried same time."

"1835, March 8. Isaac, son of Robert and Rachel Shirt, Hope. Born with one finger and thumb only on right hand."

"1868, October 22. The new church at Bradwell was consecrated. Thanks be to God for permitting me to see the accomplishment of this good and important work." C. J. Daniel.

In Wesleyan Chapel Registers:

1854. "Buried Hannah Cheetham, sister to little Isaac Cheetham."

1847. "Paid Mr. George Fox £5 borrowed money from Mr. Abraham Hill in part for his croft as burying ground. Marriage gifts paid towards burying croft £2 0s. 6d.; balance paid to Benjamin Somerset, who lent it, £1 7s. 6d."

1847. "Donation towards obtaining marriage license for the chapel, handed towards this trust account and towards paying for the croft bought for burying ground if the parties do not object and require their money to be returned, £2 0s. 6d."

1864. "Buried Hannah Hawksworth. This grave belongs to the township of Bradwell."

1864. "Buried Benjamin Barber, 19, miner, killed in the mine at Great Hucklow."

Some Curious Epitaphs of Bradwell Folk.

There is a good deal of originality in the epitaphs to be found on the gravestones of Bradwell folk. Here are a few:—

In Hope Churchyard.

To Benjamin Kirk, of Brough, who died in 1789, aged 37:

"Reader, whoe'er thou act, remember that the common lot of all mankind is the grave. Yet know that the Meek, the Charitable, and Religious shall triumph over Death, secure in a blissful Immortality."

To William Middleton, Bradwell (1824), and several children:

"Kind Reader stop and contemplate
The nature of a future State.
If Christ in judgment should appear,
Are you prepared to meet Him there?"

To Mary, wife of Ellis Middleton, of Bradwall, 1810:

"My husband dear and children seven,
Prepare to follow me to Heaven."

On a table tomb of several young children of John and Mary Fox, of Smalldale, 1754:

"The blast which nips our youth will
    conquer thee,
It strikes the bud, the blossom, and the
    tree.
Since life is short, and Death is always
    nigh,
On many years to come do not rely;
The present time learn wisely to employ
That thou mayest gain eternal life and
    joy."

To Mary, wife of Frederick Morton, 1845,
aged 25:
"Grace was in all her steps,
In all her gestures dignity and love."

Here is a curious inscription on the stone
of a former churchwarden:
"Abraham Hibberson lyeth here,
And so he must till Christ appear.
Though flesh and bones consume away
He must appear at Judgment Day "
"He departed this life Feb. 15, 1776, aged
67 years."

"Smalldale."

On the stone of John Cheetham Brad-
wall, 1768, we read:
"Man, know thyself!
All wisdom centres there."

On the monument of James and Mary
Hibbs, 1779, and nine children, there is the
following:
"With deepest thoughts, spectator view
    thy Fate,
Thus Mortals pass to an Immortal State.
Through Death's dark vale we hope
    they've found the Way
To the bright Regions of eternal Day.
Life's but a Moment, Death that Moment
    ends,
Happy, thrice happy he that Moment
    wisely spends,
For on that dreadful Point, Eternity
    depends."

On the stone of Isaac and Mary Maltby
(1802), aged 72 and 73 respectively, there is
the line:
"An unspotted life is old age."

There would appear to be doubts and
fears concerning a future state, expressed
in some lines on the stone of Benjamin
Bagshaw, of Coplowdale, who died in 1804.
At the head of the stone there is: "In hope of
a joyfull Resurrection to Enter into Life
and Glory," but beneath we read:
"Let no surviving mortal man presume,
To state my Present or my future Doom.
Let that a part for Ever to remain,
To Him who knows our hearts to be but
    vain.
So let my Ashes and this brittle Stone
Rest till i rise and be disturbed by none "

Here is another:
"Behould!
this stone stands near
upon the bones of
Martin Middleton
who Bradwell Town

Inhabited of late
and dyed near Aged
fifty E.ght.
November 16, 1753."

In Wesleyan Cemetery.

A new marble monument to Isaac Ban-
croft (1908), aged 79, erected by his daugh-
ter, says:
"Farewell vain world, I've had enough of
    thee,
And now I care not what thou say'st of
    me;
Thy smiles I court not, nor thy frowns
    I fear,
My cares are o'er; my head lies easy
    here."

On a monument to John Bradwell (39),
who died in 1896, it is stated that:
"This stone was subscribed for by the
staff and fellow cabmen at Hope Railway
Station, in loving memory of a departed
friend, as a memento of the respect and
esteem in which he was held in the district."

In Bradwell Churchyard.

On the flagstone at the entrance to the
tower doorway: " Jane Maltby Bradwell,
6, and George Edward Bradwell, 18, who
were buried on February 18, and March 6,
1889. They were the first to be buried in
this churchyard."

On headstone near entrance to vestry:
"In memory of Benjamin Giles, a native
of South Wales, but for 40 years a hawker
in this district, and resident at Bradwell,
who died February 16th, 1883, and was
buried beneath this stone February 19th,
1883, aged 81 years. Lay not up for yourselves treasures upon earth . . . . but
lay up for yourselves treasures in Heaven.
For where your treasure is there will your
heart be also."

Gretna Green Weddings.

It is well known that at Peak Forest,
often termed "The Gretna Green of the
Midlands," which was extra parochial, the
parson had formerly unique powers. He
could legally perform the marriage ceremony without previous publication of the
banns at any hour of the day or night. It
was exceedingly convenient for Bradwell
couples who were desirous of doing it on
the sly, and doubtless many patronised the
parson of Peak Forest.

Extracted from the registry of "Foreign
Marriages" are the following Bradwell
names:—

1727.

Joseph Bridbury and Lydia Wilson,
August 1st.
John Greavs and Hannah Bridbury,
License, October 18th.
Abraham Hall and Sarah Longley, March
the 9th.

1728.

Edward Dernly and Elizabeth Bray, July the 4th.

Geofrey Pearson, Ann Burroughs, September 25th.

1729.

Joseph and Elizabeth Hall, May 11th.

Thomas Elliot and Ann Eyre, December 7th.

Daniel Pearson and Elizabeth Key December 17th.

1730.

Francis Bridbury, Mary Longden, April 6th.

Joseph Dennis, Mary Key, October 11th,

Samuel Spooner, Mary Bridbury, October 12th.

1734.

John Bramhal, Sarah Littlewood, June 4th.

1735.

Samuel Edenzor, Elizabeth Greavs, September 26th.

1736.

Thomas Walker, Elizabeth Pearson, July 22nd.

Benjamin Thorp, Mary Bramhal, July 25th.

George Fox, Esther Barber, December 16th.

Abraham Ibberson, Sarah Wainwright, February 2nd.

"GRETNA GREEN" OF THE PEAK.
The Ancient Church of Peak Forest.   Demolished in 1876.

1731.

Joseph Bramhal, Hannah Allen, June 15th.

Matthew Furnice, Ann Hallam, July 20th.

John Cowper, Alice Green, August 5th.

Thomas Bridbury, Mary Adsit, August 29th.

1733.

John Bennit, Martha Morten, April 1st.

Edward Bennit, Ann Needham, July 9th.

Hugh Hill, Bradwall, Sarah Clayton, Peak Forest.

1737.

John Tricket, Mary Greavs, May 30th.

John Andrew, Mary Goodwin, May 1st.

Henry Gelly, Ruth Slack, August 31st.

John Taylor, Alice Walker, October 7th.

Benjamin Fox, Mary Elliott, October 18th.

John Onyon, Ann Elliot, February 5th.

1738.

Robert Hill, Mary Hallam, April 26th.

Benjamin Hallam, Jane Froggatt, December 31st.

1739.

Robert Barber, Sarah Morten, July 8th.
Wm. Dalton, Elizabeth Greavs, February 14th.
Robt. Hall, Betty Fox, February 21st.
Thomas Rowson, Mary Fox, March 24th.

1740.

Robert Hall, Ann Bradwell, October 26th.
Paul Andrew, Ruth Deykin, October 26th.

1743.

Wm. Deykin, Ann Bradbury, May 20th.
Thomas Morten, Elizabeth Edenzor, May 22nd.
Nicholas Deykin, Dorothy Hall, October 15th.

1744.

Benjamin Hall, Ann Hall, July 8th.

1747.

Thomas Burrows, aged 26, and Margaret Dakin, aged 25, Castleton, June ye 11.
Robt. Hill and Mary Longden, of Castleton, June ye 12th.
Thomas Andrew and Eliz. Hall (Castleton), July the 12th.
Robt. Bradwell and Margaret Hall, November the 21st.

1748.

William Longden and Hannah Needham, September ye 1st.

1752.

William Eyre and Ellen Furnace, November 2nd.

1753.

Benjamin Walker and Mary Hallam, October 19th.
John Maltby and Ann Palfryman, November 26th.

1754.

Godfrey Elliott and Susanna Barber, February 25th.
Robert Palmer and Ann Marshall, March 21st.

CHAPTER XXI.

EIGHTY ODD YEARS AGO.

Leading Inhabitants in 1829.

The population of Bradwell has varied with its vicissitudes. In the year 1801 there were 955 inhabitants, and in 1811 the population had increased to 1,074. When the census of 1821 was taken a further increase was proved, the number being 1,130. Ten years later (1831), when lead mining was very bad, the number of inhabitants was shown to be 1,153—still a slight increase—but in 1841 it was 1,273. In 1851 the population was returned as 1,334, viz., 650 males, and 684 females, this being the highest ever known. But from this period there was a gradual decline owing to depression in lead mining, and the closing of cotton mills, for in 1861 a slight decrease was shown, the figures being 1,304, but in 1871 it had further decreased to 1,141, the low price of lead having caused some of the mines to be abandoned. In 1881 there was another big decrease, the returns showing only 1,019, but in 1891 there were so many empty houses that the total number of inhabitants was but 837. But during the next decade the tide turned, mainly owing to the construction of the Dore and Chinley Railway, and the popularity of Bradwell as a resort for health and pleasure, and the census of 1901 returned 1,033 inhabitants. The returns of 1911 showed by far the greatest increase in the history of the place, the number of inhabitants then being 1,330.

When the River was Forded.

A century ago such a convenience as a bridge was not known in Bradwell, although the Brook flowed right through the centre of the place. As a matter of fact, the water had to be forded at a spot now known as Bridge End; at Town End, Town Bottom, The Hills, and other places, every water-course, whether brook or rivulet, being open. Water Lane, now Church Street, was an open stream, with a footpath by the side.

The date of the erection of Causeway Bridge, near the Roman causeway in Hope Lane, is not known, but it is the oldest structure of the kind in the district. Nor is it known by whom it was built, but it is repaired by the townships of Bradwell and Hope. In 1814 the Bridge over the brook at Bridge End was built, and in the same year two culverts were constructed over small rivulets. In 1817 the Commissioners of Common Lands built another bridge over the brook in the Holmes; in 1818 and 1829 other bridges were constructed. In 1823 three bridges were built over the Sitch rivulet on the Hills.

A Community of Eighty Years Ago.

A glance at the old town and its people eighty odd years ago—in the year 1829—cannot fail to be interesting. In those days they were a community to themselves, isolated from the rest of the world, with the carrier's cart to Sheffield the only means of communication with the outer world, a contrast to the growing, stirring place of to-day, with half the number of its inhabitants not natives. But even so far back the population of miners and weavers was almost as great as now.

The miners—men, women and children—were daily sending their lead ore to the smelting mills, of which there were several, with their tall chimneys belching forth volumes of black smoke. James Furniss and Company were the principal firm of lead smelters, and their works were extensive. Another smelting mill was worked by Isaac and Jeremy Royse, of Castleton.

Jeremy was born during some excitement at Speedwell Mine, Castleton, and became proprietor of that remarkable place. The smelting works and cupolas of the Furnisses and Royses have long been demolished, but that of the Middletons in the Meadow, is now used as farm buildings.

And this colony of miners found employment for a good number of tradesmen. As blacksmiths there were Thomas Bradbury, in Hollowgate; Wm. Bennett, George Sanderson, Thomas Bradwell, George Holme, in Netherside, and Richard Walker, who came to an untimely end. The only smithy remaining is that of George Holme, but his son is at Hope.

And as with blacksmiths, so with wheelwrights. The miners found them plenty of work. There were Benjamin and Isaac Somerset, with their big timber yard full of stacks of timber for mining purposes; Jacob Marshall, at Yard Head; and George Bradwell, but their workshops have long ago disappeared.

The hatters, too, were a force to be reckoned with, for hats were made here for the London markets, and the rough felt hats were fetched to all parts of Derbyshire. The big hatters were William and James Evans, who were people of means, indeed, William endowed the old chapel; Robert Jackson; and there was a whole family of Middletons in the same business, George, Charles, Joseph, and Robert, all in business on their own account. But the industry has long been defunct, and houses now occupy the sites of the old hat manufactories.

Handloom weaving, too, was yet in vogue, though not to the same extent as at a more remote period. But the weavers still found employment for a shuttle-maker, William Fox, whose lad, Samuel, then just apprenticed at Hathersage, was destined to become one of the greatest manufacturers England has ever known, and the founder of the famous firm of Samuel Fox and Company. The house in which the celebrity was born is still there in Water Lane, now dignified by the name of Church Street. The Pearsons, too, were finding employment for many at their cotton mills, one where the white lead works now stands —indeed, the cotton mill itself remains intact—another at the bottom of Stretfield, a portion of it converted into the farm bailiff's house, and the third, the new mill in Stretfield.

Such of the rising generation whose parents could afford to give them a little schooling were being taught by John Darnley, a famous schoolmaster in those days, and he was teaching the "free scholars" under Elias Marshall's Charity in a schoolroom in Hugh Lane that had just been built at the expense of John Birley, who still resided in the village. And the Wesleyans were conducting the only Sunday School in the place, with 300 scholars, in a schoolroom built by public subscription, now the Conservative Club.

Equally interesting it is to know who were catering for the wants of the people in those days. There was Thomas Hill, the great shopkeeper and lead ore buyer, whose shop is still there at the top of Water Lane. But there was no such thing as the Truck Act. There was also John Somerset, who did a big trade, in fact it was John Somerset who built the bridge over the brook at Town Bottom, so that carts could get to and from his shop, which is now known as "Brook House." There was Joseph Barber, who lived and carried on business in Town Gate, in the property above the White Hart, now enclosed by palisadings. One night Joseph Barber and his wife returned from a prayer meeting at the Wesleyan Chapel to find that their house had been entered and robbed, and the marauders had written with chalk across the front of the mantelpiece, "Watch, as well as pray." There was also George Middleton, Isaac Hill, Thomas Gleadhill, and Thomas Burrows, of Smalldale, who was the Sheffield carrier.

Whether or not butchers did a roaring trade is a question, but there were plenty of them, and their old shops still remain. There were John Bradwell and his son John in Town Gate; Elias Needham, next to the White Hart; and Alexander Cheetham, in Water Lane. The tailors were Joseph Elliott and his son Thomas, and Richard Kay; and the shoemakers—there were no machine-made boots then—were Robert Middleton, in Town Gate, Anthony Marshall, Thomas Elliott, William Revill (who lived in Nether Side), and Obadiah Stafford. The stonemasons were John Broadbent, George Downing, and George Walker.

But the miners were proverbial for wetting their whistles, and on their reckoning days the place resounded with their merriment. No wonder then, that there should be a good number of "houses with the picture over the door." Which is, or where was the oldest of these old inns, is not known, but certain it is that in the year 1577, Godfrey Morton and Ottiwell Yellott kept inns in Bradwell. Eighty odd years ago the White Hart was kept by Elias Needham, the Bull's Head by Ellen Bradwell, and the Green Dragon (now cottages) by Joseph Bocking. These three lived in the old Town Gate, and right in the centre, as if placed there ready to catch their victims, were the stocks, where the tipplers were made fast. At the top of Smithy Hill Robert Morton, an auctioneer, kept the Rose and Crown, while the Newburgh Arms, which had only just been built, was kept by William Kenyon, and the Bramalls were at the Bowling Green in Smalldale. William Bradwell kept the Rose Tree, a house that lost its license seventy years back, and in Nether Side there was the Old Ship kept by Thomas Gleadhill, now old cottages close to the Wesleyan Manse, and the New Ship kept by William Revill, where Crompton and Evans' Bank now stands. The Shoulder of Mutton, the

Bath Inn, and the Bridge Inn came into existence as public-houses some years afterwards.

In religious work the Wesleyans were providing accommodation for most of the people in their present chapel; the Primitive Methodists had not long built their first chapel, now a cottage; the Baptists were struggling along in their old chapel, now the Primitive School, dipping their converts in the waters of the brook, and the congregation of the old Presbyterian Chapel had by this time become Unitarian.

And there were three Friendly Societies (one a Women's Club), with a total membership of 280.

the community the latter felt under some kind of obligation to keep their instruments in tune. Jacob Hallam was fiddler at the Wesleyan Chapel, and in an account book, under date 1833, there is the following entry:—

"Jacob Hallam's Fiddle Repaired, cost with strings 15s."

"Robert Middleton 1s., Josiah Barber 1s., John Maltby 1s., John Middleton, shoemaker. 1s., Joseph Barber, sen., 1s., Thomas Hill 1s., Johnson Evans 6d., George Fox 1s., Hugh Bocking 1s., Thos. Bradwell 6d., Robert Bocking, sen., 6d., Wm. Bocking 6d., Robt. Bocking, jun., 1s., John Bradwell 1s., Messrs. Pearson 3s."

TWO FAMOUS SINGERS OF THE MIDDLE OF THE 19th CENTURY.
JOSEPH HIBBERSON and CLEMENT MORTON.

A Musical Community.

Most of the people in the Peak district are strongly attached to musical pursuits, the inhabitants of Bradwell. Castleton, Tideswell, Litton, Eyam, Hucklow, and other places in particular. Very often the whole family cultivate the taste for music, and the villages contain their choirs of singers and bands of instrumental performers. To mention those who were famous as musicians in the olden days is impossible, but it is close on a hundred years since the old Bradwell Band was formed, a mixture of brass and reed instruments, one of which, a curious instrument known as the serpent, belonging to the late Job Middleton, being still in existence, as also is the fiddle of the late Jacob Hallam, another local worthy. These musicians were looked upon as institutions in the locality, and as they rendered service to

And a glimpse at the Hope Churchwarden's accounts serves to show that Bradwell instrumentalists were to the fore quite a century and a half ago, at the old Parish Church. In 1759, "the inhabitants of the parish of Hope in vestry assembled agree to pay the sum of sixteen shillings and sixpence towards paying for a Bassoon and Hautbois to be used in the Parish Church." And no doubt William Jeffery, of Bradwell, found playing that Bassoon thirsty work, for in the accounts there are numerous entries of payments for ale and dinners for William at the Woodroofe Arms. Presumably, he spent the Sunday at Hope, having his dinner provided by the wardens between morning and afternoon services.

Other notable folk in the musical world in the early part of last century were

Joseph Hibberson, a famous bass singer;
Ambrose Gleadhill, one of the finest fiddlers
in Derbyshire; and Clement Morton.

When a Cattle Fair was Held.

Formerly a cattle fair was held at Bradwell. A century ago it was well attended,
the old Town Gate being the Market
Place. There was also all the usual paraphernalia of a pleasure fair. But half a
century ago it declined until it ceased altogether. Here are its latter years:—
1859, two cows, one sheep, and one stirk;
1860, two cows and one sheep; 1861, not a
single thing of any description; 1862, seven
cows, one sow, three pigs, and one donkey.
In 1863, six buyers turned up, but not a
beast of any description was offered for
sale, and this was the last fair.

The Wakes.

The date of the establishment of the
Wakes is a mystery. For centuries it has
been held on the second Sunday in July,
and continued through the following week,
but the bull-baiting, bear-baiting, cock-
fighting, rabbit coursing, badger-baiting,
and drinking which characterised the festival generations back have long ago ceased
and given way to a holiday for health and
pleasure.

CHAPTER XXII.

LONGEVITY AND TRAGICAL DEATHS.

Peaklanders are noted for their longevity,
and none more so than those in this district. Here are those over fourscore during
the last 100 years. These indicate the
long-lived families:—

1787.—John Barnsley, Netherwater, 101.
1813.—Widow Hannah Wragg, New Wall
Nook, 81; Widow Hannah Elliott, 95; Widow
Ann Middleton, Hazlebadge, 87.
1814.—Ann Bradshaw, 84; Widow Mary
Burrows, 86; Martin Middleton, Hazlebadge,
90.
1818.—Widow Jane Evans, Smalldale, 82;
Joseph Hibbs, 83.
1819.—Thomas Middleton, 91.
1824.—John Ellis, 84.
1825.—George Barnsley, Netherwater, 82;
Rebecca Hallam, 89; George Bramall, Smalldale, 90.
1826.—Mary Morton, 84.
1828.—Widow Hannah Ashmore, 83.
1829.—Widow Ann Hill, 81.
1831—Daniel Stafford, Smalldale, 82.
1832.—Nancy Hall, Cotes, 80.
1836.—Christopher Jackson, Smalldale, 82;
Sarah Sidebottom, Brough, 92.
1837.—Mary Middleton, 81.
1838.—Robert Middleton, 80.
1839.—John Eyre, 81.
1842.—Robert Bradbury, 83, died at Marple.
1845.—Robert Middleton, 85; Elizabeth
Elliott, Smalldale, 83.
1846.—Robert Hawksworth, 84; Betty Jackson, Smalldale, 88.

1848.—Maria Barber, 80; Ann Taylor, 87.
1849.—Thomas Middleton, 92; Edward
Middleton, Smalldale, 82.
1850.—Ellen Cheetham, 89.
1855.—Robert Middleton, 94; George Littlewood, 82; Thomas Hill, 83.
1856.—Sarah Hallam, 80; Robert Maltby,
84.
1857.—William Bramall, Smalldale, 83.
1858.—William Kenyon, 81; Adam Morton,
88; Ann Palfreyman, 80.
1860.—Ann Eyre, 84.
1861.—Edward Hartle, 94.
1862.—Jane Sidebottom, Brough, 86;
Hannah Kenyon, 82; Joseph Elliott, 83.
1863.—Durham Wragg, 83.
1866.—Isaac Middleton, 84; Robert Hall, 87.
1868.—George Goodwin, 88; Martha Elliott,
80.
1869.—George Elliott, 82; William Bocking,
87.
1871.—Charles Middleton, hatter, 83;
Richard Middleton, 88.
1872.—Betty Hall, 85; Mary Bennett, 80;
William Stafford, 83.
1874.—Mary Bradwell, 80; Charity Maltby,
83.
1875.—George Fox, Hazlebadge Hall, 80;
Martha Bocking, 81; Ellis Eyre, 88.
1876.—Robert Middleton, hatter, 82.
1877.—Betty Barber, 88.
1878.—Fanny Somerset, 81; Mary Elliott,
The Hills, 80.
1879.—John Middleton, Town Bottom, 82;
Olive Burrows, Smalldale, 85.
1881.—Rev. Joseph Hibbs, 80.
1882.—George Middleton (pinner), 83.
1883.—Nancy Dakin, 83; Mary Maltby, 87;
Robert Furness, 81; Joan Stafford, 85.
1884.—Obadiah Stafford, 87; Charlotte
Hallam, 81.
1885.—John Hallam, farmer, 81; Jacob
Hallam, 82; Ruth Bocking, 82.
1886.—Joshua Jaffrey, 82; Barbara Middleton, 87.
1887.—Joseph Bradwell, Town Gate, 83;
Deborah Elliott, 100, died at New Mills;
William Jeffery, Hill Head, 85; Wm. Longden, 80.
1888.—Mary Hallam, Smithy Hill, 88; Benjamin Giles, 81.
1889.—Rev. Robert Shenton, 83; Isaac Eyre,
87; Hannah Palfreyman, 86; Betty Hall, 83;
William Hill, 82.
1890.—Daniel Bocking, 80.
1891.—Rebecca Hall, 84; Hannah Middleton,
83.
1892.—William Jeffrey, 82; Abraham Ashmore, Smalldale, 88.
1893.—Ann Eyre, 80; Hannah Cheetham, 83.
1894.—Hannah Howe, Overgate, 81.
1895.—Hannah Pearson, died in Sheffield, 91;
Susan Cockerton, 81.
1896.—Joseph Bradwell, 80.
1897.—Joab Hallam, 82; Thomas Walker,
Hills, 87.
1899.—Job Middleton, 85; Nancy Morton, 87;
Abram Wilson, 90.
1900.—Hannah Andrew, 85.
1901.—Elizabeth Humphrey, 82; Elizabeth
Eyre, 80; Samuel Bradbury, blacksmith, 81.
1902.—Isaac Cooper, 82.
1903.—Harriett Middleton, Smalldale, 84.
1904.—Harriett Sarah Oldfield, 84; Harriett
Middleton, 80.
1905.—Robert Bradwell, 91; William Barber,
81.
1906.—Thomas Ford, The Hills, 90; Mary
Ford, his wife, 88; John Cheetham, Smalldale, 80; Mary Middleton, Gervase, 87.
1907.—Rachel Hallam, Within House, 80;
Ellen Cooper, 81.

1908.—Robert Middleton, Town Gate, 85; Caroline Brookes, 85; George Needham, Windmill, 88; Samuel Longden, 83.

1911.—Mrs. Charlotte Hill, Sheffield, 81; Joseph Bradwell, died at Longstone, 83; Charity Middleton, Smalldale, 82.

Some Tragic Deaths.

Below will be found, in something like chronological order, some deaths of a tragic character during the last century:—

1820 (about).—Wharton, found killed in a field near Eccles; supposed to have been murdered.

1838.—Thomas Bagshaw, Hazlebadge, hanged himself in a barn.
Rev. John Wright, Wesleyan minister, Bradwell, died suddenly whilst preaching at Peak Forest.

1846.—August 9th, Joseph Wright (70), killed by a horse on his farm in Smalldale.

1853.—Robert Middleton (freehold), a prominent Wesleyan, died through excitement after result of general election.

1854.—November 8th, Edwin Fox, thrown out of his cart and killed near New Wall Nook.

1858.—Mary Ann Bocking, Shoulder of Mutton Inn, died under tragic circumstances through loss of blood.

1859.—Sept. 9th, Richard Walker (62), blacksmith, cut his throat in a barn.

1860.—Martin Middleton Bland, Abney, killed and disembowelled in a horrible manner in a hayfield.

1860.—William Howe, Bradwell, both legs blown off and killed when blasting at Peak Forest.

1861.—William Hallam, Brough, drowned in River Noe.

1862.—Sarah Maltby (51), died suddenly from paralysis of the heart.
Sept. 19th, Joshua Hallam, killed by being thrown from a load of coal in Cave Dale, Bradwell. Cart overturned and killed the horse and driver.

1864.—John Kirkby (49), ruptured blood vessel and died immediately.

1865.—Dec. 2nd, William Bennett (56), miner, fell dead in Thomas Bradwell's grocer's shop, Town Gate.

1866.—Martha Middleton (73), died suddenly from fatty heart.

1867.—Oct. 10th, Charles Pearson (79), of Brough House, fell dead in the Newburgh Arms Inn, when attending a property sale.

1869.—October, Samuel Howe (63), miner, died suddenly in his chair after returning from work.

1872.—Thomas Middleton, farmer, Abney Grange, killed by lightning.

1875.—May 18th, Edward Middleton (62), Hugh Lane, died suddenly after attending a miners' meeting at the "Bull's Head."

1879.—Mary Hallam, Hill Head, died suddenly from heart disease.

1880.—May 11th, Elkanah Morton (65) Hungry Lane, died suddenly in his chair.

1881.—May, Mrs. Margaret Fox (56), Hazlebadge Hall, found dead in bed.

1882.—Sept 7th, John Andrew (67) Hollow Gate, killed by falling from a load of hay.

1883.—Oct 20th, John Hall (42), killed in a stone quarry at Dove Holes.

1884.—March 19th, Francis Palfreyman (5), died suddenly on his father's knee.
March 31st, Robert, Middleton (75), hatter, The Hills, died instantaneously.

85.—May 29th, Matthew James Buttery (47), Smalldale, hung himself in his house when the police were searching for the body of his wife. Mrs. Buttery was never found, and what became of her still remains a mystery.
Dec. 27th, Elizabeth Middleton (4), daughter of Samuel Middleton, Hollow Gate, burnt to death.

1886.—May 3rd, George Barnsley (23), Netherwater Farm, found dead in his house.

1886.—November 25th, Ann Walker (70), wife of Thos. Walker, The Hills, fell dead on the floor.

1887.—October 7th, Elizabeth Cooper (40), wife of George Henry Cooper, died from fright.

1888.—Dec. 3rd, Joseph Bland (30), killed at Abney, by his horse and cart.

1889.—Ellen Wilson (64), found dead in bed.
May 27th, John Broadbent, blacksmith, and his wife Louie, both died and were buried on the same day.

1890.—March 17th, Abraham Cooper, 36, Church Street, killed by falling from a plank into a deep cutting at Peak Forest.

1891.—February 17th, Roger Hall (54), Little Hucklow, killed by a shot on Dore and Chinley Railway.
June 27th, Elizabeth Bennett (69), killed by horse and trap at Town End.
August 29th, Thomas Harrison (69), Smalldale, killed by a cart at Peak Forest.
Oct. 10th, Miss Harriett Middleton (64), killed by falling down cellar steps at Sheffield.
Nov. 15th, Mary Middleton (70), Farther Hill, found dead in bed.

1892.—Dec. 20th, Joseph Hall (61), blacksmith, Nether Side, and Esther, his wife (63), both buried on one day.

1893.—April 7th, Mary Walker (45), wife of George Walker, The Hills, left her bed in the night and fell down Bradwell Dale rocks.
August 16th, Theresa Marsh (43), Little Hucklow, died from intemperate habits, probably accelerated by drinking laudanum.

1894.—February 28th, Mary Ann Cooper (18), found drowned in the River Wye, at Buxton.
April 4th, William Henry Draycott, late master of Bradwell Church School, and organist at church, died from alcoholic poisoning and exposure on Clifton Downs.

1895.—January 7th, Thomas Middleton (26), a native of Bradwell, fell dead when on his way to work at Peak Forest.
Dec. 25th, Benjamin Middleton (50), miner, found dead in his house in Hugh Lane.

1896.—June 12th, Hannah Bocking (63), fell dead in the kitchen whilst at work.
June 17th, George Walker (47), miner, fell dead whilst at work in his garden.
June 25th, Joseph Noble Dixon (87), Woodcroft, retired Inspector of Lighthouses, found dead in his chair with a newspaper in his hand.
John Bradwell (39), Church Street, fell dead from the seat of his wagonette in the railway station yard.

1897.—Sept. 11th, William Hayward (70), farmer, Coplowdale, run over by his horse and cart in Bradwell Dale and killed.

1898.—February 11th, George B. Hawksworth (39), Dialstone Villas, died after breaking his leg, coming from Outland Head.

Aug. 28th. Isaac Daniel Hill (62), Station Road, killed by falling out of a trap.
Sept. 25th, Emma Alice Ashton (47), Little Hucklow,, died from heart disease.
Nov. 25th, Harriett Bradwell (75), Yard Head, died very suddenly in bed.
1899.—July 13th, John Christopher Hancock (18), son of the Rev. John Hancock, Primitive Methodist, lost at sea.
Nov. 9th, Sarah Cramond (77), wife of James A. Cramond, tailor, killed by falling downstairs.
1901.—August 23rd, George Bancroft (65), stone mason, killed by falling from a new house in Stretfield.
May 12th, Robert Morton Palfreyman (12), run over by a traction engine and killed.
November 5th, Abraham Furness (75), killed by a fall of stone in Pindale Quarry.
1902.—February 23rd, Frederic Cyril Truelove (20), died suddenly.
1903.—Samuel Howe (58), killed in Bradwell Dale quarry.
1904.—February 25th, Ruth Hallam (four months). Little Hucklow, accidentally suffocated in bed.
November 4th, William H. Hallam, killed by a locomotive at Barnsley.
July 11th, Amariah Cooper (59), Little Hucklow, hung himself.
1905.—August 7th, Maria Burrows (49), died suddenly.
1907.—January 27th, Caroline Bradwell (one year), scalded to death.
February 21st, Oswald John Hill (48), "Hill Stile," died suddenly in his sleep.
June 5th, George Edward Johnson (28), butcher, hung himself.
Aaron Hallam, engine driver, killed in railway accident.

CHAPTER XXIII.

A TRAGIC VISITATION OF FORTY YEARS AGO.

Seventy Persons Mysteriously Cut Off.

A visitation of the town by a terrible fever forty years ago is considered the most terrible calamity that ever happened in the place. At the latter end of the year 1868 a fever of the most virulent type made its appearance, and in a few weeks cut off several persons, young and middle-aged. For a long time it completely baffled the skill of the medical men, and for the space of more than a year the whole place was in mourning. With the advent of 1869 the malady seemed to increase in virulence, and, in February of that year, of six persons attacked five succumbed to the disease. One of these victims was Thomas Middleton, who had served in the army and survived the climate of India, but returned to his native place to be cut off by this terrible pestilence. The same month a young married woman, Mrs. Levi Bradwell, was among the victims, and the enemy entered a house and snatched away

brother and sister, George Edward and Jane Bradwell. The church had just been built, and the churchyard had to receive the last two victims, who were the first to be buried there. Their graves are indicated by a flagstone at the foot of the tower. This month claimed another victim, a son of Mr. John Dakin, who carried on the business of optician.

There were not many cases in the month of March, but all, with one exception, proved fatal. While it cut off Mrs. William Stafford, of Smalldale, her husband and sister-in-law recovered. Another whom it snatched away was Miss Frances Hallam, a popular singer, who was to have been married shortly. Another estimable young lady, Miss Mary Barber, and Christina Middleton were numbered with the slain. The malady showing no sign of abatement, the whole populace was almost panic-stricken, and at this time the entire town was fumigated with tar, and the mouths of all the sewers with copperas.

As summer approached the disease continued its ravages, and in April, out of twelve persons attacked, five succumbed, while those who did recover were cases of a most serious character. Strange to say, the five victims this month were all in one family, four being in one house. The angel of death located itself at Yard Head, and in three weeks had snatched away Mrs. John Hallam, her daughter Alice Ann, her two sons James and William, and her sister, Mrs. Thomas Hallam. It was a pathetic sight to see the funerals of mother, daughter, and sister, all taking place at one time on the same day. The schools and places of worship were now closed so as to lessen the risk of infection, and death appeared to reign supreme.

Although there were many cases in the month of May, the rate of mortality was the lowest, for there was only one death, that of George Maltby, a fine young lead-miner, but in June the percentage of deaths was much higher, and a dreadful summer was threatened. There were several deaths this month, and no class of person seemed to escape. One of the victims was the Rev. Thomas Meredith, who then resided at Town End. He was faithful in the discharge of his pastoral duties to his suffering flock until he himself was laid low and quickly snatched away. And even the itinerant showman's household did not escape. He had pitched his tent for the coming wakes festival, and his child was snatched away.

July brought a big crop of cases, including several fatal. Thomas Meredith, junr., son of the deceased minister, was borne to his father's grave, so that the sorrowing lady had been bereft of both husband and son, and among other victims were Ann Burrows, a young woman in Smalldale, and Ada, daughter of Joshua Evans. Another pathetic case was that of Mrs. Alfred Middleton, of The Hills, who left husband and two little children, but the husband followed his wife to the grave a few weeks later, and the children were left orphans.

All the cases in August recovered, but the malady appeared with increased virulence in September, when there were four deaths—Mr. Alfred Middleton, P. Bland. Miss Dinah Ashmore, and a daughter of John Kennett, who at that time was proprietor of the Tanyard. The month of October brought sixteen fresh cases, death visiting half a dozen houses, taking away both breadwinners, their wives, and children. Those numbered with the dead this month were Michael Cheetham, a leadminer, who lived on The Hills; William Palfreyman, a fine-looking young fellow, in Smalldale; George Morton and Charlotte Bocking, who lived opposite each other on The Hills; John Prisk, who lived only a stone's throw away; and Marina Middleton. The health authorities were powerless to arrest the ravages of the disease, and a deputation from the Bakewell Sanitary Authority now visited the place and held an inquiry, consisting of Lord Denman, Dr. Fentem, and Dr. Taylor.

The inhabitants were almost panic-stricken by the virulence of the scourge, and as it continued its ravages great distress prevailed in many homes. In November there were 20 fresh cases, but only four deaths—Mrs. Slack, Miss Ruth Bramall, Smalldale, Mrs. George Bradwell, and Mr. Joseph Middleton, a well-known tradesman who carried on business in two shops, Town Bottom and top of Water Lane. The malady now appeared to be of a somewhat milder type, for although December produced another score cases there were but three deaths—Miss Hannah Hill, a son of Thomas Jennings, and Miss Elizabeth Somerset. It was a Christmas of mourning and distress, for death had stalked through the village all through the year, and continued some time during the following year.

There were several fatal cases at the latter end of 1868, Frances Taylor and Herbert Taylor succumbing to the disease; there were also a number in the early part of 1870, but the following is a list for the year 1869, from the diary of a gentleman at that time :—

January.—Recovered : Samuel Howard, Anne Howard, Alicia Evans.

February. — Recovered: John Broadbent; died: Thomas Middleton. George Edward Bradwell. Jane Bradwell, Mrs. Levi Bradwell, John Dakin's son.

March.—Recovered : William Bradwell; died: Frances Hallam, Mrs. William Stafford, Christiana Middleton, Mary Barber.

April.—Recovered: William Stafford, Nancy Stafford, Phyllis Hallam, Seth Evans, Sarah Ann Pearson, Martha Marshall, John Marshall; died: Mrs. John Hallam (mother), James Hallam (son), William Hallam (son), Alice Hallam (daughter), Mrs. Thomas Hallam (aunt).

May.—Recovered: Mrs. Charles Middleton, Dennis Evans, Maurice Evans, Richard Taylor, Thomas Bingham, Thomas Hallam's

daughter, Mrs. Joseph Hibbs, Fanny Hallam, Sydney Bradwell, Samuel Dakin, Mrs. Jacob Hallam, Mary Kay, Hannah Boyes, Sarah Middleton; died: George Maltby.

June.—Recovered: Nancy Morton, Olive Walker, Humphrey Hallam, Mrs. Jason Hallam, Josephine Middleton, Rachel Hallam; died: Rev. Thomas Meredith (Primitive Minister), Nancy Maltby's son, Travelling Showman's child.

July.—Recovered: Charlotte Middleton, Abraham Andrew, Elizabeth Andrew, Mrs. Benjamin Hall, Maggie Cramond, George Middleton's daughter, Isaac Bancroft's four children, Joseph Pearson's two children, Stephen Middleton's two children, Delia Bradwell, Thomas Hilton, Isabella Cramond; died: Mrs. Alfred Middleton, Ann Burrows, Thomas Meredith, jun., Ada Evans.

August.—Recovered: Joseph Cramond, James Henry Cramond, Thomas Burrows, Reuben Middleton, Mary Jane Marshall.

September.—Recovered: John Hallam, Mrs John Jennings, Mrs. Samuel Longden and three children, Stephen Middleton, Mrs. George Middleton, Thomas Morton, Joseph Pearson, Hugh Morton, Robert Evans' three children; died: P. Bland, Dinah Ashmore, Alfred Middleton, John Kennett's daughter.

October—Recovered: Aquilla Marshall, Reuben Bingham, Mary Jane Marshall, Samuel Bramall, Oliver Morton, Elias Palfreyman, Mrs. Jabez Morton, Ann Bramall, Betty Elliot, Betty Walker; died: Michael Cheetham, Charlotte Bocking, William Palfreyman, John Prisk, Marina Middleton, George Morton.

November.—Recovered: Mrs. Hallam, Mrs. Joseph Bramall, Mrs. Isaac Hall, Delia Middleton, Laxy Middleton, Joseph Pearson, Alice Ann Hall, Mrs. Zillah Hill. Samuel Hill, Mrs. Aaron Howe, Charlotte Hallam. Mrs. Elias Jeffrey, Emma Elliott, John Elliott, George Bancroft, Hannah Bradwell; died: Mrs. Slack, Mrs. George Bradwell, Ruth Bramall, Joseph Middleton.

December.—Recovered: Samuel Hallam, Hannah Evans, Joseph Bocking, Frank Morton, Lydia Thorpe, Hannah Bocking, Hannah Cheetham, Ann Revill, Ann Marsden, Margaret Middleton, Eliza Jeffrey, Samuel Jeffrey, John Marshall, Jane Marshall, Caroline Bocking, Frederick Archer; died: Hannah Hill, Thomas Jennings' son, Elizabeth Somerset.

Although more than forty years have passed, 55 of the above still survive. Altogether between 200 and 300 persons were attacked, and about seventy succumbed to the malady, the whole making a tragic and sorrowful chapter of local history.

CHAPTER XXIV.

SOME PLACES OF INTEREST.

A situation more delightfully romantic it would be difficult to find. Surrounded on three sides by mountains of great altitude, open on the other side to the delightful vale of Hope, with Winhill and Losehill reminders of the terrible slaughter during the Heptarchy, the situation of Bradwell is ideal for health and pleasure alike, while its curiously winding lanes are lined by the cottages that have been there for centuries, and the summit of Bradwell Edge, to which access may be gained by a gradually ascending path from the Abney Road, affords one of the most extensive and delightful views to be found on any mountain in England. One or two of the most interesting spots may be mentioned.

Robin Hood's Cross.

" I think of ages long since gone.
Of those who wrought with tools of stone;
I think of hunters free and bold,
Who dwelt up here in days of old."
—J. E. Bradwell.

Peak, one of which is of immense interest. It was prepared in the time of Queen Elizabeth, about 1590, and has small pictures or sketches outlining the churches and buildings of the principal places in the district of the forest—Glossop, Hayfield, Mellor, Chapel-en-le-Frith, Castleton, Hope, Tideswell, Wormhill, and Fairfield. There are also outlines of the various crosses, including a sketch of "Robin Hood's Cross," which is shown to be in Bradwell, but just at a point where the township of Bradwell, Hazlebadge, and Abney converge.

The remains of this monument, which has weathered the storms of a thousand years,

ROBIN HOOD'S CROSS
(from an Old Drawing); also a Stile made from the Cross.

The numerous crosses and remains of crosses met with in the Peak provide interesting study. The base and a portion of the shaft of one of these is in a field between Bradwell and Hope, but much nearer to the latter place. It is the last field before descending the hill above Eccles to Hope, and is only separated from the road by a stone wall. It is a most interesting object of antiquity that ought to be carefully preserved.

There are but few, however, who have the least idea that Bradwell possesses the remains of one of these pre-Norman crosses, for such the learned Dr. Cox concludes them to be.

In the Public Record Office there are many plans of the ancient Forest of the

may be found by following the Abney footpath up Bradwell Edge as far as the stile leading into the roadway at Abney Moor Gate. As already stated, the cross stood on the boundary line of these townships, and when the commons were enclosed the boundary wall was built over the rough base stone of the cross, which with half the squared socket may be seen in the bottom of the wall. The drawing shows the cross to have had a double base, with a shaft of considerable height.

The base of the cross is visible from the Abney Road side of the wall close to the gate, and is rendered easy of inspection by a kind of arch having been formed over it. The stone is about twenty inches square, but has been broken completely in two across the centre, probably when the shaft was wrenched from the socket. There appears to be no doubt whatever that the massive stones forming the stile leading from the first to the second field in the direction of Bradwell are the remains of the cross itself. One of these pieces is 3 feet 6 inches long, and another three feet long above the ground, but they are doubtless a great depth below the surface, while a third piece 3 feet 6 inches long lies on the ground. These would make a shaft about ten feet high. One of the pieces in use as a stump of the stile is clearly a portion of the cross, as it is L shape, showing a portion of a Latin cross. As an interesting relic of antiquity the cross ought to be restored and erected on the old base in its original position.

The Batham Gate and Roman Camp.

These two highly interesting spots have been described in the earlier part of this work.

The Bagshawe or Crystallized Cavern.

This cavern, one of the most magnificent of England's famous caves, is the property of Mr. W. H. G. Bagshawe, J.P., D.L., of Ford Hall, Chapel-en-le-Frith. It was discovered in the year 1807 by miners who, when working in the Mulespinner Mine, broke in on this splendid suite of caves. It takes its name from Lady Bagshawe, who was one of the first to visit the place, and whose husband, Sir William Chambers Bagshawe, was one of the proprietors when it was discovered.

A small building on the hillside close to the town is over the entrance to this beautiful place. The cavern is approached by 126 steps, hewn out of the rock. Here is Hutchinson's account of it when he toured the Peak in 1808, the year after the cavern had been discovered:

"There is no grandeur in its first appearance; it is rather terrific than otherwise, and is as much like going down into a deep dungeon as anything I can compare with. After descending about 300 steps, very perpendicular, you then walk, or more properly creep, on an inclined way for near a quarter of a mile, the opening being so low that it is impossible at times to get forward without going on all fours, though the road, if it be so called, is considerably improved of late; for it is not long since a gentleman of my acquaintance actually stuck fast between the rocks and was ten minutes before he could extricate himself, and then not without severely bruising his back. The different crystallizations which now attract the attention on every side, and above and below the passage, cause you to forget the irksomeness of the road and to drive away every idea of fatigue. New objects of curiosity begin to crowd one upon another. Here there is the appearance of the pipes of an organ called "The Music Chamber"; in other places the stalactites are formed into elegant small collonades,

with as exact a symmetry as if they had been chiselled by the greatest artist. Candles judiciously disposed in the inside of them gave an idea of the palaces of fairies, or the sylphs and genii, who have chosen this magnificent abode. In a recess on the left there appears the resemblance of a set of crystallized surgical instruments."

"But still you have seen nothing in comparison with what you are to expect; for in the course of 100 yards further, creeping at times, and passing down rugged places, you enter the Grotto of Paradise. This heavenly spot, for it cannot be compared with anything terrestrial, is of itself a beautiful crystallized cave about 12 feet high and 12 feet long, pointed at the top similar to a Gothic arch, with a countless number of large stalactites hanging pendant from its roof. Candles placed amongst them give some idea of its being lighted up with elegant glass chandeliers, while the sides are entirely incrusted and brilliant in the extreme. The floor is chequered with black and white spar, and altogether it has the most novel and elegant appearance of any cavern I ever beheld. This paradaisical apartment would be left with a kind of regret should you not expect to see it again on returning back."

"Still continuing a similar road to what has been passed, and entertained at various times with the curiosities of the place, and the gentle patterings of the water, which scarcely break the solemn silence of the scene, at length you arrive at the Grotto of Calypso, and the extremity of the cavern, above 2,000 feet from the first entrance. In order to see this to advantage it is necessary to rise into a recess about a yard high. There, indeed, from the beautiful appearance of the different crystallizations, some of them of an azure cast, from the echoes reverberating from side to side, you fancy yourself to be arrived at the secluded retreat of some fabled Deity. The water also running near this cavern brings a cool refreshing air which, from the exertion used and the closeness of the place, is very acceptable. The size of this grotto is something similar to that of the last, and indeed it is difficult to determine which is the most interesting. I could not restrain my imagination from composing the following little sonnet to the titular goddess of the place:—

SONNET TO CALYPSO.

Ah! Tell me Goddess, whither wilt thou fly,
  To shun the anguish of a love-sick mind;
The mocking echoes here will only sigh,
  With baffling breath, "Telemachus unkind!"

Thy grotto's sweet cirul'an hue in vain,
  To thee its dazzling lustre will impart;
Amidst thy sorrows here, thou must complain,
And pensive wreck thy deep desponding heart.

Alas! the sportive nymphs in vain allure!
  The God-like youth distains the beauteous form;

True to himself, and to his purpose sure,
  Though shipwrecked—bold, again he braves
    the storm.
Ah! Fly to Lethe's stream, Calypso, fly!
In sweet oblivion let thy anguish die.

"After returning by the same path for a considerable distance, there is another cavern to be investigated, which branches in a south-westerly direction from the one already explored. The roads here are still more difficult of access, but certainly the stalactites are more beautiful. A great many of them are pendant from the roof more than a yard long, and almost as small as the smallest reed. The top and sides

has been expended to make the exploration of this cavern easier.

There is a curious hole in the rock called "The Elephant's Throat," and in the roof a band of chert appears like the sole of a foot, with stalactites hanging on to the toes. From its enormous size, about five feet long, it is called "The Giant's Foot." In the roof of the "Bell House" are a number of holes looking like bells hanging in a church tower. In a compartment which has been named "The Bursting of the Tomb," the crystallizations are so magnificent that a visitor was once so incredulous as to apply the lighted candle to see if

The Dale.

THE DALE—ONE OF BRADWELL'S BEAUTY SPOTS.
It is here that the Ghost of Margaret Vernon is said to appear.

of this second cavern in many places are remarkably smooth, particularly the part called the amphitheatre. In general this place is of a very dark stone, to which the transparent appearances before-mentioned, with each a drop of water hanging at the bottom, form a fine contrast, and indeed this cavern is in some degree a contrast to the one before examined.

"Returning back we still admire the curiosities before noticed, and with regret leave this beautiful crystallized cavern, its representation in idea still continuing before the mind's eye, where it will remain as long as memory holds her seat."

Many additional chambers have been explored during the century, and much money

he could not detect what he thought was a fraud and not the work of nature.

"The Chamber of Worms" exactly describes the appearance of the small curling stalactites on the roof and sides, looking like worms wriggling out of the rock, and in "Tom of Lincoln's Bell Hall," a drop of water falls from the roof, which frequently changes colour from white to red, giving a beautiful variegated appearance to the stalagmite forming underneath. From "The Dungeon" other spacious openings have been found, and could a road from the valley be made into this magnificent suite of caves there is no doubt the cavern would be much more extensively visited.

The guide resides in the village.

Bradwell Dale.

This romantic ravine is considered one of the most beautiful of Derbyshire Dales. With high rocks and precipitous cliffs on each side extending about three-quarters of a mile to Hazlebadge Hall, it is a delightful walk. The rocks are of immense height, and the extensive blasting of stone of late years, whilst accomplishing the widening of the road through the dale, has not spoiled the scenery. A lead vein crosses the ravine, and here the old workings may be plainly seen. There are also public footpaths on the very summit of the rocks on one side, from which persons on the road in the bottom of the dale look like midgets, such are the dizzy heights above. From top to bottom the dale is a delightful spot.

Medicinal Waters of the Bath.

" But those hot waters were known in old
        time,
  The portway or High paved street named
        Bathgate
  Reaching for seven miles together from
        hence unto
  Burgh a little village doth manifestly
        shew."
                                —Camden, 1610.

An object of considerable interest and one that might be made a great asset to the district is the Bath at Edentree, from which "The New Bath Hotel" takes its name, but all that can be seen of a once famous medicinal spring is now a building in ruins in the Bath field at the rear of the hotel. The author of the "English Traveller" (1794), speaking of Burgh (or Brough) as "a village where there are some remains of an ancient Roman Causeway," adds, "And it is the opinion of most of the learned that those adventurers frequented the place on account of its baths."
Pilkington, in 1789, says: "I have heard of only one salt spring in Derbyshire. It is situate in the High Peak, betwixt the villages of Hope and Bradwell, and near a rock called Edintree. I have not seen it myself, though I took some pains to discover it, but am credibly informed that the impregnation is considerably strong. It is said to be useful in ulcerous and scorbutic complaints." The "Gentleman's Magazine" for 1819 mentions the "sulphurous spring" at Bradwell, and later Glover, the historian, mentions "the salt spring at Bradwell, which is worthy the attention of the faculty." About 1830 the waters were collected by Mr. Robert Middleton, of Smalldale, the proprietor, the building erected, and the bath constructed. For many years the waters were sought by many on account of their healing nature, and conveyed in barrels and vessels long distances, and thousands have derived benefit from the baths, the waters being very few degrees lower in temperature than the Buxton waters. But for the last forty years the place has been neglected. The bath itself is about five feet deep, and is approached by a descent of six stone steps, the water being conducted from the springs into the bath itself. This is doubtless a very valuable spring.

The Echo.

Although there are some notable echoes among the Peakland hills, the most strikingly curious echo ever heard, even by those who have travelled extensively, is found in Bradwell, and visitors have ravelled miles to hear it. Fortunately, t is on a public path, and any child knows "The Echo Field." Taking the field path to Castleton, it is about half a mile out of Bradwell, just before reaching Messrs. Hadfield's asphalt works. Such is the echo from the "Folly" that to describe it is difficult. The sounds produced are most uncanny in the night time, many voices responding to your own, almost close to your ear. A good story is told about a clergyman being taken along this path in the dark by a farmer. The cleric was unaware of the echo. When they were approaching the place, the farmer said, as if in fear, "There is only one spot on this lonely road where I grasp my stick a bit tighter, and we are just coming to it." The parson laughed at his dread. Presently a rough hand was placed on the preacher's collar, and a score of voices yelled, "We've got you now." It was only the farmer's joke, but the parson confessed that the sensation was not an agreeable one.

CHAPTER XXV.

FAMOUS SOLDIER IN THIRTY-SIX BATTLES.

CAREER OF THOMAS MORTON.

In a house on Nether Side, on the 12th of June, 1816, Thomas Morton first saw the light. He was a son of George and Hannah Morton, a good Christian couple, who, although Wesleyans, first opened a door for the reception of the Primitive Methodists, who held their first services in Morton's barn, which is still standing near to the house. George Morton allied himself with the new sect, but his sons, with one exception, remained with the parent body, and all their lives were prominent Wesleyans. Jacob Morton became a famous Wesleyan minister and Fellow of the Royal Astronomical Society; John Morton became a pioneer minister of the Primitive Methodists, and in the early days was thrown into prison for preaching; Frederick and Jabez Morton were prominent Wesleyan laymen all their lives, and for twenty years Thomas Morton saw more active service in the army than is given to most men in that period of time.

Thomas Morton left his home and enlisted in the 29th Regiment at Sheffield in the early part of 1838. Here is what he wrote to his distressed mother—a note scratched in pencil on a scrap of rough paper:—

"Dear Mother, it is to comfort you that I write at this time. I am quite comfortable of myself, and am fully persuaded it is for the best. Be not uneasy, for I will write at Liverpool, and every month after. I am pleased with your letter and shall be steady and look at my Bible. My respects to you all.

THOMAS MORTON."

"At Cork I met with Thomas Hibbs, and among Sheffielders in the 82nd Regiment, and at Dublin I met with Ephraim Lloyd that opened Bradwell Chapel. He has been a soldier, and been bought off."

This is interesting as having reference to the opening of the first Primitive Methodist Chapel in Bradwell (now a cottage). In the next letter in July, in reply to one from his parents, he remarks: "You said you could not understand that Ephraim Lloyd. He told me that he had been a travelling preacher in the Primitives, and that he opened Bradwell Chapel, and had slept many times with you. He had been

HISTORICAL HOUSE IN NETHER SIDE,
Where lived George Morton, who first opened his door to the Primitive Methodists.

And the Bible was his guide throughout one of the most strenuous lives even of a soldier.

In June, when he was sailing with about forty other recruits from Dublin to Plymouth, at midnight the mast-head smashed down on the boat, the engine and the compass broke down, and in this condition the boat was tossed about all night until they were picked up by another vessel and taken on to Cork, 35 miles, where they remained a week before the voyage could be resumed. In his own words, "it was a miserable scene to see, men, women and children expecting to meet with a watery grave every moment. The sailors themselves never thought of landing any more." In his final letter from Plymouth he says:

in the 99th Regiment, and was bought off. You told me to inquire about William Cheetham. He is in the same with me, and is my companion, but I am sorry to inform his uncle that he is in hospital very ill." In the same letter he gives an account of the army discipline of that day, and says: "I have seen deserters punished in a very cruel manner. I have seen one flogged and others sent to the treadmill, and many are marching up and down the bricks with a pack on their backs. One deserted out of our company, servant to the captain, and stole £170 from him. He has since been taken to Chatham, having committed another robbery of £500. I should not like to see him punished; I should not wonder but he will get shot."

But before he had been in the army a year he was tired of a soldier's life, for on Christmas Eve, 1838, the following official letter was sent to his father:—

Horse Guards, 24th Dec., 1838.

"The Adjutant General has now to acquaint George Morton with reference to his application of the 15th instant that the General Commanding in Chief has been pleased to authorise the discharge of Private Thomas Morton, of the 29th Foot, on payment of the regulated Compensation of Twenty Pounds, which must be lodged with the Paymaster of the Regiment at Devenport within one month from the date hereof, or the authority will be cancelled.
George Morton, Bradwell.

But in less than a year, he again joined the Army, for Nov. 21st, 1839, saw him enlisted in the 31st Foot, where he was destined to make his mark, for his Regiment was soon called out to the East Indies.

THROUGH THE AFGHAN WAR.

Morton had an eventful six years in the East Indies. His regiment landed at Calcutta on October 26th, 1840, and sailed up the Ganges to Chinsurah, arriving at Agra on March 3rd, 1841. In a letter at this time he mentions that he had received a letter from another Bradwell soldier, William Cheetham, who had been reduced from the rank of Corporal. Four years later he reports the death of William Cheetham.

For about a year he was in Cabul in General Elphinstone's army, when there was fearful massacre,—"thousands of human skeletons strewn all over the road, it was heart-rending to hear their bones cracking under the wheels of the guns." They had to fight all the way to Cabul, where the road for six or seven days' march was "strewn over with skeletons shocking to relate." The Massena battle was fought against the tribes that had never before been conquered, and this with the sun at 126 degrees. They destroyed 40 forts.

The letters written by Morton to his parents at Bradwell would fill a volume, and would certainly provide material for a history of the campaign in Afghanistan. He was in the East Indies from 26th October, 1840, to December, 1846, and went through the Afghanistan campaign in 1842 including the actions of Mazeena, Tezeen, and Jundallah. He was in the Battle of Dubba in 1843, when the Indians, under Shere Mohammed, were defeated by the British, under Sir Charles Napier; also at Hydrabad when the Belochees were defeated by the British, under Sir Charles. The Belochees numbered 35,000, and the British only 2,600, and this led to the surrender of Hydrabad.

He also served throughout the Sutlej Campaign of 1845-6, and was present at the Battle of Moddkee on December 18th, when the Sikhs were defeated by the British under Sir Hugh Gough and Sir John Littler, and was there when Sir Robert Sale fell. This was on the 18th December, and three days later he was in the Battle of Ferozeshah, when 16,700 British, under Sir Hugh Gough, defeated 50,000 Sikhs under Tej Sing. Six days later he was in action at Maharajapore, under Sir Hugh, when 18,000 Mahrattas were defeated by 14,000 British. He was also in the great battle at Aliwal, on January 28th, 1846, when the Sikhs (19,000) were defeated by the British (12,000), under Sir Harry Smith, and he fought in the still greater Battle of Sobraon on February 10th, under Sir Hugh Gough, when the Sikhs lost 13,000 and the British loss of killed and wounded was 2,338.

IN THE CRIMEAN WAR AND INDIAN MUTINY.

REMARKABLE EXPERIENCES.

But the most eventful period of Morton's life was that of the Crimean War and the Indian Mutiny. England and France declared war against Russia on March 28th, 1854, and his regiment, then stationed at Preston Barracks, being ordered out to active service, he made his will, sent his gold watch and other belongings to his brother Jacob, and embarked from Liverpool on the first Tuesday in April.

AT SCUTARI.

Writing from Camp Scutari opposite Constantinople, on May 21st —he had promised to write once a month—he says how glad the soldiers were to leave barracks, as they were "nearly eaten alive with fleas." There were fearful thunderstorms that flooded the tents, and two of the officers of the 93rd Regiment returning from town to camp after the storm, were washed away to sea. In his highly interesting descriptive letter, he enclosed to his Bradwell relatives some rose leaves from the Sultan's garden. He says: "Lord Raglan is gone up to Varna with the other bigwigs, French and English, to hold a Council of War, so that in a few days we expect to move towards the enemy. The steamers are all ready to take in the cavalry and artillery are just arriving." In his description of life in the camp he observes: "The men drink hard, wine and spirits are so cheap. A good many men have been flogged—one of our regiment, the first for a number of years—it is the only punishment that will answer for insubordination." Again, "the Turkish women are very virtuous, either by choice or force; if they are known to go astray they are sure of death instantly. They go about in groups more like Egyptian mummies than anything else." He concludes by wishing his friends "good health, a good spring, and a prospect of a good harvest with plenty of Hools and a good price for lead." Hools, it may be explained, is the miner's term for the lumps of lead ore got from the mine.

A month later—June 19th—writing from Camp Slojin, he tells how cholera is affecting the soldiers. Already some have died of the malady, and two were drowned while bathing. He says, "You will begin to think in England that we are a long time before we commence to fight the Russians, but I assure you that our generals, officers, and soldiers are all as anxious to be at the enemy as you are to hear of the success of our Arms, but they have to take care that they are prepared in every respect to meet the enemy. However, five or six days will bring us to the seat of war, and before another month passes we shall have measured swords with the Russians. I believe the Turks are giving them plenty to do, and when we get up there we shall bring Nicholas to his senses."

THOMAS MORTON.

With just a touch of humour the brave soldier remarks: "I don't think I shall be at Bradwell Wakes this year. but I shall think of you all if I am alive, and will drink a glass to all your very good health, and think that I am amongst you."

IN "THE VALLEY OF DEATH."

A letter of July 28th from Camp Marrartine, shows that the cholera made its appearance among the troops at Deona, and the Division lost 42 men and two women in two days, but since removing there had been only six or seven deaths. He remarks pathetically: "Poor Hogan, Quartermaster of the Seventh Regiment, was buried to-day. I think Jacob saw him at Chatham, a little man. He only lasted about 18 hours after he was taken ill. Five of our strongest Grenadiers died in a few hours. While I am writing I hear that we have two more deaths in our regiment, and if we stop at this place long I am afraid we shall have it very bad. The country is beautiful to all appearance, but it is the Valley of Death. The Russians lost 40,000 men in 1828-9 by plague and cholera, the French have had it at Varna, so have our other Divisions. It is very hot. This is worse than fighting, losing our fine men for nothing." He adds: "I drank all your healths at the Wakes, and wished I was with you for a few days."

Singularly enough, the very next day he writes a doleful letter anent the disease in the camp. The weather was boiling hot. He says: "We have lost two men by cholera up to 12 a.m., the 19th Regiment next to us lost two also. One bad case in hospital. We are to get a dram of rum to-day, which I think will do the men good. It is better than wine. When we left our last camp we left our cases of cholera with two doctors, and 21 men on guard behind. Three or four of the men died. When I wrote last I was not well, and thought it might be my last letter to you." 2nd August: "Yesterday four men died, and the officer 77th. My groom took sick last night. I have just been to hospital to see him. The tents are full, a melancholy night. Two men appear to be dying, and a number more bad cases." 3rd: "We have had no deaths yesterday or to-day, and I think this ground is much healthier than our last. All of us that are well are as jolly as possible. We want nothing but work, and it is a pity to see such a fine army sent out from England to fight the common enemy, and to be left to die in such a country as this without a sight of the Russians." "A doctor of the 23rd Regiment dead to-day."

A letter covering events from the 4th to the 8th of August is pregnant with interest. The doctors are compelling each man to take one eighth of a pint of rum daily. Large numbers of men continue to die daily in hospital and the doctor told Morton that he had over 150 under his treatment. One of his pioneers died after an hour or two's illness. He says: "There is a visible change at divine service now. Everyone seems to take a part. I hope our united prayers will be heard, and that the sickness may leave us. It is very dreadful to see fine men cut off in a few hours. Oh that we may all be ready for the great change.

7th inst.: "Yesterday we got the English Mail. I got no letters and was much disappointed. I got the illustrated and also the "Daily News" with the Bradwell postmark on it, which did me good. When I saw it I called it my "Brada Wakesing."

We have one man dead to-day in our regimen. We have lost now in our Division one Paymaster, one Quartermaster, one Doctor, and one Ensign, and about 30 men per Regiment."

8th inst.: "We had one man died last night. A captain of the artillery is dead."

The Regiment frequently removed their camp a few miles in the hope of finding a healthier site, and every day Morton dotted down a few events on a sheet of paper, and posted it to Bradwell with every mail. His next letter, which begun on August 9th, reports further deaths. Writing from a strong Turkish post, where the Turks had fortifications, garrisoned with 10,000 men, and where he had been digging wells and opening fountains to get water for the troops, he says: "I found Roman tiles cemented together with Roman cement, which must have been in the ground for ages. We have four men dead in hospital now. A captain of the 77th died the other day. Our army stores have been burned downed at Varna by Greeks, and 15,000 pairs of boots sent out for the troops were destroyed, besides biscuit and other stores. Two of the Greeks were killed on the spot, and others arrested. I don't think we shall fire a shot this year. What a miserable prospect before us for the winter."

In a hurriedly-written letter of August 29th, Morton informs his relatives at Bradwell that the cholera was still hanging about, that the assistant-surgeon was taken ill that morning and died at noon. They brought him "home" in a cart and buried him at night. Major Mackie and the paymaster were both very ill. He adds: "It took 30 native carts with two bullocks each to move our regimental sick, and 112 horses to carry the men's knapsacks, so by that you may judge in what state this country has left our men. They are not like the same men that you saw at Liverpool on the 4th of April." At the close he adds: "I was very sorry to hear of Sister Mary's death, but the will of the Lord must be done. I hope to be spared to write to you again, but if not I hope we shall all meet in Heaven."

Morton's regiment, 27 officers, 16 women, and 780 men, embarked on August 30th on the ship Orient. Major Mackie had died on the march a few days before, and one man died on board ship.

AT SEBASTOPOL.

Morton's first letter from the battlefield is a curious document. It was written "lying before Sebastopol, 3rd October, 1854," and is scribbled with pencil on narrow strips from the margin of a newspaper. At his own request he was allowed to do the duty of an officer with the men in action. Alluding to the great Battle of Alma, when the Russian army (46,000), under Prince Menchikoff, were defeated by the British, French, and Turkish forces (57,000), under Lord Raglan and Marshal St. Arnaud, he says: "On the 20th we fought a bloody battle. . . . I was slightly wounded in the right leg, but was able to continue the action till it was over. . . . We put the fear of the English and French in their hearts, but at a great loss of life on our side. I was the only officer in our regiment touched, and we were always in front of the battle. The Colonel got a ball through his pistol bolster, and it lodged in his prayer-book." On this narrow strip of newspaper he goes on to tell how they have now surrounded Sebastopol. He said: "It is tremendously strong to look at, and we must expect to lose a great number of men in taking it, but take it we shall. They keep throwing shot and shell at anyone approaching too near, and they are working like bees, throwing up fresh works. We have not fired a gun at them yet, but if any one of them come near us we try the range of our mine rifles at them. It will be four or five days before we are ready to open fire on them. What destruction of life will then commence! Thousands upon thousands must fall on both sides." "My trust is in God, the God of Battles, who is able to preserve me. I know you all pray for me; continue to do, and if we are not spared to meet again on this side the grave I hope we shall meet in Heaven."

AT BALACLAVA.

Morton was at the Battle of Balaclava on October 25th, when the Russian army (12,000) were defeated by the British and Turkish army, under Lords Raglan and Lucan. In this battle occurred the famous charge of the Light Cavalry Brigade, under the gallant Earl of Cardigan. Here the Bradwell soldier distinguished himself. In view of the historical importance attached to this famous battle, Morton's letter to Bradwell, written on November 12th, is of the greatest interest. He says: "Since I wrote last we have had some rough work to do, without mentioning the continued fire in the trenches, which causes us a great deal of loss at times. The enemy have attacked us once at Balaclava, and got nearly into the town. To drive them back we lost most of our light cavalry. . . I got a good view of the charge of the Dragoons. They did their work in grand style, but they were outnumbered and overpowered, and, poor fellows, they had to retire under a heavy fire of artillery and musketry. I went over the field afterwards, and it was a fearful sight to see men and horses strewn in all directions. I went to the Balaclava two days afterwards with Colonel Jefferys, and we saw two horses which appeared to have been blown to pieces with a shell. They were at a French post, so the Colonel asked the French officer how it happened, and to our surprise the officer told us that the horses had only been shot with musket balls, but his soldiers had cut them up for beef steaks. . . . A few days after this they made a determined attempt to turn off right flank. I mounted and rode to the place, but the balls and shell began to fall pretty thick about me, so drew back out of range of their guns, and the enemy were beaten back with a great deal of loss on their side. Our loss was trifling."

AT INKERMAN.

In the same letter Morton goes on to give his experiences at the historic battle of Inkerman on November 5th, when the British and French allied forces (14,000), under Lord Raglan and General Canrobert, were victorious over the Russians (46,000), under Liprandi, the British loss being 2,612 against a Russian loss of over 9,000. He continues:—

"On the morning of the 5th (this day week) they made a most determined attack at the same point, namely, the Heights of Inkerman, and the slaughter on both sides was tremendous. We beat them back, and their loss is estimated at 16,000 killed—I think myself about 9,000 or 10,000. I went twice over the ground after the battle, and never saw such a sight. The Russians were lying in heaps, hundreds of wounded lying with the dead, and lots of our poor fellows lying head to head with them just as they fell in defence of our camp and position. A more determined attack was never made. Our regiment went into action 346 men, and lost 131 killed and wounded, including two officers wounded, both through the left thigh. The regiment was in a most critical position. Being so weak in numbers, and having a large body of the enemy opposed to them, they fired all their ammunition away and still showed a front. When I saw them firing so much I loaded 6,000 rounds on three ponies, and went myself to the front with it, and it was very welcome. The regiment had greatcoats on, and I had not, so I was conspicuous, and I drew a heavy fire on them, so I left them when I had given them the ammunition. Our sergeant-major was killed, and the two majors both lost their horses. Colonel Shirley, with the remainder of the regiment, was on duty in the trenches and outposts. On my way to the regiment I met Sir George Brown, and he told me, if I saw any of his staff, to say that he wanted them. I answered, 'Yes, Sir George,' but turned round on my horse and saw that he was wounded, so I galloped back and asked him if he would have a doctor. He thanked me and said he would do so. I soon found one, and we got him off his horse and placed him in my greatcoat on the ground. He is wounded through the left arm. He was very cool and in good spirits, but he only just got off his horse in time. He was quite weak from loss of blood. When his arm was dressed he was taken to his tent on a stretcher, which he first refused, saying that the stretchers were more wanted for the poor men, but

he found that he was too weak, and submitted. Now we are blazing away at each other from morning till night. We have battered the town very well, but the houses are built of stone, and I think the wood and shipping in the place is fireproof, for they won't burn any length of time; besides, they have two guns for our one, and they are excellent gunners. Don't be in a hurry to hear of the fall, for we understand that we are to winter here. God help us, for we shall be miserable if any of us survive. We have now had six days' rain, men and officers drenched to the skin and no change of clothing, so how can any constitution stand it? The regiment is never in their tents more than sixteen hours out of the forty-eight. Just returned from divine service. Our numbers get weaker every Sunday. . . . Continue to write to me and pray for me. My thanks to Mrs. John for wishing to dress my wound; thank God, it does not want dressing, as it is quite well. I have only slept one night without my clothes since we have been in the Crimea, and then I got cold. We are in a sad state for want of clean linen. I paid 50 shillings for three old shirts at an auction. Our adjutant lost his arm in the trenches ten or twelve days ago. The Colonel asked me if I should like to be adjutant. I thanked him, but declined."

Three days before Christmas (December 22nd) Morton wrote home, giving a graphic description of the hardships the men were undergoing. "I don't think we have more than 400 men doing duty, and most of them would not be able to put their bayonets through a Russian's greatcoat We are getting lots of reinforcements, but lots of them are not able to stand the climate, being too young to endure the hardships, so they die in dozens, or are sent on boardship. The French assist us in removing them, and they took 1,100 sick one day from our army, 700 another day, and so on."

Other Bradwell men were in this war, and Morton says: "I inquired about the armour-sergeant of the 68th; he was well. I have not seen anyone that could give any record of Hill. If his friends write to him and tell him to call on me, I will give him a glass of grog and be glad to see him." He goes on to say that everything is very dear, flour 1s. a pound, a small loaf that would not be enough for brother Fred's breakfast 2s., and everything in proportion."

Giving his relatives accounts of the progress made from time to time during this terrible war in the camp before Sebastopol, Morton concludes a letter of March 19th with: "I hope you all continue to pray to God to preserve me and bring me safe back to Bradwell to lay my bones beside my parents, there to slumber till the great day."

In a letter a week later he says: "Last night about midnight the Russians attacked the French, also our advance post, and a dreadful conflict ensued. The French were driven out of their works with a loss of about 500 killed and wounded, together with some of their best officers. The Russians attacked our works at the same time, but they were repulsed in grand style, but not without serious loss. Colonel Kelly, of the 34th regiment, who was in command, was killed, also two captains, one of the 7th, the other of the 97th regiment, and a lieutenant of the 34th killed, besides a number wounded. We did not lose many men in proportion to officers. . . . Colonel Brownrigg came into our camp early this morning, and said that our men had behaved nobly. A Greek officer in the Russian service rushed into our 8-gun battery, followed by some desperate fellows, but they were cut down instantly. The officer had a sword in one hand and a dagger in the other. The dagger was taken by one of our officers, and it is now in my tent. Neither party dare go to collect their dead till dark."

In a further letter he says: "We opened fire on the town on Easter Monday, and we have kept it up ever since. The Russians return the fire faintly at times, but if we attempt to encroach upon them they are most vigorous, and it is with difficulty and loss that we gain any advantage over them. We have had an officer and several men killed since we opened fire, and eight or ten men wounded. My head is completely bothered with the din of guns and mortars going off every moment." In the same letter there is a reference to the kindly interest which the wife of the Vicar of Hope took in the soldiers at the front, for he says: "I received a parcel from the Colonel the other day which had been sent to the regiment from Mrs. Cave, of Hope, to be distributed to the officers and men of the regiment, and I distributed the articles, I think, in the spirit in which they were sent, and from the Colonel to the private all were most thankful for the kind feeling which prompted the gift from our native village ladies. The tracts were very nice, and I read many of them. I write to Mrs. Cave by this mail to acknowledge the receipt of parcel."

"Another Bloody Day's Work."

In a letter dated June he says: "The day before yesterday we opened fire from our trenches, which is tremendous, and yesterday, between five and six o'clock, the French went out to attack the Mamolong, which they carried in grand style, after which they attempted the Malacoff Tower, but they found it too strong, and they went back with great loss. At the same time they lost the Mamolong, and oh! what a fearful loss of life. The French did not lose less than 3,000 men, killed and wounded. However, they went at it again, and were successful, and this morning they are in possession of the Mamolong, and are reversing the works so as to open on

the shipping in the harbour, which keeps a continual fire upon them. At the same time yesterday we attacked another outwork of the Russians in front of our works. This attacking party was commanded by Colonel Shirley, and the greater part of the men and officers belonged to our regiment. They have done their work well, but at what cost! Major Bailey killed; Captains Corbett and Wray and Lieut. Webb killed; Captain Maynard, and Lieuts. Grice, Pearson, and Remy wounded. The number of killed we do not know. Other regiments lost a great many too. We are going to attack them again to-day, so that I am too much excited to write a letter. . . . You must all continue to pray for me, and I have great faith that the Almighty will spare me to return once more to my native village."

In a further letter of the 18th he says: "We have had another bloody day's work," and goes on to speak of the "fearful loss of life, some thousands and a great many senior officers"; and a week later he says that they have more than 1,000 "serious praying officers in the army; they are not the unthinking people that they are taken for."

Marked for Promotion.

With the strenuous work Morton's health suffered, but he was marked for promotion, and soon had offer as quartermastersergeant at Parkhurst. In a letter in December he says he heard from Colonel Jefferys lately, and he should be in the "Gazette" in January. As usual, he remembers everybody at Bradwell, and writing to his brother, the Rev. Jacob Morton, he says: "Will you be good enough to send them all £1 each to make them merry at Christmas—John, Louisa, and yourself included, that will be to Bradwell, Fred, Jabez, Alice, Hannah Ashmore, and Fanny, and if there is no chance of my being at home soon I will send you a cheque."

Briefly, here is the career of this distinguished man:—

Private 31st Foot, 1839; corporal, 1843; sergeant, 1844; colour-sergeant, 1845; quartermaster-sergeant, 1851; quartermaster of the 88th Regiment, 1852; quartermaster Depot Battalion, 1855.

Service: East Indies from 26th October, 1840, to 6th December, 1846; United Kingdom from 6th December, 1846, to 4th April, 1854; embarked for Scutari 4th April, 1854, and landed in the Crimea 14th September, 1854. Was in Bulgaria awhile.

Engagements: Campaign in Afghanistan in 1842, including the actions of Mazeena, Tezeen, Jungdallurk; served through the Sutlej campaign of 1845-6; was present at the battles of Mookee, Ferozeeshah, Buddiwall, and Sobraon; served through the whole of the Crimean campaign of 1854 and 1855, and was engaged at the Battle of the Alma (where he was wounded), Inkerman, and the Siege of Sebastopol.

Medal for Cabul; medal and three clasps for Moodkee, Ferozeeshah, Aliwal, and Sobraon; medal and three clasps for Alma, Inkerman, and Siege of Sebastopol; also 5th class Order of the Medfidi for distinguished conduct during the Crimean campaign.

And this distinguished soldier entered into rest at Parkhurst Barracks on the 24th of March, 1860, aged 43 years.

LATE WILFRED FISKE.
(See page 63.)

CHAPTER XXVI.

THREE HUNDRED YEARS AGO AT HAZELBADGE HALL.

Family Litigation of the Vernons. An Old Time Rhyme.

Concerning Hazelbadge Hall, in Bradwell Dale, the fine seat of the Vernons centuries ago, a volume might be written. As an addenda to the reference to the old mansion in a former chapter, a portion of a rhyme of three hundred years ago may be considered fitting for these pages.

For fifty years, at the latter end of the sixteenth and the first four decades of the seventeenth century, John Harstaff was the trusted agent and confidential clerk of the family of Vernon, and lived at Sudbury. Carefully preserved at Sudbury Hall, there is a book of paper with a parchment cover, endorsed "John Harstaff's Poetry whilst he lived at Sudbury, 1635, of the Vernon family and concerns." They are most interesting annals, showing litigation that extended over many years, dealing with various estates of the family. The first part, written in 1615, has particular reference to Hazelbadge Hall and estate, and is as follows :—

I here intend to make a true Relation,
According to my plaine and simple fashion,
Of maine troubles and incumbrances,
With sundrie suites and other grievances
Which hapt to Maister Vernon in his lyffe,
And after his decease unto his wyffe;
Which I (their servant) better can declare,
Because therein I had noe little share;
'Tis nowe noe lesse than foure and twentie years
Since first I had to doe in those affaires;
About the whiche (I truelie may affirme)
For twelve or thirtene yeares I mist noe terme.

Herein I purpose alsoe to relate,
In what great danger stood his whole estate;
And lykewyse make particular narration,
Howe he disposed his lands by declaration;
And howe his friends and servants he regarded,
Not leaving anie of them unrewarded.

First then to shewe his name and pedigree,
This worthie Esquire was Lord of Sudburie,
John Vernon called, whose father Henry Wight,
The sonne and heire of Sir John Vernon, Knight,
Of Haddon House a younger sonne was he,
And married Ellen, second of the three
Coheires unto St. John Mongomorie.

By her came Sudburie with other landes
And manie faire possessions to his handes;
Whereof to treate I do not here intend.
But onely shew they linealye descend,
From her to Henry, and from him to John,
Who being yonge did enter thereupon.

He was by suites of lawe encumb'red long,
And by his mother's meanes endured much wrong,
Who practiced by all the wayes she might
To injure him, and take away his right;
Not only in such things his father left him,
But also of his birthright she bereft him,
And gave her landes unto his younger brother;
Who can speak well of so unkynd a mother?

She was coheire unto an anncient squier
High Thomas Swinnerton, of Staffordshire;
Whose landes she with a sister did devyde;
Both Hilton, Swinnerton and much besyde
In Sharshill, Saredon, and in Essington,
In Hampton, Penkridge, and in Huntington,
Aspley and Sugnell, and in others moe,
Which I have heard of, but never did knowe.

Hilton, an ancient house, fell to her share,
A park and faire demaines belonginge are
Unto the same of which and all the rest
She John depryved, young Henry to invest,
Who after her decease the same possest.

But Henry did not long enjoy the same;
For being wedded to a gallant dame,
He leaving her with chyld did end his lyffe,
Committing goods and landes all to his wyffe.
Who shortly after had a daughter faire,
Unto her father's landes the onelie heire.

Young Henry's match did verie much displease
His elder brother John, who for to raise
Their house and name did formerlie intend,
That all his lands should after him descend
On Henry. But that marriage changed his mynd,
Soe much that afterwards he was unkynd
Both to his brother's infant, and his wyffe,
Soe that amongst them soone befell greate stryffe

And suites in lawe; All which I could declare,
For theim I sustained much toyle and care
And therfore nowe yt labour meane to
spare.

By these he was exasperated more,
And (which did also discontent him sore),
One Justice Townsend from ye Marches
came,
And did espouse the young and loftie Dame.

They sell and cut downe woods, great waste
they make,
But then, whether it was redresse to take,
Or for his owne avayle, or else of grudge,
To them, it fitts not me thereof to judge
He went about, and by all meanes prepar'd
To fynde his brother's heire the Prince's
Warde
And to that end he quicklie set to worke,
One Wakeringe then, who for such praies
did lurke,
And was as faythfull as a Jewe or Turke.

Betweene theim two I think it was agreed,
That if in this affaire they hapt to speede,
The Wardship should to Vernon granted be,
And Wakeringe should in money have his
fee.
All their proceedings here for to repeate,
Would be but little worth (thought labour
great)
Short tale to make (which was of all ye
ground)
She was prov'd Ward a tenure there was
found.
How truly, here I list not to decyde
Theirs be yt change by whom yt poynt
was tryed.

The Wardship Maister Vernon looked to
have,
But Wakeringe (since made knight) proved
then a ——
Alledginge that it lay not in his handes,
Unto their first accord as then to stand;
And good cause why, for Justice Towns-
end's purse
Did open wyder, and more crownes dis-
burse;
He therefore got ye wardship of the chylde,
And Vernon by Sir Gilbert was beguyled:
Who made himself the Farmer of her
landes,
And during nonage kept them in his
handes,
And here might Maister Vernon well repeat
His labours ill-employ'd and money spent.

But oftentymes we see it come to passe
When men of malice, seeke their neigh-
bour's losse,
Or Worke their owne revenge. It pleaseth
God,
To beate themselves, they make a smart-
inge rod;
As in this case it afterwards befell,
Both to himself, and those he lov'd right
well.

For nowe forthwith newe suites they doe
commence,
I'th Court of Wardes against him with pre-
tence
To right the Ward, whose tytle in such
sort
Was favour'd be ye friendship of that
Court,
That they recover'd there out of his handes,
A manie parcells of his mother's landes;
Which for some yeares before he had
enjoy'd
As copi-holde, nor sought they to avoyd
Him from ye same, nor doe I thinke they

could,
Had not ye Court of Wardes therein con-
troul'd.

Besydes they sued him in the Channcerie,
For certaine summes of money formerlie
Recover'd by him for landes which by his
mother
Had beene convey'd unto his younger
brother
In sale wher of they joy'd the one with th'
other.

Which sumes amountinge to nyne hundred
pounde
As debte yet due to Henrye's will were
founde.

They charged him further with six hun-
dred more,
Which they alledg'd he had receav'd before
His brother's death, who mortgag'd for ye
same,
A farme he held called Haselbach by name.

Concerninge which gith thus it comes i' th'
way,
I thinke it not amisse something to say;
This farme of Hazlebach whereof I speake,
Is situate nere Castleton i' th' Peake;
And worth (as by ye rentall did appeare)
But little less than seavin score pounde a
yeare;
Part of the Vernons landes long had it
beene.
As in their anncient Deedes is to be seane,
Sir George who of ye Vernons was ye last,
That helde those goodlie landes, from whom
they past
By two Coheires out of the Vernons name
(For which great Talbott was ye more to
blame)

Sir George I say of whom yet manie speake
(For great houskeepinge termed King o' th'
Peake),
Was much directed in his younger yeares,
In all his causes and his greate affaires,
By's uncle, Sir John Vernon's, good advyse,
Who was a learned man, discreete and
wyse;

Wherfore Sir George to shew yt he was
kynd,
And to his uncle have a thankfull mynd,
Of Haselbach he granted then a lease,
To him and his assignes which should not
cease,
Untill ye terme of four score yeares were
spent,
Reserving thereupon a pennie rent.

Sir John until his death possess't ye same;
And afterwards this farme to Henry came
His onlie sonne who held it during liffe
But after his disease there fell great stryffo
About it, through ye practise of his wyffe.

This Henry Vernon was of great esteeme
A man both wyse and learned (as may
seeme),
Who in his cuntrie also bore great sway,
And kept a worthie house, as old men say,
Who often talke of him even to this day.

It chanced (manie yeares before his death)
He went and served in the Warres at Leath
In Scotland, where he was a Captaine then,
Ore some three hundred of his cuntrimen
But he had thought it meete before he
went,
For to ordaine his will and testament;
Wherein to John, his sonne, he did be-
queath,
The farme of Haslebach after his death
When eyghteene yeares of age he did
attaine

The one tyme ith mother's handes ʒt
should remaine
And after yt as seemeth true and plaine,
He never altered it, but left it soe ;
But what's soe foule yt mallice will not
doe?

He sicke or deade his ·wyffe found out ye
will,
(And to her elder sonne intendinge ill)
She secreatlye ye name of John did race,
And put ye name of Henry in ye place;
That this is true I know not who will
sweare,
Yet strong presumptions make ye case too
clear
For it was knowne not long before he dyed,
His will did in ye former state abyde,
Which was by oath of witnesse testifyed :
Besydes it was too manyfestlye knowne,
She used means to get herself alone,
Into his Studie, when she did desyne,
And for that purpose had a crooked wyer,
Wherwith she easlie could unlock ye door,
And leave it in such order as before;

And when in private she resorted thither
Both pen and inke some tymes she did
take with her,
And set a maid to watch whyle she staid
there
Where both his will and other wrytings
were,
Some servants too who were acquainted
best
With both their hands did on their oath
protest,
They thought it not his hand, but her's
much rather,
As by the forme oth' letters they did
gather.

These things and manie other being
brought
In evidence on John's behalf, who sought
To right .himself herein against his
mother
Who holde ye Farme, and also gainst his
brother
(Whom she defended) gave such satisfaction
Unto a jury (charged to try the Action)
(Ith' Court of Comon Pleas) that they had
greed
On John's behalf their verdict should pro-
ceede.

But too much cunninge all the cause did
marre ;
For as the Jury unto to the Barre,
A juror (by a compact underhand)
In private lett a servant understand
Gainst Vernon would their present Verdict
passe ;
But Goodman Blockhead, lyke a drunken
asse,
Forgetting that his Maister's right was
tryed
Ith' name of Buck against Vernon forth-
with hyed,
And tould his Maister yt the truth was soe
A present Verdict would against him goe;
Who caused Buck be non-suite thereupon;
And lost the cause which else with him had
gone.

This suite as by ye copies doth appeare,
Did happen in the two and twentyth yeare
Of our late soveraigne Queene Elizabeth :
About tenn yeares after ye father's death;
In all which tyme and two or three yeares
after,
Continewed suits twixt mother, sonne and
daughter,
For she did practize lykewyse to defeate
Her elder daughter called Margarett,

Of some fyve hundred marks left by her
father,
Which she by changinge of ye names, had
rather
Should come unto her yonger daughter
Mary,
About which point oth' Will they long did
varie,
I dare not say, that it was verie sooth,
Though manie did beleeve it for a truth;
For she was cunninge, could both read and
wryte,
And to her elder children had much spyte,
But on ye yonger sett her chiefe delight.

This farme of Haslebach did still remayne
Ith' mother's handes till Henry did
attayne,
To eighteen yeares and thenceforth he
possest it,
For soe (they say) his father's will exprest it,
But after it once came to Henrye's handes,
In that he had noe other state or landes,
Nor other Lyvelihood did as then enjoy,
His elder brother would not him annoy;

But shortlie to atonement with him grewe,
And then good friendship twixt them did
ensewe;
Soe that young Henry held it without
stryffe,
From thenceforth duringe all his term of
lyffe,
And by his will he left it to his Wyfe
And Chylde unborn; Whereon this suite
they ground,
Gainst Maister Vernon for six hundred
pounde.
From which I have digressed somewhat
longe
Onely to shewe in part his mother's
wronge,
But now I will returne unto the same,
And here declare what end thereof became.

The several sumes demanded did amount
To fifteene hundred pounds, by their ac-
count ;
To wit, for sale of Aspley and Sugnell, nine,
And sixe for Haselbach, which made
fifteene.

Gainst which then Maister Vernon went
about
For to declare and sett his tytles out,
Both to ye landes were sould, and to ye
lease
Of Haselbach; and how he did in place,
Permitt his brother to enjoy them still,
During his lyffe of friendship and goodwill,
Intending to have beene to him more
kynde,
If hee had matched according to his mynd,
Even soe farre forth as to have made him
heire
To all his landes. Besides it myght appeare
That Henry's state was not so absolute,
But verie manye had ye same in doubt,
Soe much that he to whom those lands
were sould,
To deal with them would not have been so
bould,
Had John not joyned with his yonger
brother,
And given securitie as well as th' other.

For Haselbach himself did mortgage it,
With whom his brother joyned (as was fitt)
And both had equal power it to redeeme
But be best right (if conscience they
esteeme).

Thus eyther partie laboured for to prove
Their causes good, as it did theim behoove;
Yet by the labour of some frendes at last,

Some motion of agreement mongst them
  past,
To put this matter to arbitrement,
Where to ith' end both parties gave con-
  sent.

The arbitrators at th' appoynted day
Awarded Maister Vernon for to pay
To Justice Townsend there demannds to
  clear,
Upon's owne bonds, one hundred markes a
  yeare,
Untill one thousand marks were fullye
  paid;
Which was not hard (one thought) all
  things were maid,
Yet Maister Vernon thought it was too
  much,
But nothwithstanding since th' award was
  such,
He gave ye poundes and soe did end ye
  stryfe
And made one payment onely in his lyffe,
For ere ye second payment did ensewe,
It pleased God, he yealded nature's due.

The "rhyme" goes on at great length, but
this is the part of it having particular reference to Hazelbadge Hall.

CHAPTER XXVII.

HOW PROTESTANT NONCONFORMITY ROSE IN THE PEAK.

The Ejected Clergymen of 1662.

The light of the gospel had penetrated to
this remote and at that time wild region
long before the ejection of the two thous-
and. Churches are said to have been
built in various parts of the Peak which
dated from the first century of the Conquest. The chosen parishes of the High
Peak were Glossop, Eyam, Castleton, Hope,
Hathersage, Tideswell, Bakewell, and Youl-
greave, to which were afterwards added
Chapel-en-le-Frith, Edensor, and Darley.
In addition to these there were about
twenty-three chapels, but these were built
during the time which covers the period
between the Reformation and the passing of
the Act of Toleration in 1689. To the
people of to-day it seems strange that
clergymen of the Church of England at the
period now spoken of were not necessarily
preachers, indeed, some of them never attempted to preach, but only read the homi-
lies insisted upon by authority. This called
into existence a body of itinerant or temporary abiding ministers, men of great zeal,
and doubtless possessed of an eloquence
adapted to the times, who went about from
parish to parish, and soon obtained great
influence in the country. The labours of
these lecturers were one principal origin
which led to the prevalence of dissent.

For many of the following facts we are
indebted to an express treatise written by
one of the fathers of Derbyshire Nonconformity, the Rev. William Bagshawe, the
Apostle of the Peak, who in his old age

set down to recall to his memory those who
had been his fathers and brethren in the
ministry, and who had been, like himself,
zealous preachers of the word among the
people of the Peak. The title of this little
volume is "De Spiritualibus Pecci, notes
(or notices) concerning the Word of God and
some of those who have been workers together with God in the Hundred of the
High Peak in Derbyshire." The date is
1702. We have also had the privilege of
perusal of Hunter's M.S. in the British
Museum, on "The Rise of the old Dissent in
the Peak of Derbyshire," which was intended as a specimen of a new Nonconformists' memorial, 1851. We have also consulted Mr. Greaves-Bagshawe's "Memoir"
of his distinguished and saintly ancestor,
and various other works, and have also had
the opportunity, by the kindness of Mr.
Bagshawe, of perusing the diary of the Rev.
James Clegg. With this additional and
reliable information, no apology is needed
for a supplementary chapter to the somewhat meagre sketch given earlier in these
pages.

In the reign of James the First, two of
these itinerant preachers, Mr. Dyke and
Mr. Tyler, were sent into the Peak by Lady
Bowes, who lived at Walton, near Chesterfield, an old seat of the Foljambes, to one
of whom she had been united in her first
nuptials. She outlived Sir William Bowes,
her second husband, and at last became
Lady D'Arcy, by her marriage with John,
Lord D'Arcy, a nobleman of the same religious spirit with herself. They were married at Chesterfield, on May 7th, 1617, which
serves to fix the era of this lady, who may
be regarded as having been, more than any
other, the nursing mother of the Noncon
formity of these parts.

Queer Parsons in the Olden Times.

It was Lady Bowes' rule not to intrude
these lecturers into any parish where there
was no call for them, but some idea may be
formed as to the necessity for some such
agency as this from a description of the
character of some of the clergy. It is
particularly interesting, inasmuch as the
letter was written to Lady Bowes by Adam
Slack, on October 12th, 1609. This Adam
Slack was a Peakland notability of that day.
He was a man of considerable property,
was a wealthy yeoman of Tideswell, a landowner in Bradwell, and at that time was
Lord of the Manor of Thornhill, which he
had ten years previously purchased from
the Eyres of Hassop, but which he sold to
them again a few years later. His influence, therefore, counted for something.
Ralph Clayton, of Burton, then a chapel of
ease to Bakewell, is described as "a clergyman of the worst sort, who had dipped his
finger both in manslaughter and perjury."
In the same letter he alludes to "the Bad
Vicar of Hope," and states how one of the
justices would have licensed the "vicar to
sell ale in the vicarage, and a special rule
was made to prohibit him from either

brewing or selling beer on his premises," and he is further charged with some "of the most contemptible and loathsome crimes." At that time William Leadbeater was the vicar of Hope, for he succeeded Rowland Meyrick in 1604. But whatever might be Vicar Leadbeater's character his signature as vicar appears in the Hope Register as late as 1634.

But unfortunately this was not the only "bad" vicar of Hope, for Meyrick's predecessor, Edmund Eyre, appears to have died under Church censure, as may be inferred from the following entry in the parish register: "1602, April 15, buried Edmund Eyre, Vicar of Hope, without service or bell, in the night."

These were strange times, but they were still more strange at an earlier period, judging from another Vicar of Hope, John Dean, who was appointed to the sacred office in the year 1395. At that time Sir Thomas Wendesley was knight of the shire in Parliament, and on the Rolls of Parliament there is recorded of him a strange incident, about the year 1403. Godfrey Rowland, Esq., was living at Longstone Hall, when Wendesley, only a few weeks before he was slain at Shrewsbury, together with John Dean, Vicar of Hope, and others, made a raid upon his homestead with force and arms, and carried off goods and stock to the value of two hundred marks. They took Rowland prisoner, carrying him to the Castle of the Peak at Castleton (which at that time had become a prison for the detention of criminals), where they kept him for six days without food, beside which they cut off the vile outrage of cutting his right hand off. Rowland petitioned the Commons for redress, but no light seems to be thrown upon so dastardly an act by a brave soldier and a reverend gentleman.

Bradwell Men Fight in Church.

Any bloodshed in or about a church in former times was regarded in a very grave light, even when accidental. There is on record a case where a man was killed by an accidental fall from the summit of the tower, and the blood from his nostrils flowed under the west door of the church. Service was not allowed to be resumed until the Bishop had held an inquiry. There are records where blood has been shed violently within Derbyshire Churches and one of these comes within the scope of this work.

It is evident that then, as now, folks were occasionally in anything but a prayerful mood, even when at church. But whatever their feelings they were compelled by law to be present at the services. It was in the beginning part of the year 1530—probably in February—when a couple of Bradwell men created a most unseemly scene in the parish church at Hope, and even before the altar of St. Nicholas. One would have thought that these two Bradwell kinsmen would have settled their differences at any rate on the road to or from church, but we are told that "Robert Elott maliciously struck Edmund Elott on the nose, before the altar of St. Nicholas, and that blood was effused upon the altar." No time was lost in certifying such a terrible thing to the Chapter, the three who took the oath as having witnessed the outrage being Otwell Bamford, Curate of Hope, Nicholas Smyth, and Helia Staley. Having had his revenge, Robert Elott confessed, whereupon the Chapter appointed Canon Edmund Stretehay to act as their commissary, and Robert was brought to his knees in more ways than one, for the Canon ordered him to submit to corporal punishment, kneeling before him. When blood had been shed in the church there was a great to do—the sacred edifice having been defiled service was not allowed until that defilement had been wiped out—and in this case the church was closed for something like two months. The Bishop's Chancellor was informed of the circumstance, and he inhibited the curate from celebrating in the church until episcopal "reconciliation" had been obtained. And so matters went on—the Bishop caused an inquisition to be held as to the circumstances, and on the 4th of the following May he removed the interdict, and the services were resumed.

The Nonconforming Parsons.

BAKEWELL PARISH.

But to return to the subject. Amongst the clergy who, in the reign of Charles the First, held livings in the Peak, were Isaac Ambrose and Charles Broxholme. Ambrose lived to be ejected, but in another county, and Broxholme died before the Act of Uniformity was passed. There were also two Rowlandsons, father and son, who were Puritan ministers in the time before Puritanism became Nonconformity. Mr. Bagshawe bears honourable testimony to the Rowlandsons, who were in succession vicars of Bakewell, but when the great day of trial came the father conformed and remained in the church, although he is said to have benefited largely in his income by the property confiscated from the Royalists.

In the neighbouring Church of Edensor, the incumbent, Richard Archer, was returned by the Parliamentary Commissioners in 1650, as "reputed disaffected," and as having been formerly in Prince Rupert's army. The two incumbents at Darley, John Pott and Edward Payne, are passed over with the remark concerning Mr. Payne, that he was "a hopeful man." He had been recently placed there. In 1651, Samuel Coates was the minister of Youlgrave, described as "a godly minister." Mr. Cantrell, the minister at Elton, was reported by the Commissioners "scandalous and insufficient." Robert Craven, of Longstone, and Anthony Mellor, of Taddington, were among the best-known and highly respected ministers of that day. Mr. Bagshawe speaks very highly of Parson Mellor, and relates how he was dragged to the sessions at Bakewell for his Puritanism, his offence being "his strict observance of the Sabbath, and the holding of prayer among his family." John Jackson, who was at Baslow in 1650, but went to Buxton on account of his health, remained here till he was turned out on Bartholomew's Day. At Fairfield, Thomas Nicholson, who had a wife and five children, occupied the living, and was content to leave all for conscience sake, and suffer with the rest. Mr. Payne, one of the most remarkable of the ministers ejected, when he was assistant minister of Sheffield Parish Church, continued a non-conforming minister in that parish till his death in 1708. He was born at Wheston, near Tideswell.

HOPE.

Coming nearer home, in connection with Hope parish there is not much more recorded, only that a Thomas Bocking was vicar in 1650, that he was a Royalist who had borne arms on the side of the King, and that he was reported "a scandalous minister" by the Parliamentary Commission. His name is carved on the front of the handsome oak pulpit in Hope Church.

CASTLETON.

In the neighbouring Church of Castleton, Samuel Cryer was the minister when Mr. Bagshawe wrote on the spiritual things of the Peak. He had then been more than forty years the vicar, and "is now most a father of any minister in the High Peak." He was the son of an elder Cryer, one of Mr. Bagshawe's predecessors in the living of Glossop. Mr. Bagshawe appears to have had great esteem for Mr. Cryer, of Castleton—"May they who have heard his elaborate and eloquent discourses, evidence that they have heard God speaking through and by him." Mr. Cryer was here as early as 1650, and he was a conformist in 1662.

"It was a privilege," said Mr. Bagshawe, "to Mr. Cryer, that he was, though not immediately, the successor of the thrice worthy Mr. Isaac Ambrose, a star of the first magnitude, for a time fixed at Castleton. I had not the time to converse with or indeed see this saint of the Lord, save once at Manchester. At that time his love to Castleton at the mention of it revived, tears shot into his eyes, and from his mouth fell the ingenious acknowledgment, "It was my sin and is my sorrow that I left that place when the Lord was blessing my ministry in it." Mr. Ambrose was a Nonconformist in 1662, retiring from the vicarage of Garstang, in Lancashire. At Castleton, he succeeded Ralph Cantrell, was buried at Hope in October, 1626.

EDALE.

There was a very learned and godly minister of Puritan sympathies at the chapel at Edale, then a chapelry in the parish of Castleton. Of him, Mr. Bagshawe says, "I have not only heard of, but in my childhood heard worthy Mr. Cresswell, one who drew as his first, so his last breath in our parts. He was some time chaplain at Lyme Hall, and preached at Disley, not far from it. . . . . The Lord called this, His servant, from his work when that black night was come or coming. Surely Edale was a dale or valley of vision in his days. May their posterity show their profiting by others, as many did that were profited by him."

Mr. Cresswell was succeeded by Mr. Robert Wright, a very earnest and sincere, though a less learned man than Mr. Cresswell. He refused to conform, and was, therefore, turned out of the Church. It is said that he afterwards conformed, but he was a Nonconformist when he died. He appears to have been a warener. However, he was silenced by the persecuting Acts, and he never took out a license to preach after the declaration of indulgence, and died between the year 1672 and 1675. The chapel in Edale was founded by the devotion of the Protestant people inhabiting that "valley of vision" the names of fifteen of the chief of whom are preserved in the Deed of Consecration, which bears date August 3rd, 1634.

TIDESWELL.

At Tideswell the parson at this time was William Greaves, "a man whose very plain words were directed against the vices of his hearers, and he used that unusual exercise of catechising." What the folk of Tideswell thought about him, especially the catechising part of his ministrations, is not stated, but he was there many years, while his successors, Christopher Fulnetby and Nicholas Cross, were there for a few months only. In 1636, Ralph Heathcote was given the living, and held it for twenty-six years. Mr. Bagshawe says he "could not be charged with falling short as to conformity before the war, whatever is charged on him for siding with the two Houses of Parliament in it."

In Mr. Fletcher's "Guide to Tideswell," Isaac Sympson is given as the vicar in 1662, but Mr. Bagshawe mentions others, and his notes on them are as follows: "After some vacancy that followed that minister's (Heathcote's) death, followed for a time (alas! a short time), reckoned not by years, but by months, and those not many, the labouring of one whose attainments were far above his years, with an eye to the preserving of whose memory, as well as that of others, this piece is penned, to wit, excellent Mr. Anthony Buxton, of him take the following account:

"This person derived from parents, well-esteemed at Chelmorton, where the water that serves it springs at the upper end and sinks at the lower end, so in other parts of the country. His noted studiousness and seriousness when a schoolboy were as hopeful buddings of a fruitful tree."

After giving an account of his college career, Bagshawe says of Buxton that "not long after his commencement he was prevailed with to preach at Hayfield, a parochial chapel within my beloved parish of Glossop, where he showed that none were to despise his youth, and to my knowledge some to this day bear impressions of the precious truths which with much exactness he delivered." . . . "He was, through the importunity of friends, and, I believe, through hopes of being a more useful instrument of furthering the work of the Lord, prevailed with to remove to Tideswell, but, alas, he saw little more, if so much, as a quarter of a year there." Mr. Bagshawe relates how "grave, reverend and tender Mr. Stanley," the ejected minister of Eyam, attended Mr. Buxton on his death bed, how he (Bagshawe) was a bearer at his funeral, and preached his funeral sermon.

After him came Mr. Beeby. "He was here and elsewhere," says Mr. Bagshawe, "particularly in the latter end of his time at Cirencester; industrious, apt to teach, and well esteemed. One thing was less satisfactory to his brethren, that he married his brother's widow, and defended his so doing from an order which did, as they believed, concern the Jewish nation and Church only." Dr. Calamy says that he left Tideswell at the Restoration, and took charge of the chapel at Sheldon, when he was ejected. After him were Mr. Bryerly, and Mr. Creswick, a native of Sheffield, both Nonconformists.

HATHERSAGE.

The living at Hathersage was held by Robert Clarke, who was presented by the Earl of Devonshire, in 1627. He must have professed himself a Puritan, because in 1646 he had his living augmented by the Committee for Plundered Ministers, with £30 a year out of the rectories of Duckmanton and Normanton, sequestered from Francis Lord Denicourt, and £9 from the tithes of Abney and Abney Grange, sequestered from Rowland Eyre, papist and delinquent farmer thereof, under the Dean and Chapter of Lichfield, also £5 from the tithe of Litton, and the glebe there. We have no evidence that he lived to the critical year, 1662, but though he had largely partaken of the spoils of the suffering Royalists, he did not abandon his church at the last.

The chapel at Derwent lies far remote from the parish church of Hathersage, and the Parliamentary Commissioners in 1650 recommended that Derwent should be constituted an independent parish. A Mr. Burgess was then the minister, of whom nothing more appears to have been handed down.

They also recommended that Stoney Middleton should be made a district parish. There was a chapel, 400 communicants, and not above £10 maintenance for the minister. Richard Thorpe, the minis-

ter, is reported to be "scandalous for drinking," and when the Committee voted an augmentation of £40 out of the tithe of Glossop, sequestered from the Earl of Arundel and Surrey, and the Countess of Arundel, his mother, a Recusant, they voted it for "such minister as they shall approve." Mr. Thorpe, however, received at least a portion of it in 1650, and there is no account of his resignation of the benefice.

But though Mr. Bagshawe has nothing to say of the ministers who lived in the Puritan times in the parish of Hathersage, he speaks with great respect of a gentleman who lived at Highlow Hall, who belonged to the class so often spoken of as the Moderate Conformists. This was Mr. Robert Eyre, who was a magistrate for the county, a man of considerable estate in this district, as well as of very ancient descent. He had been left a minor by his father, and considered that he had suffered something in his wand-time, "yet God in wisdom and favour ordered that he should match into the family of Mr. Bernard Wells," by which his estate was so much advanced. This Mr. Eyre was a good man, and notwithstanding the satisfaction he had as to the point of conformity, he was far from persecuting Nonconformists. As before stated, he was a magistrate, and he so highly esteemed the Apostle of the Peak that informations were not given against him, and "in times of bondage precious liberties for labour were indulged in by me."

This Mr. Eyre was the head of one of the principal families of the name and stock of Eyre, that very old and widely ramified family in the Peak. His mother was a Jessop, of Broomhall, Sheffield, who, like himself, belonged to the class of moderate Conformists.

EYAM.

The living at Eyam was held by Thomas Stanley. He succeeded Shoreland Adams, who held two livings, and was dispossessed at Eyam for his strong sympathy with the Royalist cause. He was of a very turbulent and selfish disposition. He was restored to his living in 1660, and Stanley acted as his curate till the ejection in 1662. It is said that Adams, when speaking of a clergyman who had left his living in Sheffield, said: "Fowler is a fool, for before I would have sacrificed my living for a cause like that I would have sworn that a black cow was white." This contrasts greatly with the disposition of Stanley, of whom Mr. Bagshawe writes at length.

Stanley was removed from Ashford to Eyam in 1644, from which place he was ejected in 1662. After his ejection he continued to reside at Eyam, and was a worthy helper to the Rev. William Mompesson during the terrible visitation of the Plague in 1666. After his ejection some of his bitterest enemies tried, but failed, to induce the Earl of Devonshire to remove him out of the village, and in reference to this a witness of that time says: "It was more reasonable that the whole country should in more than words, testify their thankfulness to him who, together with the care of the town, had taken such care as no one else did to prevent the infection of the towns adjacent." It would seem from this statement that to Thomas Stanley is due no small share of the honour which history pays to the people of Eyam for their heroism and self-sacrifice during that dreadful visitation.

In the year 1670 Thomas Stanley was seized with the sickness that resulted in his death. William Bagshawe was called from his bed to visit him. Stanley had suffered very greatly from his Nonconformity, but he rejoiced on his death bed that he had been permitted to suffer in such a cause, and within three days, on the anniversary of his ejection, viz., on "Black Bartholomew's Day," he went to his reward. He had been supported by the voluntary contributions of two-thirds of the inhabitants of Eyam. He died and was buried at Eyam, but there was no monument raised to this remarkable man until nearly 120 years afterwards, when it was done by a private individual.

The Apostle of the Peak.

In the year 1662, good William Bagshawe was quietly and effectively ministering to his parishioners of Glossop, reverenced and loved by all. He was content to remain there, doing his duty without any noise or ostentation, proof against all temptations to worldly advancement which would involve his severance from his beloved people. Such was his condition when that eventful 24th of August arrived, which taught so many ministers and congregations what a bitter thing it was to part who had lived and toiled and worshipped together.

William Bagshawe was born at Litton, on January 17th, 1627-8. He received his education at several country schools, where his diligence enabled him to attain to greater proficiency than many of his contemporaries. Under Mr. Rowlandson, minister at Bakewell, and Mr. Bourne, of Ashover, he imbibed very deep religious impressions. He subsequently went to Cambridge University, where he took his B.A. degree in 1646. He possessed a strong desire for the ministry, but his wish was opposed by some of his friends, who desired him to follow some other pursuit, but he carried his point, and preached his first sermon at Wormhill, where he remained for three months. Being desirous of finding a wider field of labour he went to Attercliffe, Sheffield, and became an assistant minister to Mr. James Fisher. On New Year's day, 1651, he was ordained by the presbytery at Chesterfield by the laying-on of hands, and the confession of faith he then made, and the sermon he preached on Christ's purchase, was afterwards published.

In the following summer he married Agnes, daughter of Peter Barker, of Darley. Early in the year 1652, he was appointed to the living of Glossop. Here he laboured with very great effect for 10½ years; he was happy and contented in his work, he refused all offers of preferment, and was contented to live in the heart and affections of his people. But when he was called upon to make a sacrifice for truth he freely gave up for conscience sake what all the offers of worldly advancement could not tempt him to part with. For this he was willing to sacrifice friends, and to sever the ties of love and sympathy that bound him to his people and his people to him. When he preached to them the last time before his ejectment, the tears of sorrow that fell from the eyes of his people testified to the affectionate regard in which he was held, more eloquently than words. On being compelled to lay down his work at Glossop, his father placed Ford Hall, Chapel-en-le-Frith, entirely at his service, and he made this his regular residence until his death, nearly forty years later.

But although Mr. Bagshawe was no longer allowed to minister to people inside the Church, he still continued to be a minister of the Church of Christ. He went from village to village, and even from house to house preaching the word to such as would listen, and his labours were crowned with abundant success. It is recorded that through his ministrations a spirit of seriousness, repentance, and faith pervaded these wild regions that had never been witnessed before, and his energy in preaching, and in all Christian work was such that he was called by his contemporaries "The Apostle of the Peak," by which name he is known to history to this day. Through his untiring and self-denying labours he established Presbyterian congregations at Malcalf, near to his own home (who afterwards built the chapel at Chinley), at Great Hucklow, Bradwell, Charlesworth, Ashford, Middleton, Chelmorton, Bank End, and some accounts add Marple Bridge and Edale. He was called upon to suffer much and severe persecutions, but in all his trials his faith in God never wavered, and there are many stories on record which give an account of the very remarkable way in which he was delivered from the plots of his enemies.

For a considerable time after his removal to Ford Hall, he was compelled to act with very great caution. Every Sunday morning and afternoon, accompanied by his family, he attended the church at Chapel-en-le-Frith, but in the evening he held service privately in his own house and elsewhere, and he also delivered an address to a few friends on the Thursday evening. In this way there passed another ten years, but after the Declaration of Indulgence in 1672 he entered upon a more active public work. He went to his beloved people at Glossop once a month on a week evening, where the people flocked to hear him. He preached at Ashford once a fortnight, and very great caution being necessary in order not to expose his hearers to the severity of the persecuting laws then in force, he used to change the scene of his labours almost every Sunday morning so as to baffle the enemies of Nonconformity and the various bands of informers who were ever ready to give information to the authorities. His whole ministerial life was one continued act of suffering for conscience sake. Because of his choice of the Christian ministry as his profession in opposition to his friends' wish he was partially disinherited, and after the ejection he was for years in constant danger of fine and imprisonment.

Concerning his private life, he kept a constant guard upon his heart at all times, and he is said to have attained to such a degree of grace that few arrived at. The hearts of the poor were by him made glad, and with his readiness to give of his substance, he combined a rare faculty for giving wise counsel to those to whom he gave temporal aid. As a son he was most dutiful to his parents even after he had a family of his own; as a master he was kind and considerate; as a husband he was loving and affectionate, and as a father he was anxious for the moral and spiritual welfare of his children.

The bulk of the Apostle's journeys were made on horseback—a difficult task at certain seasons of the year—in fact, there are frequent references to these difficulties and dangers in his diary, and he states how on one occasion he and T. Barber were lost in a mist between Castleton and Bradwell. In this diary, too, are very many allusions to Bradwell and Great Hucklow, which are very interesting. Some of these are given in the chapter on the old chapel, Bradwell. The entries in his diary also prove how thorough was the self-examination which the Apostle of the Peak continually applied and how dissatisfied he was with his own efforts. Referring to his preaching he writes:—" I cannot get my eyes down to the people, nor preach as though I were talking with them." Of a petition that was being sent round by the Bishops soliciting subscriptions for the poorer clergymen, Mr. Bagshawe writes:—" Is it of good aspect that bishops take this course?" He replies to his own query by saying:—" It does not appear so to me, they themselves going away with so large a part of the Church's revenue. What kind of creatures in their eyes are the poor nonconformists, for whose relief no motion was made these 33 years." And he adds:—" O, the meanness of mean measures."

There is the entry:—1695, August ye 25th. " One fruit of my poor labours ye last year is ye poor people of Bradwell have prepared a more meet place to meet in, and they are more than willing that my younger brethren should take their turns in preaching there."

August ye 25th " Flocked in."

Another entry reads: " I preached and prayed in ye new meeting-house at Bradwell, where very many heard and I was assisted."

Again he writes:—1695, Sept. ye 11th. " It was said at Bradwell, where ye people hear me and others attending yt my poor endeavours in ye evening of one Sabbath on ye 4th had this good effect, that since then every Sabbath has been less profaned."

1695-6. " When on February the 23rd I preached at Hucklow on meekness (1), and on the blood of the covenant (2), many persons seemed much affected, and when, on the Tuesday following I preached at Bradwell, in the former discourse (1), relating to the diligent keeping of the soul, tears shot into many eyes, and I hope the following one (2), concerning coming, and recourse to the waters, or ordinances, especially as dispensed publicly, was not unaffecting."

"Divers and those whose judgments I most value, say that my taking so much time in preaching is best for writers and for those who desire to be edifyers. It is said and hoped that there is some reformation wrought by the word at Bradwell."

1697, July 19th. " My preaching at Bradwell hath, through mercy, had this effect and influence, that many flocked to hear Mr. Parker on the last Lord's Day save one, and Mr. Haywood is thereby encouraged to go and preach to them, and I shall wait to hear what effect my sermon the last Sabbath, which was about sanctifying the Sabbath, had amongst them."

In the year 1697 and 8 are several entries in his diary which tell how acutely he felt the infirmities of age weakening his body and interfering with his labours. On the 30th January in the former year he wrote: " I was carried through the cold to Hucklow and there led others in mourning and prayer." It was his custom at this time to preach at Hucklow every Sunday morning and at Malcalf in the evening. On March 20th, 1698, he wrote: " I went to Hucklow, taking in a sort, my leave there."

Speaking thirty-five years after his ejection, he said " I have now been an ejected minister for so many years, and have had much time to review my position and weigh the reasons of my nonconformity, and upon an impartial and serious consideration of my case, I see no cause to change my mind. But, some of you may perhaps say, but others have better eyes than you. I readily grant that, but I must see with my own." So long as physical strength would permit this faithful son of God and earnest disciple of Christ continued to labour incessantly in God's vineyard but at last his growing infirmities compelled him to shorten his journeys and lessen his toils. For a time he had to confine his ministrations to Malcalf, and for the last winter of his life he was confined to his own house, but even then he did not cease his ministry, for he conducted service there, and only for a single Sunday before his death was he unable to deliver God's message to the people. He died on April 1st, 1702.

The care of his Peak congregations, and the work that was so dear to his heart, fell into the hands of John Ashe, his nephew, of Ashford, and James Clegg, who succeeded him at Malcalf. Both these men lived very near to the Apostle's heart, and their names appear in the Trust Deed as the joint ministers of Bradwell Chapel.

Churchwardens since opening of St. Barnabas' Church, Bradwell, in October, 1868 :—

1868 & 1870.—Dr. Joseph Henry Taylor.
1870 & 71.—Robert Hill, Benjamin James Eyre (Brough).
1872 & 3.—Robert Hill, Thomas Bradwell.
1874 -6.—John Dakin, Thomas Bradwell.

early days. On one occasion a young man in Bradwell had committed suicide, and as his mental condition was laid at the doors of the Methodists, William Green, of Rotherham, one of the earliest preachers, was prevented from entering the town by friendly outposts at the various entrances, fearing he would be killed as the enemies of the cause had vowed vengence on the next Methodist preacher who should visit the place.

It has already been said that the first chapel—now a cottage—was built in 1768. At the conference the following year a grant

THREE NOTABLE CHURCHWARDENS.

| WM. J. BRADWELL, 1881-93. | THOS. BRADWELL, 1872-77. | JOHN DAKIN, 1874-93. |

1877-8.--John Dakin, Thomas Bradwell, Caleb Higginbottom (Great Hucklow) and Henry Eyre (Abney).
1778-80.—John Dakin, Thomas Elliott.
1881-93.—John Dakin, Wm. John Bradwell.
1894-5.—C. E. B. Bowles (Abney), Francis Harrison.
1896-7.—Joseph A. Middleton, Abram Morton.
1898-1905.—Abram Morton, William Eyre.
1906.—Abram Morton, Harvey Hallam.
1907.—Harvey Hallam, Wm. B. Prisk.
1908-10.—Harvey Hallam, Durham Wragg.
1911.—Durham Wragg, Wm. John Harrison.

CHAPTER XXVIII.

WESLEYANISM'S ESTABLISHMENT IN THE BRADWELL CIRCUIT.

Early Local Preachers.

In the previous chapter the introduction of Wesleyanism is briefly touched upon. There were many exciting times in those

of £9 was made towards the building, and in 1772 there is the record " Brada £5," and a similar amount the following year. When the present chapel was built in 1807, Bradwell was in Bakewell circuit, with the Rev. William Midgley, a famous man in those days, as the minister, but in 1812 Bradwell became the head of a circuit with a membership of 450. The first superintendent was the Rev. Wm. Bird who had Joseph Lewis as his colleague. At the end of ten years the membership had fallen to 388. Later, even a lower ebb was reached, but in the thirties there was wonderful activity and growth. Chapels were built in the smaller villages, and in 1834 the membership had reached 580. In 1851 the membership had reached 600, the highest ever recorded. At this stormy period of the " Reform " agitation, John Bonsor and Henry Cattle were in the circuit, and it is a remarkable fact that although the neighbouring circuit of Bakewell suffered very seriously, only two local preachers remaining on the Wesleyan plan, such was the loyalty and devotion of the Methodists of the Bradwell circuit that there is not, nor ever has been, a single "Reform" cause within its boundaries. Owing, in a great measure, to the gradual decline in the lead mining industry the membershp declined during the fifties to 409, but during the ministry of Richard Smailes in 1860-1 it increased 157 in one year. On the first Bradwell circuit plan in 1813 there were nine local preachers —Barber, Shaw, Robinson, S. Cocker, Bradwell, Fletcher, Walker, John Longden, and

been added to the preaching places. William Blundell was the minister and the other preachers were Booth, Bennett, Wilson, Chapman, Frost, Longden, Cocker, Bradwell, Handley, Somerset, John Frost, Middleton, J. Longden, Eyre, Wheater, Dakin, Clayton, Goodwin, and M. Goodwin, with H. Eyre, J. Harrop, and W. Birchell "on trial."

By 1862 Derwent Dale and Litton Slack had been added as preaching places and the local preachers were: John Longden, Snake

BRADWELL WESLEYAN CHAPEL.

Crook. These nine local preachers were fully employed, as the preaching places were Bradwell. Hathersage. Hope, Abney, Hucklow, Tideswell, Edale, Castleton, Thornhill, Gillot Hay, Hag Lee, Peak Forest, Sparrowpit. Litton, Wardlow, Rider House and Fair Holmes.

By the year 1837 Cressbrook, Cockbridge (now known as Ashopton), and Brough had

Inn; Jonathan Longden, Hope; Ralph Handley, Tideswell; Benjamin Somerset, Bradwell; John Frost, Grindlow; Thos. Middleton, Brough; James Dakin, Castleton; Matthew Goodwin, Peak Forest; Francis Hall, Ashopton; John Eyre, Castleton; Thos. Royles, Litton; Thomas Bramwell. Tideswell; John Darvil, Hathersage; Wm. Roscoe, Priestcliffe; Joseph Robert

Cocker, Hathersage; Henry Fletcher, Sparrowpit; Wm. Oldfield, Hucklow; George Robinson, Thornhill; John Andrew, Bamford; Thos. Hancock, Hucklow; Edward Howard, Tideswell; Jonathan Eyre, Alport; John Barber, Bradwell; Joshua Evans, Bradwell; Ebenezer Bradwell, Bradwell; with Stephen Dakin, Bradwell; Robert Somerset, Bradwell; and Benjamin Bradwell, Bradwell, "on trial." Only Mr. Stephen Dakin and Mr. E. Bradwell are now living of these local preachers of half a century ago.

Tideswell Methodists Horsewhipped.

These were trying times at Tideswell for early Methodists there. Such was the feeling there that on one occasion they were publicly horsewhipped by a local magnate named Captain Wyatt. But the cause grew and the first chapel was built in 1810, and served nearly eighty years until the present chapel was built on the site. The chapel at Litton was built in 1834. The chapel at Hucklow was built in 1806.

First Chapel in a Farm House.

But the mother church of the circuit was that at Sparrowpit, where the seed of Methodism was first sown about 1738 by David Taylor, who, when crossing the wilds of the Peak, called at the house of Mrs. Amy Taylor, and there preached. From that day a barn on the farm was thrown open for the Methodist services and the first class meeting in the Peak was thus formed. For more than fifty years the house was thrown open for the public service of the Methodists until a small chapel was built in the adjoining little hamlet of Sparrowpit. The historical farm house is still there. Peak Forest built its chapel in 1852 and it gave to the Methodist ministry Edward White, who died in harness in the United States.

Pioneer's Adventure in Edale.

The story of how Methodism got a foothold in Edale is interesting. Quite a century and a half ago, when David Taylor was travelling late at night through these wills in a blinding snowstorm, fatigued and almost perishing, he and a companion reached a solitary house, knocked at the door, walked in, and began to shake the snow off their clothes. Thinking the strangers were influenced by evil intentions, the good man of the house, Joseph Hadfield, reached down his sword which hung over the mantlepiece with other armour which had been used by him as a soldier in the Battle of Preston Pars a few years before. But his fears were soon dispelled when David Taylor, stepping up to him, exclaimed "Peace be to this house." Methodist services were commenced in that house forthwith, and a society formed, of which Joseph Hadfield was the first member. In that house, at Barber Booth, James Ridal, a travelling preacher, was born, and a farmstead across the valley is the birth-place of Daniel Eyre and Peter Eyre, both Wesleyan ministers. The house has since been pulled down, but the chapel, built in 1811, stands close by.

Bradwell Preachers Mobbed at Castleton.

The first Wesleyan service at Castleton, in 1765, was held in a house there, by Matthew Mayer, of Stockport, and Benjamin Barber, of Bradwell. It was disturbed by a mob, one of whom beat a drum. After service the preachers and their friends from Bradwell retired for refreshments to the house of Mrs. Slack, but the mob burst into her house, making hideous noises, and as they refused to go when requested, the lady cut their drum end with a large knife. They climbed on the roof of the house, threw offensive matter down the chimney of the parlour where the preachers were at supper, and finally waited on the road leading to Bradwell, and in the dead of the night made such a furious attack with stones on the preachers as to place their lives in danger; indeed, Benjamin Barber was stoned almost to death, and carried the marks of his wounds to the grave. It is remarkable that two days afterwards the leader of the mob, who broke in his master's young horses and trained them to the use of firearms, placed a loaded pistol in his pocket, which by some unknown means went off in the stable and killed him on the spot. Such was the dismay caused by this sad occurrence, and it was so regarded as a judgment from God, that the Wesleyans were never again subjected to such brutal usage. The first chapel at Castleton was built in 1809.

Hope Vicar's Wife at Wesleyan Class-Meetings.

Although the Wesleyans had a society at Hope from their earliest days, it was not until 1837 that the chapel was built. From 1843 to 1856 the Rev. Wilmot Cave-Browne-Cave was Vicar of Hope, and his wife, Mrs. Cave, was a regular worshipper at the Methodist Chapel, and frequently sat on one of the forms in the bottom of the building. Indeed, the lady often took an active part in the services, and sometimes attended the class-meeting. Hope gave to the Wesleyan ministry one of its natives, John Kirk.

Prayer Meetings in the Snake !

The famous lovefeast at Alport in the Woodlands has been connected with Bradwell Wesleyanism for a century and a half. John Longden, a local preacher, kept the Snake Inn, and held prayer meetings in the public-house. One Sunday in 1815 he went to preach at Tideswell, fourteen miles distant, but finding on his arrival there that nearly all his congregation had gone to see Anthony Lingard hang in the gibbet at Wardlow Miers, he followed and preached to the multitude beneath the gibbet post. When Cockbridge collapsed and killed several men, their bodies were removed to the nearest farmhouse, which was the Wesleyan Preaching House, and as they lay there John Longden preached from Christ's words in reference to the Tower of Siloam—"Think ye that these men were sinners above all men?" Its powerful effect was marked by converting power in the crowded company gathered together under such solemn circumstances. Woodlands Chapel was built in 1862 by the Duke of Devonshire, a monument of the good work done by the Methodists of his territories. The first chapel at Ashopton was built in 1840, and the new chapel in 1897.

A Bamford Centenarian Methodist.

One of the pioneers of Methodism at Bamford was George Wainwright. When 100 years old he worked at his trade—a weaver—at Dore. At the Jubilee of George the Third fifty old men were gathered out of the town and neighbourhood of Sheffield, whose separate ages exceeded that of His Majesty, and to these coats and hats were given as a memorial of the day. George Wainwright was the oldest, and a subscription was opened to have his portrait painted for the Cutlers' Hall, but though the picture was executed it never reached its intended destination. The Methodists of Bamford built their first chapel in 1821, and the new chapel came twenty years ago.

Persecuted at Hathersage.

Hathersage was the place which was first stirred into active opposition to the advances of the Methodist movement in this direction, and it is on record that "a preacher, through violence of persecution, was driven out of Hathersage," but he and by the seed took root, and in 1807 the chapel was built in the centre of the main street, followed by a Sunday school. The Cocker and Darvill families were among the principal Wesleyans here for more than a century. It was mainly through the liberality of the Cockers that the chapel at Thornhill was built.

Pelting the Methodists at Eyam.

After Mr. Matthew Mayer, of Stockport, had preached at Bradwell one night in 1765, he was invited to preach at Eyam. He went there, and stood by the side of a barn in the presence of a multitude of people who had gathered from different motives. The ringleader of the mob, who had sworn to his companions that he would pull the preacher down, was so struck with the sermon that, as he confessed afterwards, "he had not the power to stir hand or foot," and Mr. Mayer got off scot free. But there were stirring times when, the following Sunday, Mr. John Allen, of Chapel-en-le-Frith, attempted to preach at the same spot. Joseph Benson, who was nicknamed by his neighbours "Bishop Benson," was the first to receive the preacher into his house, as an outrageous mob had assembled to have some fun with the Methodists. Stones were hurled through the windows into the midst of the little congregation, and the preacher narrowly escaped serious injury. Mr. Allen and his friends applied to a magistrate for redress and protection, but without avail, and, encouraged by their attack, the mob again congregated the following week. A narrator of that time says that when the preaching was over "the crowd seemed like lions and tigers let loose," and as the Methodists dispersed they were pelted with dirt and mud along the streets. "The preacher particularly was the target for mud, stones, and brick bats, but he was stoutly defended by a brave little bodyguard, and providentially escaped unhurt." Next morning it was resolved, if possible, to punish some of the ringleaders, and the Methodists went to a magistrate who resided at Stoke Hall. But he was a clergyman, and all the advice he could tender to John Allen was "to get ordained and enter the Church." Joseph Benson was ejected from his cottage for harbouring the new sect, but it was there to stay, for when John Wesley visited the village the year following he wrote: "The eagerness with which the poor people of Eyam devoured the Word made me amends for the cold ride over the snowy mountains."

There was still opposition from the clergyman, or rather from the Rev. Peter Cunningham, who was curate of Eyam, who succeeded for a time in driving the Methodists out of the place to Grindleford. He went round the parish and prevailed upon many to sign an agreement "not to hear the Methodists any more," and in a letter to the Vicar of Eyam, the Rev. Thomas Seward, at Lichfield, in 1776, he said: "No more Methodist preachers appear in the chapel at Eyam; the few that resort to them at Grindleford Bridge are such as an angel from heaven would have no influence with. And as I suppose you do not expect me to work miracles, since nothing less will convert them, they must even be left to prey upon garbage, and follow the wandering fires of their own vapourish imaginations."

There are now two Methodist Chapels at Eyam, and one at Grindleford. Wesley visited the latter place and preached there. The house is still standing.

A Century's Ministers.

The circuit is now in the North Derbyshire mission. Here are the Bradwell circuit ministers from its formation to the present time:—
1812-13.—William Bird, Joseph Lewis.
1814-15.—James Johnson, Thomas Hall, John Smith.
1816-17.—Isaac Keeling, Christopher Newton, James Mortimer.
1818.—Thomas Gill, Joseph Brougham.
1819.—James Hopewell.

1820-1.—William Brocklehurst.
1822-3.—Benjamin Barrett.
1824-5.—John Poole, George Chambers (re-
signed), Thos. Henshall.
1826.—William Rennison, Joseph T. Milner.
1827-8.—Isaac Muff, James J. Topham.
1829.—John Leigh, Henry Wilkinson.
1830-1.—William Scholefield.
1832.—John Gill.
1833.—John Roadhouse.
1834.—Thomas Rought, Hugh Jones
1835.—Henry Tuck.
1836-7.—William Blundell.
1838.—John Wright, died suddenly whilst
preaching at Peak Forest.
1839-40.—Robert Totherick, John B. Dyson.
James Emery.
1841-2.—John Felvus, James Emery.
1843-4.—Thomas Catterick, Joseph Garrett.
Thomas H. Hill.
1845-6.—Richard Greenwood, E. R. Talbot (re-
signed).
1847-8-9.—Moses Rayner, John Nowell (2 years)
Joseph Sutton.
1850.—David Cornforth, Henry Cattle.
1851-2-3.—John Bonser, Henry Cattle (2 years),
S. T. Greathead.
1854-6.—Thomas Brown, S. T. Greathead (2
years).
1857.—William Exton.
1858-9-60.—Thomas Burrows.
1861-2-3.—Richard Smailes.
1864-5.—John Archer, George Chambers
1866-7.—John E. Doubleday.
1868-9.—Henry M. Ratcliffe.
1870-1.—Jonathan Barrowclough.
1872-3-4.—Edward Russell.
1875-6.—Joseph Hirst
1877-8-9.—Cornelius Wood.
1880-1-2.—George S. Meek.
1883-4-5.—William R. Dalby.
1886-7-8.—James Clegg.
1889-90-1.—William Henry Hill.
1892-3-4.—William Dawson Watson
1895-6-7.—William Wandless.
1898-9-1900.—Samuel Goodyer.
1901-2-3.—James Foster.
1904-9.—Marmaduke Riggall.
1910-11.—William Fiddian Moulton. M.A.

CHAPTER XXIX.

EARLY PRIMITIVE METHODISM.

The Bradwell Pioneers.

In a previous chapter the introduction of
Primitive Methodism is touched upon very
briefly. Since that was written the first
account book of the newly-formed body has
been placed at the disposal of the writer,
and is highly interesting as showing the
work of the pioneers, under the most trying circumstances.

The very first entry is one of eighteenpence "for small rules given to members
by Brother Ingham," under date January
12th, 1822. This shows that James Ingham was the pioneer. During the first
three months the town was invaded by
preachers, who were paid small sums for
their work. The chief of these was Susan
Berry, who, on arrival in Bradwell, was
given three shillings, and during the quarter was paid 11s. 5d. for her work. Messrs.

Beeley, Fletcher, and Barber were also
pioneers this quarter. They were paid a
few shillings each. These first preachers
were fed and lodged by William Evans, in
Smalldale. The only other items of expenditure were for glazing the windows of

JAMES INGHAM
The Pioneer Primitive Methodist.

George Morton's barn so as to make it suitable for a chapel, and numerous payments
for candles, in addition to 16s. 8d. for
sacramental wine. The total expenditure
for the quarter was £7 1s. 11½d., but such
was the success that attended the missionaries' work that the receipts were £16 8s.
6¾d. from the classes that were formed at
Bradwell (£8 15s. 6d.), Little Hucklow,
Castleton, Tideswell, Curbar, Calver, Eyam,
Bamford, Hope, Edale, Wardlow, Foolow,
Taddington, Flagg, Peak Forest, Chinley,
Wash, and Chapel Milton.

The movement spread, and during the
second quarter, Abney and Rowarth were
added to the list of societies, then Grindleford Bridge, Bugsworth, Mellor, Stoney
Middleton Great Hucklow, Bagshaw, Pindale, Chapel-en-le-Frith, Monyash, Chelmorton, Thornsett, New Mills, Aspinshaw,
Derwent, Furness Vale, Litton Slack,
Bretton, Sheldon, Buxton, Simmondley,
Whitfield, Kettleshulme, Stone Heads
(Whaley Bridge) Marple, Longstone, Hayfield, Glossop, Brookhouses, Birch Hall
Houses, Compstall, Mottram, Tintwistle,
and Marple Bridge. When, in 1826, this
big circuit had a membership of 430, it was
divided, and New Mills (with Glossop, etc.)
constituted a separate circuit, for on June
26th there is the entry: "New Mills was
made into a circuit, and Bradwell took the
household furniture and the debt which
was £6 14s. 0d., New Mills one half of the
books."

TRAVELLING PREACHERS AT FOURTEEN SHILLINGS A WEEK.

Goldsmith's Vicar of Wakefield was rich on forty pounds a year, but these early travelling preachers were obliged to fancy themselves rich on much less. Amos Ogden and Joseph Hibbs (who became the Rev. Joseph Hibbs and was known as the Primitive Methodist Bishop of South Wales), had to be content with a shilling a day, while Thomas Fletcher, Samuel Beeley, Humfrey Goddard and Elias Oldfield had two shillings a day. The first regular minister was Jeremiah Gilbert, who had charge of this big circuit at the princely salary of fourteen shillings a week, and he had as his assistant, John Hallam, at seven shillings a week. Hallam was a Bradwell lad, who went out into the regular ministry, as also did Joseph Middleton,

REV. JOHN HALLAM.

another native. No wonder that with such salaries there was occasionally a "present" of a few shillings to the preachers. But as things improved and the cause made its way these regular preachers were employed at 14s. a week each, and they were assisted by a number of local preachers, who were paid two shillings a day while the Peak was being missioned. But when the New Mills circuit was formed in 1826, Bradwell had to be content with one minister—Josiah Partington—at 14s. a week, and Robert Shenton a young man, whose quarterly wage was £3 10s., and £1 10s. was paid "for Robert Shenton's meals." Robert Shenton was only here one year, for he entered the Unitarian ministry, and remained a minister here half a century, as noticed in a previous chapter.

As there was a rapidly increasing adverse balance every quarter, it was found necess-

ary to reduce the expenses, and so Robert Hewson became the preacher in 1827, at the magnificent wage of twelve shillings a week, and he lived in a house at £3 a year rent. But things improved, for his successor,

REV. ROBERT SHENTON,
Who left the Primitives and was Unitarian Preacher 63 Years.

George Tindal, was put up to the fourteen shillings standard, but in order to pay him up when he left, the hat was sent round, private collections made, and the accounts squared up by selling blankets and bolsters out of the house. John Graham was the next preacher, and he had to be content with being paid on account each quarter until there was £11 due to him as arrears, and in order to clear it off when he left the circuit, £8 3s. 3d. was "collected in New Mills circuit."

JOHN VERITY, THE STONEMASON PREACHER.

When the famous John Verity made his appearance in 1831, he stirred things up There was a great revival, and the increased membership meant an improvement in the finances, so that the deficiency became a thing of the past, but only for a time, for when two preachers were engaged, financial troubles re-appeared.

John Verity was a most popular preacher. By trade he was a stonemason, and he carved the inscription stone over the old chapel at Castleton. He also preached the opening sermons of that chapel. Here is an interesting entry we came across: "Castleton Chapel was opened Castleton Wakes Sunday, 1833. There are nine Trustees. The debt upon the chapel is £42 10s. The names of the Trustees, and the sum each finds on interest of 5 per cent. is to be received at Christmas are as follow:

Anthony Gilbert, Tideswell, £5; Wm. Bennett, Tideswell £5 10s.; Geo. Bennett. Tideswell, £5; John Kitchen, Calver, £5; Mary Andrew, Hathersage, £5; Francis Ayre, Abney, £4; George Rose, jun., Abney, £4; William Derwent, jun., Thornhill £4; Thos. Hadfield, late of Sittinglow, £5; £42 10s. 0d. The deed is kept at George Bennett's, of Tideswell."

FEMALE PREACHERS.

In 1834 there is a minute "That we try to get a female preacher to travel in this circuit as a Second Preacher." The application was successful for Sister Ann Noble made her advent into the circuit, and remained a year at 3s. a week and her "meat bill," and she was succeeded by Sister Robotham, who was paid £2 10s. a quarter.

There were, in the early days of the movement, many women amongst the local preachers of Primitive Methodism, and an occasional glimpse is got at the earliest of these, who tramped over the Peak in hail, rain, wind or snow. In 1833 there is the entry "that Sister E. Bradshaw's name come off the plan, she having left the circuit."

1834. "That Mary Hawkins be upon the plan, and be represented by a star."

"That R. Swift and wife have their credentials sent to Macclesfield circuit they having removed thither."

"That a star be upon the plan for the young females, and they have an appointment or two."

"That Mary Hawkins have a few appointments on the plan, signified by a star."

1835. "That we pledge Sister Noble at the ensuing District Meeting."

"That Sister Noble stop till Christmas, 1835, and that we have a female the last six months."

"That Hannah Howe be exalted to a full and Credited Local Preacher."

"That Ann Bradwell's initials come on the plan."

"That Mary Hawkins Do."

"That Ann Bradwell's full name come on the plan."

"That Elizabeth Handford be received upon the plan."

"That Sister M. Potter have a note of liberty from this meeting to preach amongst us."

"That the initials of Violet Hill come upon the plan."

These are sufficient as showing some of those women who occupied the pulpits in the early days of the movement.

REFRACTORY MEMBERS.

The new body was jealous of the conduct of its members and did not hesitate to call them to account at the Quarter Day for any breach of discipline. Thus, the minutes for the "Full Quarter Day," March, 1833, contain an entry, "That George Maltby's name be left off the plan, he having voluntarily declared that he, the said George Maltby, had left the body, and immediately on his own accord left the Quarter Day." And the same minutes, which are signed by Thomas Jennings and John Hallam, go on to say: "This is to certify that we have now laid before us every Class paper in the Circuit, and after the most strict examination find them to contain, according to Rule, 206 Full Members and 20 on Trial."

There seems to have been trouble with another, who had for some years done a great d l of preaching, for at the December meeting in the same year it was determined "that Richard Hamilton be no longer a member nor preacher in our Society, in consequence of professing and preaching Antinomist Doctrines, and dooming all to misery who dissent from him." Evidently Richard had joined the Antinomians, who thought that the law was of no use or obligation, that virtue and good works were unnecessary, and that faith alone was sufficient to insure salvation. It is easy to imagine what a flutter he would create, and how promptly he would be expelled. But everybody were under the strictest obligation to keep the proceedings of these meetings a profound secret, and as somebody had been letting the cat out of the bag—perhaps Richard the delinquent —it was resolved "that every member of this meeting keep secret the business of this and all other official meetings on pain of censure." Some of the members, however, had no dread of censure, for at the very next meeting there is another resolution that if anyone divulge to others the business of the meeting or any part thereof his case should forthwith be placed before the General Committee.

SOME COMICAL PREACHERS.

There were no college men among these early pioneers, they were men who had to earn their daily bread by the sweat of their brow, hence they had to bear with the gibes of fastidious people. But they were urged to improve themselves, and in 1834 the Quarterly Meeting decided "that it be the standing rule of this Society that Local Preachers on Trial preach trial sermons at their Exaltation," and "that all our Local Preachers be affectionately requested to improve themselves by reading, study, &c., so that there may be no complaints against them, and that their profiting and usefulness may appear unto all."

One of the local preachers William Wagstaff, caused a deal of trouble at this time. Whether he had preached Antinomianism or how he had kicked over the traces is not stated, but he did not wait for expulsion, for "as William Wagstaff has withdrawn himself from our Society we therefore cannot enter into the charges alleged against him." There had been trouble also with John Hawksworth, for we have it "that J. Hawksworth's name come off the plan in consequence of NEGLECT of PLAN and CLASS." This is written in capitals, underlined, as if to serve as a warning to posterity.

One of the brethren appears to have been rather long-winded in his sermons. Of all religious bodies the Primitive Methodists tried to avoid this, hence in 1835 it was decided "that Joseph Taylor have a note sent to him from this meeting, requesting not to exceed 20 minutes in his exhortations." At the same meeting one or two preachers who did not exactly come up to the standard were taken to task, for we read "that James Howe have a note sent to him cautioning him in the regard of his future conduct." It is not said what his past conduct had been, but that a Calver worthy was not strictly teetotal is evident from the entry. "That Nathan Cocker, of Calver, have a note sent to him, informing him that in consequence of his repeated acts of drunkenness we cannot allow him to meet as a member in our Society. This entry clearly shows the attitude of the denomination in relation to intemperance 80 years ago.

THE FIRST PIONEERS.

Among those who were local preachers, prayer leaders and officers in this circuit during the first fourteen years of the existence of the denomination in this district, from 1821 to 1835, were Susan Berry, Thos. Fletcher, J. Barber, Joshua Beeley, Humfrey Goddard, Elias Oldfield, Joseph Hibbs, John Hallam, James Oven, Samuel Silvester, Richard Hamilton, John Oldfield, Samuel Beeley, Henry Ellis, Thomas Stocks, Israel Brown, Robert Marshall, Thomas Jennings, George Morton, Robert Morton, Ruth Morton, George Holme, George Maltby, Thomas Jennings, William Cocker, J. Howson, George Bennitt (Tideswell), Anthony Jennings, Henry Middleton, Christopher Broadbent, J. Andrew, J. Howe, Thos. Middleton, Robert Calvert, George Gyte (Hope), Benjamin Hill, Joseph Wilson, Mary Hawkins, William Bennett (Tideswell), William Parrett, Thomas Hadfield, Elizabeth Kirk (Castleton), Anthony Gilbert, J. Slack (Tideswell), Joseph Ashton, Wm. Wagstaff, J. Hawksworth, John Cheetham, John Hall, Hannah Howe, Ann Bradwell, Joseph Taylor, Thomas Ashton, Edward Howard (Tideswell), Nathan Cocker, Mary Potter Violet Hill, Elizabeth Handford, John Clayton, Elias Rowarth, John Bocking Derwent, Wm. Cheetham, Thomas Palfreyman, and Thomas Mosscrop.

John Morton, who entered the ministry, was thrown into prison for preaching at Hereford. He was the author of "The wife that will suit you, and how to win her"; "The Husband that will suit you and how to treat him"; and "Lectures to the Young Men."

COMPLETE LIST OF MINISTERS.

Here is a complete list of ministers to the present time:—
1822—James Ingham, formed first Society.
1822 & 1823—Jeremiah Gilbert, Jas. Ingham, Joseph Brook.

1823 & 1824—Thomas Holloday, John Hopkinson, Joseph Hibbs, John Hallam.
1824 & 1825—Andrew Robshaw, Paul Sugden, Abram Harrison.
1825 & 1826—John Britain, Joseph Buckle, James Bilson, Joseph Middleton, Robt Shenton.
1826 & 1827—Josiah Partington, Henry Stepney.
1827 & 1828—Robert Hewson.
1828 & 1827—George Tindal, Ruth Morton.
1829, 1830 & 1831—John Graham.
1831, 1832, & 1833—John Verity.
1833, 1834 & 1835—Jonathan Clewer, Ann Noble, John Hallam.
1835 & 1836—Joseph Hutchinson, Miss Robotham.
1836—Robert Hill, Jesse Ashworth.
1837—Robert Hill, Thomas Moscrop.
1838—G. W. Armitage, Thomas Moscrop.
1839—G. W. Armitage, J. Cheetham.
1840—S. Atterby, J. Cheetham.
1841—Thomas Charlton, James Openshaw.
1842—Thomas King(James Openshaw.
1843—Thomas King, David Holdcroft.
1844—David Tuton, James Bottomley.
1845—David Tuton, James Bottomley & John Eastwood.
1846—S. Smith, J. Davy, J. Taylor.
1847—J. Lawley, T. Aspinshaw, Obadiah O. Britain.
1848—J. Lawley, J. Unsworth.
1849—John Judson, John Standrin.
1851—John Judson, John Standrin.
1851—John Judson, William Wilkinson.
1852—W. Inman, George Smith.
1854—James Peet, Joseph Graham.
1855—James Peet, James Openshaw.
1856—David Tuton, James Openshaw.
1857—David Tuton, — Sutcliffe.
1858—David Tuton, William Harris.
1859—Thomas Doody, Edward Kershaw.
1861—Thomas Doody, John Turner.
1862—Thomas Doody, John Turner and David Thomas Maylott.
1862—Thomas Parr, John Turner and David Thomas Maylott.
1863—Thomas Parr, David Thomas Maylott.
1864—Thomas Bennett, Thomas Wilshaw.
1865—Thomas Bennett, R. B. Howcroft.
1866—Thomas Bennett, Robert Middleton.
1867—Thomas Meredith, Robert Middleton.
1868—Thomas Meredith, S. Kelly.
1869—Thomas S. Bateman, John Glass.
1870—Walter Graham, George Morris.
1873—Walter Graham, John Glass.
1874—Walter Graham.
1875—James Hall.
1876—William Smith.
1878—William Smith and J. Cleaver (Special Missioner).
1879—John Hancock.
1880—John Hancock.
1881—John Hancock.
1882-3-4 & 5—George Smith.
1886-7-8 & 9—William Henry Mason.
1890 & 1—Robert W. B. Whiteway.
1892-3 & 4—John Edmund Jones.
1895-6 & 7—John Prince.
1898—John Hancock.
1899—John Hancock.
1900—John Hancock.
1901—John Hancock.
1902—John Hall.
1903—John Hall.
1904—John Hall.
1905—Edward Quine.
1906—Edward Quine, John Hancock (supernumerary).
1907—Edward Quine, John Hancock (supernumerary).
1908—Ralph H. Gent, John Hancock.
1909—Ralph H. Gent, John Hancock (supernumerary), Mr. Hillard, H.L.P.

1910—Ralph H. Gent, John Hancock (supernumerary), John T. Pratt. H.L.P.
1911—John T. Goodacre. John Hancock (supernumerary), Luke Stafford (supernumerary).

CHAPTER XXX.

FAMOUS VISITORS OF A CENTURY AGO

And Their Impressions.

Bradwell has often been honoured with the visits of men of letters, who have given their impressions of the place and its people. Some of these are curious reading in these days.

AUTHOR'S AMUSING EXPERIENCE.

When Hutchinson made his tour of the Peak a hundred years ago the Bagshawe Cavern had just been discovered in 1807. Going down Bradwell Dale he inquired for the newly discovered cavern, and here is his own version of his experience :—Several of the country people answered that they knew nothing of it; and it was some time before I found that they did not understand the meaning of the word cavern; for upon changing my question to that of a place underground, information was immediately given; observing one person more simple than the rest I could not help asking him a few further questions.
"Is it two miles, my good fellow, to Hope?" said I.
"Aye," answered he.
"Is it twelve o'clock?"
"Aye," answered he.
"Is that Bradwell before me?"
"Aye, mester."
"These ayes being still answered to several other interrogations, I asked him, as he seemed between forty and fifty years of age, whether to the best of his knowledge and belief he had ever said yes in his life."
"The simpleton immediately scratched his head, produced the following candid and ingenious answer : 'Why mester, to tell yo th' truth, for its now use telling a lie, I believe I ne'er did.'"

HISTORIAN ON EARLY MARRIAGES.

Glover, the Derbyshire historian, who visited Bradwell (1829), appeared to be particularly impressed with the early marriages here, and handed down to future generations the information that "The young people here of both sexes generally marry at the age of 18." With these few words he dismisses the subject.
William Wood, the historian of Eyam, with whom Bradwell was a favourite spot, said (1862) that "Like all other mountain-hid villages, it contains a population strongly marked by peculiarities of custom,

retaining notions of a highly superstitious nature, and most pugnaciously tenacious of their numerous time-honoured, antique usages. Here, to a deplorably excessive degree, inter-marriage exists, and have existed for ages."

"STERLING WORTH AND INTEGRITY."

Bernard Bird, in his "Perambulations of Barney, the Irishman" (1850), alludes to this trait of character, for he observes: "The attachment of the inhabitants of Bradwell to their own people is very strong; they seldom or never inter-marry with strangers, and are a community of relations, consisting of about 300 families, or 1,500 inhabitants. . . . I have traded with the inhabitants for 38 years, and in justice to them must say that I have always found them (without exception) of sterling worth and integrity."

JAMES MONTGOMERY'S EQUESTRIAN FEAT.

James Montgomery, "The Christian poet," his friends Ebenezer Rhodes. author of "Peak Scenery," Sir Francis Chantry, the eminent sculptor, James Everett, the Wesleyan historian, and John Holland, were frequent visitors to Bradwell in the early part of last century, and in the life of the poet. written by Holland and Everitt, there is an interesting and curious reference to Bradwell.
On April 26th, 1823, Montgomery being then 51 years of age. he took tea with Mr. Holland and Mr. Molineaux, of Macclesfield, at the house of Mr. Cowley, a Sheffield manufacturer, whose place of business was in Pinstone Street. In the course of the evening the conversation turned on the writing of epitaphs for tombstones. Montgomery spoke of the reluctance he felt in composing them, though they were often extorted from him. "I have an order to write an epitaph on a good woman at Bradwell by next Tuesday," said the poet. "If Mr. Holland pleases. he shall write it."
Holland's reply was "I might surely venture to do it for an obscure burying-ground in the High Peak. Did you ever visit Bradwell?" asked Holland.
"Yes," replied Montgomery, "on one occasion many years ago, and I have good occasion to remember the visit. The entrance into the village amidst the rocks is by a very steep descent. When my horse reached a certain part of the road he suddenly went down upon his knees, pitching me as suddenly over his head upon the stones. I was not, however, much hurt, and got up again as well as I could, unassisted by any one of half a dozen petrifaction of men who stood and witnessed the accident apparently with as little emotion as the limestone crags around us."
"Then they offered neither assistance nor commiseration?" observed Holland.

"Not they," replied Montgomery. "Such an occurrence appeared to be not strange to them; for I heard one of the fellows say 'Aye, that's where everybody falls.'"

The lines of the epitaph sent to Bradwell on this occasion were as follows :—

"The wicked cease from troubling here,
And here the weary are at rest;
Henceforth, till Christ their life appear,
The slumbers of the just are blest,
The saint who in this silent bed
Waits the last trumpet from the skies,
Shall then with joy lift up her head,
And like her risen Saviour rise."

HOPE VICAR'S WIFE AT WESLEYAN CLASS MEETINGS.

Nearly quarter of a century afterwards— on July 31st, 1847—the two poets, Montgomery and Holland, had the following conversation on Holland's return home after spending a few days at Hope.

"I am glad to find you have escaped safely from the caverns and all the other perils of the Peak," said Montgomery.

"I shall not soon forget the alarm of one of my nieces on being ferried over the little lake in the celebrated Castleton cavern," observed Holland.

"Nor shall I ever forget my sensations under similar circumstances," said Montgomery. Indeed I never felt so powerfully the combined impression of awe and sublimity as when I lay in the shallow boat on my back, and my breast nearly in contact with the under surface of a mass of thousands of tons of rock that only appeared suspended, as it were, by a hair, while the number of immense blocks lying about me reminded me that these portions of the roots of the mountains had at some period been actually detached. When I used to visit that neighbourhood on the annual recurrence of Bible Society and missionary anniversaries. Dr. Orton was vicar of Hope, and the Methodists, placed as they were, between the noted preaching-stead of Bradwell and the famous love-feast locality of Woodlands, were exceedingly zealous and flourishing. Did you you go to the church or to the chapel?"

"We went to both," replied Holland, "to the church in the morning and afternoon, and to the Wesleyan Chapel in the evening. The present worthy vicar of Hope is the Rev. W. C. B. Cave, and I was equally surprised and gratified to recognise his excellent wife sitting on the lowest form among the poor women in the Methodist Chapel. Indeed, I was more struck with the rare fact—for rare it is now-a-days—of a lady in her position affording such evidence that her religion raised her above mere church or chapel prejudices than I was by the magnificent mountain masses of Mam Tor, Winhill, Losehill, and the Winnats, which I could see from the chapel windows. I have mentioned to two or three clergymen, since I came home, the fact of the frequent attendance of good Mrs. Cave

at this little hill-side conventicle,, with all the circumstantial aggravations of the case —such as the vehemence of the rustic preacher, the loud and indecorous responses of the humble mountaineers, the great number of them present, the hearty singing of Wesley's hymns, with which the lady in question was evidently provided—nay, that she had been known to go into a class meeting! and, above all, the consideration that she is, in all other respects, an active, intelligent and excellent woman. And my good clerical friends not only expressed their surprise at my statement, but regarded such conduct in a vicar's wife as highly scandalous—the morning attendance of those Peak Methodists at church notwithstanding!"

'The more shame for them," exclaimed Montgomery. "Her conduct as a Christian woman is highly to her credit. Why should she not join in social worship with her Methodist neighbours when there is no service at the church? And why should she not make herself personally acquainted with, and even encourage those good men who are engaged in preaching the gospel to scores of persons in the parish who might not come to hear her husband? I warrant she is not on that account less active in the discharge of her other position and proper duties."

'Not she, indeed," replied Holland, "if I may judge from the reports of the villagers as to the way in which she labours among them, and from what I saw of her activity in shepherding up all the boys and girls who were old enough, to be examined and instructed preparatory to their confirmation by the Bishop."

CHAPTER XXXI.

FRIENDLY SOCIETIES OF THE PAST AND PRESENT.

Some Curious Records.

When a complete history of the Friendly Society movement in this country comes to be written — not the history of one particular Order, but covering the whole ground right back to the days and doings of the ancient Guilds—it will form a highly interesting contribution to the literature of the country. And not the least interesting portion of it will be that relating to the many small, self-contained, and independent societies established for mutual help in the towns and villages during the eighteenth century, before the establishment of the big incorporated Orders, such as the Oddfellows, Foresters, Druids, Shepherds, etc. Certain it is that the men—and women too —of Bradwell, then an isolated but populous place in the Peak, consisting mainly of lead miners and weavers, and tradesmen dependent on those workers, were among the first to set up those organisations, which served their day and generation exceedingly well. In the latter part of the 18th century there was an "Old Men's Club" and an "Old Women's Club." Unfortunately, the interesting records and chronicles of the oldest of these societies are not to hand, but it is a fact that one called "The Old Club Friendly Society" was established in Bradwell very early in the eighteenth century. This is clear, because there appears to have been some defection of members in 1789, when the disaffected brethren formed a society of their own, which they designated "The New Club Friendly Society." But the weakest went to the wall, and that happened to be the "New Club," which after a struggling existence for thirty-four years decided to dissolve itself and again unite with the parent body. Hence it was that "The United Society" was established on the 3rd of July, 1813, "in consequence of the New Club Friendly Society in Bradwell (which commenced the seventh day of March, 1789) having agreed to dissolve the same, and unite with the Old Club Friendly Society, for the better benefiting and assisting each member in the time of sickness and infirmity, and for the further aid and improvement of the stock."

"CHARITABLE AND BROTHERLY."

To members of present-day Friendly Societies, at any rate, the "articles to be observed by the charitable and brotherly members of the United Society in Bradwell" will be both interesting, instructive, and amusing, as showing how their forefathers conducted their business. The governing body consisted of a master, two stewards, and twelve assistants. The first master was Joseph Hallam; the first stewards were Robert Middleton and Obadiah Stafford; and the assistants were Robert Middleton (Dale End), Isaac Palfreyman, junr., Philip Barber, junr., Benjamin Morton, Robert Bradwell, Isaac Palfreyman, senr., Benjamin Somerset, Thomas Morton, Isaac Furniss, William Bradwell, Charles Middleton, and William Jeffery. The "articles" had to be "perused and approved" by two magistrates—Samuel Frith, the famous "Squire Frith of Bank Hall," the popular sporting squire, and Marmaduke Middleton Middleton, of Leam Hall; and after these two dignitaries were satisfied with them they were "exhibited to and confirmed by the Court" at the Michaelmas Quarter Sessions, 1813, and signed by A. L. Maynard, clerk of the peace.

The society, curiously enough, had two classes of members, and each class was dealt with differently both as regards payments and benefits; the entrance fee varied from 1s. 8d. to 3s., according to age, which

varied from 15 to 30 years; the subscription was a shilling a month for the first class and 6d. a month for the second class, the rate of sick pay being proportionate to the subscription. And the funeral benefit, too, was on a sliding scale; for instance, a member of the first class dying after having been in the society two years, his representatives received £2, for four years £4, and for seven years £5, the benefit of the second-class member being exactly half those sums.

That they were kept up to the scratch in their payments is evident, for a first-class member had to forfeit twopence, and a second-class member a penny, if he neglected to pay; the amount was doubled for a second neglect, and for neglecting to pay a third time the member was publicly exposed by notice being given in the club-room, and excluded from the society—a rough-and-ready way of doing things. Evidently there was no such thing as suspension in those days; rigorous expulsion was the penalty for those who neglected to pay up.

This old society existed before the days of banks in this district. It is not said whether the officer who held the cash was accompanied by a bulldog, armed with a revolver, and guarded home by the constable, but certain it is that he was provided with a box—a big, strong chest with three locks and three keys to it, one for the Master and one each for the stewards. In this box the "cash, deeds, bonds, notes, books," etc., were kept.

The Master continued in office one year only, when the head steward was promoted to the position, "provided he behave himself as he ought to do." By this we are led to infer that they were not exactly perfect a century ago. Who were to be the judges as to whether he "behaved himself as he ought to do" we are not told. This "Master" was an important individual, something approaching a little god in the place—at any rate in the society. For instance, he had two votes on every question that came before the meetings, while the stewards and assistants had only "single votes." And the whole of the business was conducted by these fifteen important personages, who "shall sit together in one room on all occasions, neither shall any interrupt them nor enter therein, but upon business of their own. If any offend herein, shall forfeit sixpence, or be excluded." Rather a wide difference between "forfeiting" sixpence and being expelled.

THOSE PINTS OF ALE.

This society of "charitable and brotherly members" flourished in the days long before the temperance movement took hold. Those were the times when most folk brewed their own peck o' malt, when brewers' drays were unknown, when every publican was his own brewer, and when it was thought the proper thing to give

" ale " to children at Sunday School festivals. The officers of this society loved their pint pot, or its contents, because while a "forfeit" of sixpence had to be made by any one of them who dared to be absent from any business meeting, "everyone who attends shall have a pint of ale allowed him, to be paid for out of the box."

BRIDLING THE TONGUE.

That there were occasional "scenes" at the meetings is not to be wondered at, and some of the language used was not too choice. When drink was in wit was out, and the calling of "nicknames" was quite the order of the day. In the days of the old society there had been many a lively time in the club-room, so that when the amalgamation came these "charitable and brotherly" folk agreed to put the bridle on themselves by declaring:—
"That there shall be strictly observed the following orders in the club-room during club hours, viz.: First, if any member of this society shall come in disordered with liquor, so as to be a disturber, and incapable of discharging his office or duty as a member, shall curse, swear, talk profanely, or call anyone present by any other name than to which he answers, he shall forfeit twopence, but if he continue to offend he shall forfeit sixpence or be excluded. Secondly, after the Master or stewards shall demand silence, if anyone speak, until liberty be given him by the Master, he shall forfeit twopence, and no more than one to speak at once on matters of business. Thirdly, if any member plays or promotes playing at any game or games, he shall forfeit twopence or be excluded. Fourthly, every member shall keep his seat during club hours, except he change to oblige his brother; in default thereof he shall forfeit twopence."

FOOTBALL UNLAWFUL.

Here is another curious "article," showing that football was among the "unlawful exercises" in those days: "If any member of this society has received pay from the stock, and sufficient proof be given that he has caught the venereal, or has been working at any trade or calling, drinking to excess, wrestling, fighting, football playing, or any unlawful exercise whatever, he shall be excluded."

THE WHITSUNTIDE JOLLIFICATION.

The members had a right good jollification every Whit Tuesday, when they held their annual feast, when beer and the Bible appeared to be the order of the day. Under pain of exclusion all the forfeits and arrears had to be paid off on the club night before the feast, and for neglect to do this there was a further forfeit of a shilling, to be paid on the feast day. And at the same time honorary members paid what they pleased, all the money being thrown into the feast, which was held at the public-house after the members had attended service at the Wesleyan Chapel. Sometimes, however. John Barleycorn had got hold of some of the members before they went to chapel, and in order to preserve some sort of decorum a rule was made to the effect that "every member that resides within two miles shall attend where it (the feast) is held; the master, stewards, and assistants at ten o'clock, or forfeit threepence each, and the members at eleven in the forenoon, or forfeit twopence; they shall attend in good order to hear divine service, and every person who quits his ranks, either going or coming, shall forfeit threepence. If any member shall fight, challenge to fight, strike, threaten to strike, or in any wise disturb the harmony of the society, he shall forfeit two shillings and sixpence or be excluded." But apparently a good many kicked over the traces when the taps were turned on later in the day and the fine was no longer operative. "Likewise if the master, or some member appointed by him, does not wear the club hat girdle at the funeral of a member, and upon the Sunday preceding every club night, he shall forfeit sixpence."

And a member of this society could not even be buried without ale, for when a member died whose residence was within two miles from the place of meeting, "the master, stewards, and assistants shall attend at the house of the deceased, and thence attend their brother's corpse to the grave, for which they shall receive five shillings for ale." The custom survives to-day, for in the Bradwell Friendly Societies there are what is known as "The Twelve"—a dozen members who are appointed every year to attend the funeral of a brother, but, of course, the "ale" is missing.

After all, the members of this old-time Friendly Society were very jealous of each other's honour and integrity. If a member was proved to have "upbraided" another without cause, for having received money out of the box, he had to forfeit half-a-crown or be excluded, and anyone convicted of felony was expelled from the society "for ever." As will be seen in a former chapter, these were the days when every man between 18 and 45 years old was liable to be called upon to serve in the Militia, and in Bradwell a certain number were ballotted every year. Even this was provided for in the articles of this society, for—

"If any member shall voluntarily enter into His Majesty's regular forces, and continue therein three months, he shall be excluded from this society. But if a member be impressed into His Majesty's service, or be obliged to serve in the Militia, and be maimed and incapable of work, he shall receive such allowance as the club shall think fit, but if he be entitled to any pay or pension from the Government, then he shall receive nothing from our stock."

By way of closing the notice of this society of bygone days, it may be stated that, by rule, "every member shall use his endeavour, both by example and admonition, to suppress and discourage vice and profaneness in general, to promote the faith and practice of our true religion in particular, with good neighbours, to cultivate the peace and happiness of this society to the glory of God and the honour of our country."

With the advent of the Oddfellows, and the establishment of other benefit societies, this club gradually dwindled in membership and funds, but it struggled on until about 1880, when the few remaining members, all aged men, divided the funds and dissolved the society.

THE UNITED SOCIETY DISUNITED.
NAMES OF THE SECEDERS.

The first defection from the ranks of this United Society was in the year 1821. Apparently they were neither so "united" nor so "charitable and brotherly" as their name seemed to imply, for there were ructions in their ranks. In those days young children and old people earned just a trifle at "winding bobbins" for the weavers, and when old John Wragg's pay was stopped because he earned eighteenpence a week at this job there was a big rumpus. The section who sympathised with old John formed a club of their own, and were joined by many young men, who constituted themselves "The Independent Union Sick Society." Those who met and constituted themselves a new society were Thomas Jeffery, Thomas Fox, George Fox, George Elliott, Thos. Andrew, John Bradwell, junr., John Pearson, John Hallam, John Middleton (smith), George Bradwell, and Thomas Middleton (meadow). And although nearly a century has passed since then, the descendants of these men remain as members to-day. Here are the members of the new club who joined the first day, December 8th, 1821:—

Mark Ashton.	Robt. Hallam, junr.
Ellis Ashton.	Edward Hallam.
Thomas Ashton.	Samuel Hallam.
John Ashmore.	Jacob Hallam, junr.
George Ashmore.	William Howe.
Benjamin Barber.	Thomas Howe.
John Barber.	Robert Howe.
Wm. Bradwell, senr.	Samuel Howe.
Edward Bennett.	Robert Hilton.
Robt. Bocking (Hills).	Henry Hill.
William Burrows.	Adam Hill.
William Cooper.	John Hall, senr.
John Cooper.	John Hall, junr.
John Cheetham.	Micah Hall.
William Cheetham.	Wm. Hibbs, junr.
Richard Cheetham.	Robt. Jackson.
Emanuel Downing, senr.	Thos. Jeffrey, junr.
	Richard Kay.
Emanuel Downing, junr.	Geo. Maltby, senr.
	Geo. Maltby, junr.
George Downing.	Thomas Middleton (Smith).
Abraham Dakin.	Thos. Middleton, jun.
Johnson Evans.	John Middleton (Asters).
Edward Evans.	
William Evans.	George Middleton (Hatter).
James Evans.	
Robt. Elliott, senr.	

Robt. Elliott, junr.	George Middleton (Hill Top).
William Elliott.	
John Elliott.	Robert Middleton (Meadow).
Isaac Furness.	
Robert Furness.	Robt. Morton, junr.
William Fox.	Robt. Pearson.
Jeremiah Gilbert.	Isaac Pearson.
Thos. Hallam (Hills).	Joseph Revell.
Richard Hallam.	Thomas Revell.
John Hallam (New-Nook).	William Revell.
	Richard Walker.
Adam Hallam.	Jacob Worsley.

Thus the United Society was shaken, and the present Independent Union Sick Society formed. Jeremiah Gilbert was the pioneer of Primitive Methodism, and his membership of this club fixes the date of his first appearance to mission for the new sect.

The rules of this new club would doubtless be curious composition, but the earliest copy we have is dated 1849, when they were registered by Act of Parliament, and signed by Joseph Hall, George Bradwell, Frederick Morton, and Robert Howe.

There is nothing mentioned about prosecuting members who might embezzle money belonging to the society, but if he refused to make the same good the club night after his fraud was found out he was to be excluded from the society.

NUTTING FORBIDDEN.

The reference to "nutting" in the following rule is interesting: "If any member of this society, having received pay from the stock, and proof be given that he had, at the time, caught the venereal, or had been working at any trade or calling, drinking to excess, fighting, football playing, nutting, making bargains, etc., or any other unlawful exercise whatever, he shall be excluded."

Provision was also made for cases where members enlisted in the army or were balloted in the Militia. If he was balloted into the Militia, and happened to be called out, he received no pay during the time of his "servitude," but on his return he was re-admitted, but if a member either enlisted into the army or into the Militia as a substitute he was expelled.

In those days imprisonment for debt was common, but in such a case the unfortunate member was excused payment of his contribution, nor did he receive any benefit whilst in prison, but when he was liberated he was received into membership.

A rule of interest to present-day societies was, doubtless, made after a good deal of trouble. A sick or infirm member who was so reduced in circumstances that he could not subsist on the society's allowance was permitted to apply for parish relief, but if he entered the poorhouse his benefit ceased, and if he died there funeral expenses were not allowed, but if he was removed from the poorhouse and paid off all arrears due he was again received into the society.

Conviction of murder, felony, perjury, or larceny was attended with exclusion from the society, and if he was convicted of any other offence on account of which he was subject to imprisonment or corporal punishment, he had to pay ten shillings or be excluded.

BEER AND THE BIBLE.

Of course, the members had to have their feast day, when there was a good deal of festivity, in which ale played a prominent part. This "general feast day," "to commemorate our brotherly love and affection towards each other," was held on the 16th of May every year. The members "walked in rank" to hear divine service, and any member refusing to walk, or going out of the rank, was fined. The declaration, "every member shall pay one shilling per ale if he partake thereof," seems to imply that teetotalism was just taking root. That some of those who did "partake" did so freely may be gathered from the fact that for fighting or challenging another to fight on the feast day a fine of five shillings, or expulsion, was inflicted. The expenses of the feast had to be paid by those who partook of it, as the funds were not allowed to be drawn upon for that purpose.

Beer and the Bible again seem to be mixed up, for "every member shall endeavour, as well by admonition as example, to discourage and suppress all vice and profaneness, to promote the faith and practice of our true and holy religion, together with good neighbourhood in general, and to cultivate the peace and happiness of this society in particular, to the glory of God and the honour of our village, that it may be said unto us at the last day— 'Come, ye blessed of My Father, inherit the kingdom prepared for you from the foundation of the world, for I was sick and ye visited me.'"

The society appointed arbitrators to settle all disputes that might arise among the members. These arbitrators were men who were not interested in the funds. They were seven in number, but only three acted in each case of dispute, and they were appointed in a somewhat extraordinary way. The first arbitrators appointed were Robert Hill, Robert Hallam, George Fox, Robert Hill, senr., John Hallam, Samuel Bocking, and Jabez Birley Somerset. When a case of dispute arose the names of the arbitrators were written on separate pieces of paper, and placed in a box or glass, and the three whose names were drawn out by the complaining party decided the matter in difference.

This old society was in the meridian of its days in 1881, when it had 168 members and a capital of £1,760. Since then it has gradually declined in numbers, for there has not been a member initiated for the last thirty years, the roll now containing 39 names, with some £900 in the funds.

THE ODDFELLOWS.

The "Welcome Traveller" of the Peak Lodge of the Manchester Unity of Oddfellows was established on July 20th, 1829. In the box there remains to-day an interesting relic of the past in the shape of a couple of swords that were held over the heads of the newly initiated, when the ceremony took place in a darkened room, but the skull and cross-bones have long ago disappeared. Here is a complete list of those who have held the office of Noble Grand since the formation of the lodge:—

Thomas Bocking.	Joshua Walker.
William Burrows.	Zachariah Walker.
George Downing.	George Walker.
Thomas Broadbent.	Philip Bradwell.
Benjamin Hallam.	John Fox.
William Taylor.	Jas. Allan Cramond.
Charles Howe.	Abram Morton.
Thomas Barber.	John Wragg.
William Cheetham.	Arthur John Baker.
Edwin Bradwell.	Thos. Hy. Middleton.
Robert Hallam.	Jabez Bradwell.
Joseph Hy. Taylor.	John E. Jennings.
Samuel Howe.	Arthur Burrows.
Ernest Morton.	Samuel Hibbs.
Charles Bradwell.	Walter Howe.
John Kay.	Benjamin Hallam.
Benjamin Walker.	Isaac Andrew.
Robert Burrows.	Willoughby Bradwell.
Isaac Bancroft.	John Dakin.
Christopher Broad-	Albert Elliott.
bent.	Anthony Middleton.
John Bancroft.	Isaac Palfreyman.
George Ashmore.	Albert H. Walker.
George Middleton.	James Middleton.
George Bancroft.	Ernest Hilton.
Philip Middleton.	Ralph Middleton.
John Hall.	Charles A. Bancroft.

The lodge is No. 373 in the Unity. For many years the meetings were held at Ellis Needham's, the White Hart; then at the Bull's Head, afterwards at the Primitive Methodist School, and now at the Board School. There are 132 members, and £2,185 in the funds.

Within recent years a Rechabites' Tent and a Druids' Lodge have been established.

CHAPTER XXXII.

SOME TRAGIC DEATHS.

A Remarkable Chronology.

There will be found compiled below from various sources, in something like chronological order, tragic events that have occurred in towns and villages within a few miles of Bradwell. Though far from complete, the list will, so far as it goes, doubtless be interesting to the inhabitants of the places which they concern. It will be noticed that a large proportion of the fatalities during the last half century have been in the quarries and limeworks of Dove Holes, Peak Forest, and Millers Dale, and a considerable number of other casualties were during the construction of the Midland main line in the early sixties, and the Dore and Chinley line thirty years later.

1685—Feb. 28th. Thomas Carnal, killed by falling from the Torrs, Eyam Dale.

1689—Sept. 12th. Samuel Ratcliffe, shot in Highlow Wood by Martin Robinson, of Offerton.

1692.—Feb. 4th. Elizabeth Trout, starved to death in snow on Sir William.

1694.—Feb. 18th. John White, found dead in Eyam Dale.

1711—Dec. Woman starved to death near Edale End.

1711—Dec. Old man at Hope crushed into the fire by a falling beam in his house and roasted to death.

1729—July 10. William Hibbert, killed by a cart at Eyam.

1730. Man and woman starved to death in snowstorm on Ronksley Moor, Derwent.

1736—Jan. 26th. William Ainsworth, killed in Litton Dale.

1744—William Bradshaw, Castleton, drowned.

1748—Feb. 5th. Stephen Broomhead, starved to death in the snow on Eyam Moor.

1748—May 16th. Hannah Millward, killed by falling down Eyam Dale Rocks.

1750—Nicholas Dakin, drowned at Castleton.

1752—July 12th. Edward Mortin, drowned in a well on Eyam Edge.

1758—May. Lady and gentleman murdered in the Winnatts, Castleton.

1759—Rebecca Cock, drowned at Castleton.

1762—Joseph Flinders, run over by a cart and killed at Castleton.

1764—Samuel Blackwell, killed by fall down a rock in Eyam Dale.

1767—June 27th. Thomas Brettener, burnt to death in a lime kiln in Middleton Dale.

1768—James Blackwell, killed by a horse at Eyam.

1771—Ellen Hall, killed by fall from a horse at Castleton.

1773—Oct. 12th. Joseph Bradshaw, killed by a cart at Eyam.

1775—Aug. 21st. Sarah Mills, drowned herself at Eyam.

„ Aug. 30th. Wm. Furness, drowned in a well at Eyam.

„ Dec. 30th. John Hadfield, found dead in a field at Eyam.

1778—Joseph Staveley, killed by falling from a hay-loft at Castleton.

1780—June 16th. William Beeley, killed by a horse at Eyam.

1784—Oct. 14th. Joseph Archer drowned in Middleton Mill Dam.

1785—Jan. 26th. Joseph Vernon drowned in the Derwent near Hathersage.

1787—May 24th. Mary Hall, Bretton, killed by lightning.

1788—Thomas Dain, carrier, of Castleton, killed.

1790—Sept. 8th. George Froggatt, died in a ditch at Eyam.

1791—Oct. 30th. Kirk's Cotton Mill, Bamford, burnt down, damages £5,000.

1792—July 14th. James Ridgeway, cut his throat in Bretton Clough.

„ Aug. 2nd. Thomas Bagshaw, a child, killed from some steps at Eyam.

1794—John Hall, Castleton, committed suicide.

1796—Dec. 1st. Edmund Cocker, died suddenly in Eyam Church.

1802—July. John Ridgway, killed at Eyam.

„ Aug. 28th. Edward Dooley, musician, died suddenly on Eyam Edge.

1804—April 28th. Mary Brittlebank, Eyam, burnt to death.

„ Joseph Marrison drowned at Castleton.

1805—Feb. 1st. George Sheldon (47), Tideswell prison keeper and tax collector, starved to death in a snowstorm on Tideswell Moors.

1807—June 11th. Jonathan Fullwood, dropped dead in Eyam Dale.

1808—Longsden, found dead in Magclough.

1809—Samuel Slack, Castleton, committed suicide. Not read over at graveside.

1810—William Shaw, killed by a bull at Eyam.

1811—James Hall, found dead in a field at Castleton.

1812—June 26th. John Wildgoose found dead at Green Lee Barn, Eyam.

1815—Anthony Lingard, Tideswell, executed for the murder of Hannah Oliver, at Wardlow Miers, and gibbetted at Wardlow.

1819—Hannah Bocking (16), executed for poisoning her cousin, Jane Grant, at Litton Lane End.

1820—Three workmen killed by collapse of Cock Bridge, Ashopton.

1823—July. William Wood, of Eyam, murdered near Whaley Bridge.

1854—Mary Unwin, Eyam, fell dead while dancing at a public house.

„ July 20th. Wm. L. G. Bagshawe, Esq., Wormhill Hall, murdered by poachers in the river Wye.

1855—Alice Webster, Derwent, killed by horse taking fright when crossing the river Derwent and throwing her into the river.

„ Joseph Wyatt, killed by falling out of his cart at Eyam.

„ Sarah Handley, drowned in a well at Peak Forest.

„ Mary Ann Howe, burnt to death at Tideswell.

1857—Mytham Bridge washed down by a great flood; present bridge built.

1858—William Colman, Castleton, died suddenly from apoplexy.

„ Mary Needham, Litton, found dead in bed.

„ John Drabble, Foolow, burnt to death.

„ Samuel Priestley, Hathersage, found dead on the Moors.

„ John Froggatt, Hope, whilst in drink and quarrelling, got into a rage and fell dead.

„ Ann Hadfield, Edale, bled to death.

„ Thomas Gregory, Wardlow, fell dead.

„ John Henry Morten, Dove Holes, killed by a cart.

„ John Vernon, Sparrowpit, killed on the Peak Forest tramway.

1859—William Furness, of Hathersage, killed by an overdose of poison.

„ John Dakin, Castleton, run over and killed by horse and cart.

„ William Darwent, Thornhill, found dead in the road.

„ Polycarpe King, Derwent, fell dead.

„ Thomas Taylor, Wormhill, killed by a horse and cart.

„ John Dakin, Castleton, run over and killed by a horse and cart.

1860—Wm. Howe, Bradwell, killed by a shot in New Line Quarry, Dove Holes.

1861—Thomas Fox, hung himself at Ashopton.

„ Frances Hall, Hathersage, committed suicide by hanging to bedpost.

„ Selina Skidmore, killed by a cart at Wormhill.

1862—William Farmer, Litton, killed on Midland Railway construction.

„ Ann Wild, Tideswell, found dead in bed.

„ Joseph Warhurst, Litton, hung himself in a plantation on Tideswell Moor.

„ Richard Robinson, found drowned in the River Wye at Cressbrook.

„ John Fox (62), killed in a quarry at Dove Holes.

1863—Sarah Garlick, Grindleford Bridge, burnt to death.

,, Sarah Ellen Hudson, Tideswell, found dead in bed.

,, Samuel Stone, Litton, killed in Dove Holes Tunnel making.

,, John White, Eyam, drowned in a tub of water.

,, William Dakin (42), Tideswell, ruptured blood vessel and died.

,, Henry Knowles, Litton, killed on Midland Railway construction.

,, William Sutton, Tideswell, killed on Midland Railway construction.

,, Thomas Birchenough, killed by a shot in Warhurst's Quarry, Dove Holes.

,, June 26th. Sarah Beeson, Ann Beeson, John Beeson, and Ann Hampton, who lived in a hut formed in the lime ashes hillock in Dove Holes Dale, were killed by the hut falling in. Owing to the swelling of the hillock the sides closed together, the roof fell in and all four were buried alive and suffocated.

1864—Richard Turner (62), Wardlow Miers, fell dead.

,, George Wilson (66), Tideswell, died instantaneously.

,, John Charles Robinson, Tideswell, accidentally suffocated.

,, Jonathan Wall, killed in a stone quarry at Calver Sough.

,, Thomas Hibbert, Litton, accidentally shot himself.

,, Mary Blackwell, Eyam, found dead in bed.

,, Thomas Hibbert, accidentally drowned in the Derwent at Calver Bridge.

,, Thomas Kirk (68), Hope, died through excessive drinking.

,, Thomas Somerset (45), Wardlow Miers, killed by falling through the floor of his hay-loft.

,, Jeremiah Brown (36), killed on the Midland Railway works at Dove Holes.

,, James Jodrell (18), killed on the Midland Railway works by a wagon at Dove Holes.

,, John Wildgoose (37), killed on the Midland Railway works at Dove Holes.

,, John Daffin (19), killed on the Midland Railway works at Dove Holes.

1865—John Wright (59), Thornhill Moor, died through excessive drinking.

,, Richard Hartley (45), Dove Holes, killed by excessive drinking.

,, Thomas Brough (59), Dove Holes, killed by a fall of stone on Midland Railway works.

1866—Edith Barber (13), Castleton, thrown out of cart and killed.

,, Henry Kay (18), Hathersage, killed by a fall from a horse.

,, George Hall (60), Castleton, hung himself whilst insane.

,, John Murphy (25), killed by a fall of stone on the Midland Railway works, Dove Holes.

,, Elizabeth Barnes (1), Dove Holes, died from exposure and want.

1867—Abraham Frude (55), Hathersage, fell dead.

,, George Fisher (22), killed in a stone quarry at Hathersage.

,, William Ashmore (58), killed by falling out of a cart at Thornhill Moor.

,, James Taylor (77), Eyam, found dead in bed.

,, Catherine Hobson (66), Hathersage, died by the visitation of God.

,, Hannah Dakin (3), Tideswell, found drowned.

,, Luke Needham (69), Wormhill, fell dead through over-exertion.

1867—Mary Robinson (44), Foolow, died by the visitation of God.

,, Martha Vaines (12), killed on the railway at Peak Forest Station.

,, Alfred Fletcher (16), killed in a quarry in Dove Holes Dale.

,, George Garlick (24), killed in a stone quarry in Dove Holes Dale.

1868—John Slinn (62), Grindleford Bridge, died by the visitation of God.

,, Peter Unwin (66), Eyam, found dead in bed.

1869—Thomas Holme (56), Bamford, hung himself whilst insane.

,, John Garlick (12), Grindleford Bridge, (drowned when bathing).

,, Dinah Marsden (6), Grindleford Bridge, burnt to death.

,, Thomas Drabble (75), Hathersage, died in a fit of apoplexy.

,, William Swindell (70), Windmill, died by the visitation of God.

., Francis Palfreyman (84), Litton, when returning home from prayer meeting at Wesleyan Chapel, fell into a quarry and was killed.

,, Sarah Ann Schofield (38), Hathersage Booths, died instantaneously.

,, Elizabeth Elliott (81), Hathersage, killed by falling downstairs.

1870—Francis Millward (30), killed by falling down rock at Millers Dale.

,, George Broomhead (13), Foolow, killed by horse and cart.

,, Ann Shakespeare, Hathersage, found dead in bed.

,, George Hibbs (50), Little Hucklow, killed crossing railway at Peak Forest.

1873—Joseph Fox, killed in stone quarry at Dove Holes.

,, John Frith, killed in a stone quarry at Dove Holes.

1875—August 7th, Henry Vines, fell down rock at Blackwell Mill Junction.

,, Nov. 5th, James Garside, killed in a lime kiln at Potts and Jackson's, Dove Holes.

1876—March 31st, John Hayward, killed in a lead mine at Peaks Hill, Peak Forest.

.. April 26th, John Storer, fell into a lime kiln at Potts and Jackson's, Dove Holes, and was burnt to ashes. Nothing was found but his knife blade, a few buttons, and one or two small bones, and these were interred in a cigar box in the Primitive Methodist burial ground, Dove Holes.

,, June 7th, Edwin Taylor, killed in Chee Tor Tunnel, Wormhill.

,, August 8th, Robert Potts fell dead in the street at Dove Holes.

,, Nov. 24th, Sarah Fletcher died instantaneously at Peak Forest.

1877—January 22nd, Rachel Harrott died suddenly at Dove Holes.

,, March 13th, Thomas Cartwright killed whilst shunting at Millers Dale.

,, May 12th, Ellen Mullins, fell dead in Dove Holes Dale.

,, Nov. 28th, an unknown man found drowned in Barmoor Clough.

1878—January 11th, Henry Lomas killed whilst shunting at Bibbington, Dove Holes.

,, May 3rd, William Catlin cut his throat at Hargate Wall, Wormhill.

., June 12th, Dr. Alfred Cottrill fell dead in the road at Millers Dale.

1879—March 22nd, George Clayton, killed in Great Rocks Quarry, Peak Forest.

,, March 27th, Samuel Barber killed by falling from a plank at Wainwright Works, Peak Forest.

1879—June 6th, Moses Sheldon found drowned in Barmoor Clough.

„ Nov. 8th, Joseph Heath, killed by the explosion of a pistol in Bibbington's Smithy, Dove Holes.

1880—January 12th, George Pearson killed by a stone at Wainwright's Works, Peak Forest.

„ April 1st, John Mosley shot himself in a railway carriage near Millers Dale.

„ June 16th, Owen Evans hanged himself in a barn at Perry Foot, Peak Forest.

„ July 27th, Thomas Derbyshire fell dead at work at Dove Holes.

„ Sept. 10th, Benjamin Mycock, crushed to death by waggons on the tramway at Dove Holes.

1881—March 11th, John Brown killed by a train in Dove Holes Tunnel.

„ Oct. 8th, George Mellor killed by a horse and cart in Barmoor Clough.

1882—June 6th, Francis Garlick killed by falling down cellar steps at Upper End.

„ June 6th, James Lomas crushed to death by waggons at Beswick's, Peak Forest Station.

„ August 4th, Thomas Hawley found dead in a lane at Upper End.

„ Nov. 6th, Ada Dicken drowned in a reservoir at Upper End.

1883—In July, Robert Clayton (28), killed by falling down Wainwright's quarry, Peak Forest.

„ August 16th, John Kenyon (56), Grindleford Bridge, fell dead in Marquis of Granby, Bamford.

„ Sept. 8th, George Berrisford, run over by a waggon at Bibbington's Works, Dove Holes.

„ Oct. 22nd, John Hall, of Bradwell, killed in M S. and L. Quarries, Peak Forest Station.

„ Nov. 23rd, James Dakin (57), Castleton, died from hydrophobia caused by a dog bite.

„ Dec. 1st, Annie Wheeldon, died suddenly in bed at Higher Bibbington, Dove Holes.

„ Dec. 12th, Mary Ball, found dead in bed at Dove Holes.

1884—Jan. 2nd, Martin Mullins (50), Dove Holes, killed by falling down Bibbington's quarry, Dove Holes.

„ May 24th, John Bower, found dead in bed at Laneside Farm, Peak Forest.

„ June 23rd, John Brough, killed by a railway train at Dove Holes.

„ Oct. 5th, Walter Gould, Spring House, Hope, killed by fall from his horse at Hathersage.

1885—Dec. 27th, George Platt, Bamford, found dead in a cowhouse.

„ Dec. 27th, Samuel Austin (53), killed by falling down Bibbington's quarry, Dove Holes.

1886—Jan. 1st, Isaac Wilson (40), killed by falling over a wall at Hathersage Booths, when "letting the new year in."

„ Jan. 4th, Joseph Longden (30), killed by a fall of stone at Great Rocks quarries, Peak Forest.

„ Jan. 5th, John Bagshawe (10), Wormhill, fell when crossing a bridge over the River Wye, and was drowned.

„ Jan. 12th, John Lomas (16), killed by machinery in Beswick's blacksmith's shop, Peak Dale.

„ Feb. 10th, John Bocking Darwent (74), Thornhill, a well-known Primitive Methodist local preacher, found dead on the sofa.

„ Feb. 12th, James Goddard (36), killed by a fall of stone in the Great Central Quarries, Dove Holes.

1886—April 9th, Robert Howe (54), Litton, killed by a runaway horse at Millers Dale.

„ May 26th, Thomas Fox (45), killed by falling down the rock in Furness's Quarry, Eyam Dale.

„ June 12th, Allen Walker ((35), Tideswell, accidentally thrown down the shaft at Norwood Colliery and killed.

1887—Samuel Cock (40), found dead in bed at Castleton.

„ July 26th, Hannah Longden, found dead in her chair at the Clown Inn, Dove Holes.

„ Aug. 17th, Sissie Gaunt, Yorkshire Bridge Inn, Bamford, accidentally poisoned by sucking lucifer matches.

„ Aug. 31st, William Boothby (14), Higher Bibbington, Dove Holes, killed by lightning whilst reading the Bible. Five other persons injured.

„ December, Charles Hodkin (74), starved to death on Froggatt Edge Moors.

1888—Jan. 6th, William Hall (59), postmaster, Castleton, died suddenly.

„ July 26th, Walter Hall Walker (17), Riding House Farm, Derwent, killed by an avalanche of snow falling upon him whilst shepherding.

„ Oct. 15th, William Webb, Bamford, found dead in bed.

„ Oct. 31st, John Hibbert (32), killed by a waggon at Heathcott's quarry, Dove Holes.

„ Nov. 26th, Rev. Charles Smith (56), rector of Bamford, fell unconscious in the Post Office, and died in a few hours.

„ Dec. 2nd, Hugh Isaac Cooper (7), died as a result of swallowing a halfpenny at Peak Dale.

1889—Feb. 4th, Joseph Harrott (20), shot in Bibbington's quarry, Dove Holes.

„ May 18th, Samuel Simpson (11), killed by a fall whilst bird nesting, at Dale Head Farm, Tideswell.

„ May 14th, Eyre, of Great Hucklow, killed on new railway works at Dore.

„ July 24th, Thomas Millward, Litton Mill, killed on the railway at Millers Dale.

„ Aug. 12th, Benjamin Clayton, accidentally shot with his own gun in his house on Tideswell Moor.

„ Nov. 5th, Richard Green, killed in Grindleford Tunnel.

1890—Jan. 31st, John Wm. Bradbury (13), Tideswell, killed by falling down the face of a quarry at Millers Dale.

„ March 7th, John Thomas Cooper (3½), of Eyam, burnt to death.

„ March 8th, John Marsden, killed by a fall of rock in a quarry at Peak Dale.

. March 19th, Abraham Cooper, killed by fall at a Peak Dale lime kiln.

„ March 26th, Wm. Bland, Farnley Eyam, died suddenly.

„ March, Jonathan R. Hall, killed on the L. and N.W. Railway, Dove Holes.

„ May 28th, John Daniel Hodson (31), poisoned himself at the Snake Inn, Woodlands.

„ June 18th, Sidney John Rosewell (28), killed in Edale railway cutting.

„ July 8th, George Chappell (8), killed by falling down rocks at Peak Forest.

„ Aug. 11th, William Slinn, killed by machinery on Dore and Chinley Railway works, Edale.

„ Sept. 5th, John Higginson, water bailiff, Mytham Bridge, fell dead on the banks of the Derwent.

1890—Oct. 29th, Thomas Hartle (34), Dove Holes, killed on the railway at Manchester.

1891—Jan 10th, Walter Mosby (28), killed in Edale Tunnel on railway works.

,, Jan 24th, Mary Pickford, Litton, died from exposure, consequential on a fall during a fit.

,, Feb. 4th, Job Hodgkinson (67), run over and killed in Peak Forest Tunnel.

,, February 22nd, Samuel Eyre, Great Hucklow, burnt to death.

,, April 30th, John Marriner (32), cut his throat at Hathersage.

,, Aug. 15th, James Storer fell into a lime kiln and was burnt to death at Dove Holes.

,, Sept. 17th, Thomas Smith (26), killed by a shot in Great Rocks quarry, Peak Forest.

Oct. 4th, Rev. A. B. Camm, Blackpool, fell from a train in Peak Forest Tunnel.

, Nov. 19th, Martha Dawson, Cressbrook, drowned herself.

,, Dec. 1st, Albert Schofield, killed by a fall of clay from the side of the cutting on the Dore and Chinley Railway works at Padley Wood, Hathersage.

,, Dec. 3rd, Herbert Twiner crushed to death between two waggons on railway works at Padley Wood.

,, Dec. 8th, Ethelbert Swindell (23), Bamford, killed at Oughtibridge Railway Station.

1892—January 13th, Joseph King, killed by a waggon at the railway works at Padley Wood.

,, Feb. 24th, John Moulson, Peak Forest, killed by an explosion in Ashwood Dale Quarries.

,, Walter Gilbert, Tideswell, killed at Edgeley Station, Stockport.

,, April 11th, Roger Barber (37), found killed in Bibbington's Quarries, Dove Holes.

,, April 22nd, Charles Ronksley (21), Hathersage, killed on Dore and Chinley Railway works.

,, May 21st, James Millward (60), Stoney Middleton, cut his throat.

,, May 30th, Anthony Potter (27), Castleton, killed in Cowburn Tunnel, Edale.

,, June 3rd, Bernard Robinson, Tideswell, fatally injured in Buxton Lime Firm's quarries at Millers Dale.

,, June 16th, an unknown man, tatooed "E.J.P., found drowned at Peak Forest.

,, June 16th, Whitfield Watson (30), run over and killed by waggons on the new railway works, Edale.

,, Nov. 8th, Isaac Watts, drowned whilst crossing over stones in River Derwent, Hathersage.

,, Nov. 10th, Mary Ann Hunstone (64), Tideswell, committed suicide with a razor.

,, Nov. 1st, James Fletcher, Peak Forest, burnt to death at Beswick's Lime Kilns.

1893—Jan. 18th, William Tym, Hope, killed by fall from a cart.

,, Jan. 22nd, Henry Jones, Hathersage, killed by falling into a culvert at Padley Saw Mills.

,, Jan. 22nd, John William Gerrard (14), killed by a fall of refuse from a lime kiln at Small Dale Lime Works, Peak Forest.

,, May 18th, William Wainwright, killed by wagonette at Hathersage.

,, May 27th, Harriett Townsend, drowned in the river Wye at Litton.

1893—June 16th, — Edwards, killed by a runaway horse on railway works at Edale, at Dove Holes Station.

,, July 1st, William Barker (70), fell dead

,, July 8th, Reuben Leech, Tideswell, killed by a train on the railway at Peak Forest.

,, Sept. 9th, Benjamin Mansbridge, killed by a locomotive in Midland cutting near Peak Forest.

,, Sept. 16th, Percival James Wallington, drowned at Hill Farm, Wormhill.

,, Sept. 21st, Mary Alice Porter (2), scalded to death in a bucket of hot water at Great Rocks Farm, Wormhill.

,, Sept. 26th, Gertrude Howe, Brook Bottom, Tideswell, burnt to death through dress catching fire at a candle.

1894—Jan. 22nd, Joseph Eley (48), Millers Dale, died suddenly.

,, Feb. 6th, Reginald Broom, accidentally killed by a fall at Taddington.

,, March 7th, Mary Ann Cooper (18), Peak Dale, drowned in Wye, Buxton.

,, March 21st, Jonathan Howe (34), shot himself at Castleton.

,, May 26th, Mary Walker, a native of Castleton, died very suddenly at Bakewell.

,, June 14th, John Oag, killed on railway at Edale.

,, July 5th, Henry Lawton (43), run over and killed at Hope.

,, Oct. 24th, Martha Unwin, Stoney Middleton, accidentally suffocated.

,, Dec. 20th, Dr. George Sibley Hicks, of Eyam, died from an overdose of laudanum.

1895—March 17th, George Hardy (56), Castleton, ruptured a blood vessel when fighting with another man and died.

,, April 16th, John Cheetham (82), formerly chemist, found dead on his house floor at Hope.

,, July 18th, Elizabeth Roebuck, found killed in Dove Holes tunnel, having fallen from a train.

,, July 25th, John Wilson (65), Thornhill, cut his throat whilst temporarily insane.

,, Aug. 5th, William Tingle, found dead in Burbage Brook, Hathersage.

,, Sept. 23rd, George Maltby (35), crushed to death by dray at Monsal Dale.

,, Oct. 7th, Fredk. Slack (26), Tideswell, killed by jumping out of a trap when horse was running away.

,, Nov. 18th, Mrs. Pearson, widow of Jos. Pearson, of Little Hucklow, fell dead at Upper End, Peak Dale.

,, Nov. 25th, Ann Wain, Eyam, burnt to death.

1896—July 2nd, Elizabeth Cooper (23), a visitor from Manchester, killed by falling from Peveril Castle into Cave Dale, Castleton.

,, July 3rd, John Power, found dead on the railway at Peak Forest.

,, October 11th, Mary Ellen Johnson, drowned at Upper End, Peak Dale.

,, October 12th, Charles Neath, killed on the L. & N.W. Railway at Dove Holes.

,, Nov. 5th, John Woollen found drowned in the river Derwent near Hathersage.

1897—Jan. 16th, Robert James Hallam, Stoney Middleton, hung himself.

,, Jan. 31st, John Fletcher (43), Ivy House Farm, Peak Forest, hung himself in a barn.

,, Feb. 10th, James Bennett, Dove Holes, killed by a fall of stone in "Victory" Quarry.

1897—March 9th, Thomas Wm. Ludlow (36), signalman, Peak Forest, when knocking twigs from telegraph wires, wall collapsed and he was killed.

,, March 30th, James Shallcross (32), found drowned in Litton Mill dam.

,, April 19th, John Ward West (66), Bamford, died from heart disease after a fall.

,, July 29th, Herbert Gilman (17), Litton Mill, shot himself in Marple Hall Park.

,, Aug. 27th, Harry Leech, Tideswell, killed by a fall of stone in Millers Dale quarry.

,, Sept. 8th, Richard Brown Berry, a Bolton visitor to Castleton, died very suddenly.

,, Oct. 27th, Samuel Hodgkinson (48), Tideswell, killed on the railway at Millers Dale.

,, Nov. 19th, Abraham Yeomans, killed by falling downstairs at Stoney Middleton.

1898—March 18th, James Ashmore, Tideswell, killed by a fall of clay at Great Rocks quarries, Peak Forest.

,, April 23rd, John Henry Mosley, killed by being thrown from a cart at Millers Dale.

,, July 5th, William Hoyle, Peak Forest, died in Holding's quarry, Dove Holes.

,, July 5th, Edmund Bennett (29), shot in Great Rocks quarry, Peak Forest.

,, Nov. 5th, Mary Hannah Vernon (39), killed by falling downstairs at Dove Holes.

1899—April 14th, Elizabeth Grace Broome, suffocated in bed with her parents, at Poynton Cross Farm, Hucklow.

,, April 15th, George William Goodwin, killed by fall of stone in a quarry at Dove Holes.

,, June 15th, Mrs. James Carrington, Edale, found dead in bed.

,, Aug. 25th, Mrs. Lily Middleton (25), Bamford, found dead in bed.

,, Sept. 30th, Chas. Wm. Bowden, drowned in Litton Mill dam.

,, Oct. 20th, James Lewis (62), fell dead at Great Rocks kiln, Peak Forest.

,, Dec. 29th, William E. D. Palmer, killed by an engine at Millers Dale.

,, Nov. 8th, Hugh Stafford (32), killed by an explosion in Holderness quarry, Dove Holes.

1900—March 18th, funeral at Stocksbridge, both on one day, of Charlotte Evans and Wilfred Evans, mother and son, formerly of Bradwell.

,, Mar. 26th, Esther Ellen Lee (3), scalded to death in a bucket of hot water at Dove Holes.

,, Sept. 6th, Esther Mycock, burnt to death at Taddington.

,, Oct. 15th, Martha Green, killed by a fall at Wormhill.

,, Dec. 23rd, Gladys Broome (1½), crushed to death by a cow at Hucklow.

1901—Jan. 9th, George Jackson, Peak Dale, found hanged.

,, Mar. 15th, Samuel Booth, Hathersage, found hanged.

,, May 12th, Samuel Gibson, Litton, found hanged.

,, May 22nd, George Jackson, Tideswell, drowned himself at Peak Forest.

,, Aug. 13th, George Hodkin (58), fell dead in a quarry at Peak Forest.

,, Oct. 12th, Emily Sellars, and her daughter, Emily, found drowned on the Hall Farm, Litton.

1902—Jan. 10th, Joseph Walton (60), Tideswell, fell back in his chair and died.

1902—Jan. 13th, John Jackson, John Flint and Henry Swindells, of Tideswell, knocked down and killed by an engine when walking on the railway at Millers Dale.

,, Jan. 13th, John Samuel Berrisford (18), killed by a wagon at Bibbington's Works, Dove Holes.

,, Mar. 12th, Isaac Hadfield, killed by an engine at Great Central Railway Co.'s quarry, Peak Dale.

,, May 12th, Annie Gertrude Hepworth, Tideswell, strangled herself.

,, July 17th, Charles Smith Herrington, killed by a fall at Eyam.

,, Aug. 20th, William Greenhalgh, killed by a pole falling on his head at Tideswell Gas Works.

1903—Feb. 12th, William Brewster, killed by a wagon running down an incline at Bole Hill Quarries, Hathersage.

,, April 23rd, A child, named Robinson, suffocated in bed with its parents at Stoney Middleton.

,, May 1st, George Furness, drowned in the Delph, at Eyam.

,, May 4th, John Webster, killed by a train at Peak Forest Station.

,, Aug. 31st, John Marsh Robinson (45), thrown from his horse and killed at Bamford.

,, Sept. 6th, John Hill, killed by a fall in New Lime quarry, Peak Forest.

,, Oct. 14th, Henry Watson (47), killed by fall from a hay-loft at Castleton.

1904—May 17th, John Robinson Gregory hung himself at Hathersage.

,, May 20th, Matilda Rawles (26), found dead on the house floor at Hope.

,, June 25th, John Evans killed by a fall at Derwent Valley Water Board's quarry, Hathersage.

,, July 4th, Charles Henry Bullard, killed by a crane balance weight falling upon him at the quarries, Hathersage.

,, July 13th, William Allen Guthrie, found drowned in the river Derwent at Hathersage.

,, July 8th, Frederick Garlick, killed by an explosion of cheddite in Bibbington's quarry, Dove Holes.

,, Oct. 19th, Sarah Dean, Tideswell, died suddenly during an operation under chloroform.

,, Nov. 22nd, John Brown (55), found starved to death at Bamford.

1905—Jan. 2nd, An unknown man found starved to death on Hathersage Moors.

,, Jan. 24th, Jane Ann Blackwell, killed by a fall at Tideswell.

,, June 23rd, Herbert Lomas, Litton, drowned himself.

,, July 4th, James Sheldon, hung himself at Hathersage.

,, Aug. 26th, Mary Elizabeth Jones (21), drowned herself at Bamford.

,, Dec. 9th, an unknown man hung himself at Bamford.

1906—June 12th, Thomas Barker (37), drowned himself at Bamford.

,, Sept. 10th, Andrew Henry Dungworth, poisoned himself at Hathersage.

,, Dec. 4th, James Allcock (3), burnt to death at Dove Holes.

1907—Jan. 2nd, William Wilson, hung himself at Peak Dale.

,, Mar. 6th, Edward Kirk, killed by being thrown from a cart at Dove Holes.

,, Aug. 12th, Joseph Vernon (54), Sparrowpit, killed by an explosion in the quarry at Peak Forest.

,, Sept. 4th, John Thomas Heath and William Fletcher, blown to pieces by an explosion of gunpowder whils blasting in Great Rocks quarries, Peak Dale.

1907—Nov. 4th, Thomas Gibson, killed by a fall of stone in Great Rocks quarry, Peak Dale.

,, Nov. 12th, Joseph Martin, killed by a train on the railway at Peak Forest.

1908—March 11th, Reggie Walker (2), burnt to death at Tideswell.

,, April 21st, Robert How (81), barmaster, of Castleton, died from an accidental fall.

,, July 20th, Thomas Gould, drowned whilst fishing in the river Derwent at Hathersage.

,, Aug. 7th, an unknown man jumped in front of a train at Thornhill and was cut to pieces.

,, Aug. 27th, Kathleen Mary Revill (3), drowned in the Hay Brook, Hathersage.

,, Nov. 26th, Arthur Bingham (2), burnt to death at Peak Dale.

1909—Jan. 1st, Samuel Blackwell, died from concussion of the brain at Eyam.

,, Jan. 5th, Tom Peel, was felling a tree at Hathersage, when a branch fell upon him and he was killed.

,, Jan. 18th, M. Strickland accidentally suffocated at Hathersage.

,, Feb. 12th, John Iredale, killed by falling downstairs at Tideswell.

,, March 13th, Isaac Makinson strangled himself at Hathersage.

,, April 7th, Edith Annie Rowbotham (3), drowned at Bamford.

,, April 20th, Hannah Bramwell, death accelerated by a fall at Tideswell.

,, Aug. 12th, Archibald Jerram drowned whilst bathing in the river Derwent at Froggatt.

,, Aug. 9th, John Wells, killed in a collision of a bogey and engine at Bole Hill quarry. Hathersage.

1910—Mar. 11th, Teresa Biggin (11), killed by a fall at Hathersage.

,, April 21st, William Garlick, killed by a fall of stone in the Buxton Lime quarries, Peak Dale.

,, April 27th, Fred Vernon, shot in an explosion whilst blasting at Dove Holes.

,, June 11th, Annie Furness, strangled herself whilst not responsible for her actions at Tideswell.

,, Sept. 29th, Robert Bingham, Peak Dale, died from blood poisoning from an injury to his fingers whilst quarrying.

,, Oct. 22nd, Robert Cotterill (58), fell dead from his chair at Bamford.

,, Dec. 23rd, Mary Jackson cut her throat at Eyam.

1911—Feb. 20th, Thomas Beverley. Castleton, cut his throat in a stable during temporary insanity.

,, May 1st, Hamlet Tattersall, electrocuted at Great Rocks Siding, Peak Dale.

,, June 23rd, Blanche Wilkin cut her throat during insanity at Hathersage.

,, In June, William Hulley (60), killed by a waggon at Holderness lime works, Dove Holes.

,, June 14th, William Hawley Mycock, killed at Calton Hill quarry, Taddington.

,, Aug. 25th, Herbert Brooks killed by a waggon at Perseverance Lime Works, Peak Dale, Dove Holes.

,, Oct. 16th, Andrew John Roche (63). steward for the Duke of Norfolk. fell into the River Derwent and died from exposure.

1911—Dec., Mrs. Amelia Seaman (83). Tideswell. died from shock after accidental burns.

CHAPTER XXXIII.

SOME MEMORABLE SNOWSTORMS.

Tragedies of the Snow.

Although Bradwell is situate in a deep valley, sheltered from the stormy blasts, the hills that surround it on all sides are of such an altitude that snow will remain there for several months. and these severe storms that visit this part of the Peak in the winter, have been responsible for many tragedies, a few of which may be mentioned here

"THE LOST LAD."

Tradition has handed down through four hundred years the story of the lost lad of the Woodlands, a few miles from Bradwell, which gave the name to the mountain still known as "The Lost Lad." A lad of 13, who lived with his parents in one of the neighbouring villages, ventured too far from home one winter's day, and when darkness approached. he was terrified to find himself on the moorlands—lost, ah and lost in the snow! He shrieked until he lay down to sleep,' completely exhausted, and his father searched all night in vain. Living on wild berries from the bushes for several days, the father searching for him miles away on the severest night, the poor lad, on the summit of one of the highest hills, far away from any dwelling, had just sufficient strength left to pile up a few stones and inscribe his fate thereon. Here marked with the aid of a sharp stone, were particulars of his fate, and on another he wrote in big characters "LOST LAD," sank beside his own self-erected monument. and on this lonely eminence slept his last sleep.

Many years the remains of the poor lad lay on these heights undiscovered, until some sportsmen, seeing the pile of stones. went thither and found the skeleton, which was removed and interred. With difficulty they deciphered some inscriptions on the stones, but very plain, in big capitals, was "LOST LAD." For many generations the heap of stones remained entire, and the hill is still known as "The Lost Lad."

STARVED TO DEATH ON WINHILL.

Such was the severity of a snowstorm in the winter of 1674, that a man named Barber, a grazier, and his maid-servant, crossing the shoulder of Winhill, a little over two miles from Bradwell, were lost in the snow, and remained covered with it from January to May, when they were found, and the bodies being too offensive, they were buried on the spot in their clothing.

In his "Additions to the Brittania," as detailed from the Philosophical Transactions, Gough alludes to this, and says: "About twenty-nine years afterwards some country men, probably having observed the extraordinary properties of this soil in preserving dead bodies, had the curiosity to open the ground, and found them in no way altered, the colour of the skin being fair and natural, and their flesh as soft as that of persons newly dead. They were exposed for a sight during the course of twenty years following, though they were so much changed in that time by being so often uncovered. In 1716, Mr. Henry Brown, M.B., of Chesterfield, saw the man perfect, his beard strong and about a quarter of an inch long; the hair of his head short, his skin hard and of a tanned leather colour, pretty much the same as the liquor and earth they lay in. He had on a broad cloth coat, of which the doctor in vain tried to tear off a skirt. The woman was more decayed, having been taken out of the ground and rudely handled; her flesh particularly decayed, her hair long and spongy, like that of a living person. Mr. Barber, of Rotherham, the man's grandson, had both bodies buried in Hope Churchyard, and upon looking into the graves some time afterwards, it was found that they were entirely consumed. Mr. Wormald, the minister of Hope, was present at their removal. He observed that they lay about a yard deep in moist soil or moss, but no water stood in the place. He saw their stockings drawn off, and the man's legs, which had not been uncovered before, were quite fair. The flesh, when pressed by his finger, pitted a little, and the joints played freely, and without the least stiffness. The other parts were much decayed. What was left of their clothes not cut off for curiosity, was firm and good, and the woman had a piece of new serge, which seemed never the worse." ··

PERISHED ON SIR WILLIAM.

The winter of 1692-3 was notable for very heavy snowstorms in these parts. A woman named Elizabeth Trout was overtaken in one of these storms crossing Sir William, and was starved to death.

FROZEN TO DEATH AT EDALE END.

The winter of 1711 was most severe. There was a big snowstorm in December, and a woman walking over the hills from the Woodlands, perished in the storm near Edale End, and was found starved to death.

STARVED TO DEATH ON EYAM MOOR

In the early part of 1748 there was another big storm, and many people perished in different parts of the country. On the 5th of February, a man named Stephen Broomhead, was found starved to death in the snow on Eyam Moor.

PERISHED IN THE SNOW ON TIDESWELL MOOR.

It was on Tideswell Moor, on the verge of Bradwell Moor, where more than a hundred years ago George Sheldon, of Tideswell, lost his life in a snowstorm. He was the keeper of the prison at Tideswell, as well as tax collector, and it was in the exercise of the duties connected with this office that he lost his life. The Bradwell and Tideswell moors were not then enclosed, and when Sheldon was returning from Peak Forest on the night of February 1st, 1805, he was overtaken by a terrible snowstorm, lost his way, fell into a snowdrift, and perished. And on his memorial tablet on the outside wall of Tideswell Church we read :

"By depth of snow and stormy day,
He was bewildered in his way;
No mortal aid did him come nigh,
Upon the snow he there did lie
Helpless, being worn out with strife,
Death soon deprived him of his life;
But hope he found a better way
To the regions of Eternal Day."

A HATHERSAGE HERO.

Occasionally snow accumulated in immense drifts on the hills above Hathersage, obliterating all traces of the road, rendering it not only dangerous but impassable. In the old coaching days, when the journey from Bradwell to Sheffield had to be made by "'bus," the passengers had exciting experiences, as many can well remember. In the winter of 1813 the carriages that attempted to cross this bleak part of the moors either returned, or were left buried in the snow. A young man from Brookfield, near Hathersage, was the means of saving several persons from perishing in this severe winter. Near Burbage Brook he found a sailor and his wife who were exhausted with fatigue, and unable to proceed on their journey. The poor man had fallen under his exertions to support his wife, and was nearly dead, but the young man carried him on his back to the only house he could find, nearly a mile distant and then returned and carried the woman in the like manner, as she was laid starving to death in the snow. At this time the coach from Manchester was overturned and nearly buried in the snow, where it remained for several days. All the passengers were females, and among them was a woman with her two-year-old child. The young man carried the child to Hathersage, and the woman, in attempting to follow, fell into a snowdrift and was almost starved to death, when the young man extricated her and restored her to her child. The remaining two ladies he released from their perilous situation.

HOUSES BURIED IN RECENT SNOW-STORMS.

Remarkable Experiences.

The great snowstorm of 1888 was considered to be the most furious that had raged over the district for at least half a century. Edward Hall, who drove the mails from Castleton to Sheffield, had some remarkable experiences. He was accompanied on the journey by William Eyre, and it was a case of cutting through the huge drifts for thirteen miles, but when Brough Lane Head was reached, about a mile below Bradwell, they were fairly beaten. The roads were completely blocked by huge drifts, and one, 150 yards long and six feet high, it was impossible to get through, so the cart had to be left fast in the snow, and 21 men engaged to cut a track just wide enough to let the horses pass, when, taking out the mail bags, Hall and Eyre put them on the horses' backs, and left the cart embedded in the snow. The Bradwell conveyances remained at home, the whole place being completely snowed up with drifts, in some places twelve feet high. Old inhabitants declared that they never knew so much snow as there was at that time on the roads around Bradwell, extending several weeks in February and March.

In the old toll-bar house at Slack Hall, on the Castleton Road, near Chapel-en-le-Frith, there resided Mr. and Mrs. Samuel Revill, an elderly couple, natives of Bradwell. On the Sunday night the old couple retired to rest, little thinking what a terrible experience was in store for them. About 1 o'clock the husband was awakened by a suffocating sensation. Feeling very ill, and not knowing what to do, he wandered about for some time in search of an inlet for air. But in vain. He endeavoured to procure a light, but the candle burned only with great difficulty owing to the want of air. Both husband and wife feeling they were suffocating, and naturally expecting an outlet at the chimney, they proceeded to light a fire, when the house was filled with smoke, almost to suffocation, and in this terrible situation they passed the night.

The house was buried; their cries were unheard and unavailing, but a band of workmen cut a road to the door, and at nine o'clock the imprisoned couple were released, almost suffocated, but thankful indeed that they had been rescued from the jaws of death.

At Sparrowpit there was a remarkable scene. The Devonshire Arms public house was snowed up to such a degree that to cut through the snow was considered an impossible task, and a tunnel was driven underneath as an approach to the house. But even this appears to have been equalled, for in the old coaching days this house was completely buried in a snow-storm, and for some time the coaches ran over the top of the building.

BURIED BY AN AVALANCHE.

It was in this storm that a sad fatality occurred at Ashopton. Some of the sheep belonging to Mr. Mark Walker, of Riding House Farm, were out in the snow, and two youths, sons of the farmer, set out to look for them. Knowing how sagaciously the sheep seek for what shelter is available, they went to look behind a mass of rock, which overhung a portion of the hillside pasture, being accompanied by the dog.

Time passed by, and when the dog returned alone alarm was occasioned. Their mother went out to look for them, and to her horror found that they were buried under the snow near the rock. The heavy avalanche of snow which lay upon its upper surface suddenly slid down upon them and buried them. The terrified mother at once sought for help, and one of the young men was rescued, but the other, Walter Hall Walker, a youth of 17, was dug out a corpse.

There were snowstorms of unusual severity in 1889 and 1892.

In January and February, 1895, there was a long and very severe storm, when the roads were blocked for weeks. Leaving Bradwell at seven o'clock one night, Mr. Bramwell, a Tideswell greengrocer, reached Collins Farm, a mile distant, after three hours' snow cutting. Here the cart was left behind, and home was reached after midnight. Even the snow plough, although drawn by five horses, was unable to get through the drifts near Tideswell Lane Head, and Mr. Slack, another Tideswell greengrocer, had to leave his cart stuck in the snow, although drawn by three horses. All the villages in the district were snowed up, and all the working men available were employed cutting tracks through the snow.

This district was visited by another terrible storm in December, 1901, when many persons were dug out of the snow in an exhausted condition. A farmer named Webb, who had died at Abney Grange, was to have been buried at Bradwell, but the whole district was snowed up, and the funeral had to be postponed for some days. In fact, the coffin could not be got to the place, and 42 men were engaged all weekend cutting a road so that the funeral could take place at Bradwell on the Monday. A Peak Dale man fell exhausted in the snow, and was there 17 hours before being rescued. A Sheffield traveller, with his boy and horse, stuck fast in a drift near Tideswell, and were out in the storm all the night. They were dug out of the snow next morning by a young man from a neighbouring farm, who found them nearly dead.

SKELETONS FOUND ON THE MOORS.

In some instances people have been lost

in snowstorms after wandering far off the beaten track, and their skeletons found years afterwards. Many such cases could be cited.

On the 3rd of July, 1778, the skeleton of an unknown man was found on the moors in Hope parish, and buried in the churchyard. On Monday, the 17th of February, 1886, Charles Hodkin, a medical botanist, of Pyebank, Sheffield, set out to visit his sister, who lived at Froggatt Edge. Although 74 years of age, he was in the habit of taking long walks into Derbyshire in search of herbs, and on this morning it was his intention to walk all the way. Soon after he had left his home, snow began to fall, and hopes were entertained that he would turn back and defer his visit, but he seemed to have no fear of continuing the journey. He reached the "Peacock" at Owler Bar in safety, and asked the landlord to direct him the nearest route to Froggatt Edge. He called for no refreshment, and the landlord, noticing that one of his shoes was unlaced and the tongue hanging down, that he looked tired, and that there was every prospect of a wild and stormy night, suggested that he had better not attempt the journey, but he thanked him for his advice and walked on.

But as he neither reached his sister nor returned home, the terrible suspicions came to the family that he had lost his way, and had by that time perished in the snow, which on the night he travelled had fallen heavily, and in places on the roads and moors had drifted several feet deep. Search parties were organised, including the police, the Duke of Rutland's keepers, with their dogs, and others, and for several days a diligent and exhausting search was made everywhere about the moors where he was likely to have strayed, but not a trace of him could be found. It was then decided to abandon the search until the snow had disappeared, when it could be prosecuted more thoroughly—for by this time all hope had been abandoned of finding him alive. The snow melted away but slowly, and when it was gone, search parties went out again, but not a trace of poor Hodkin could be found, and what had become of him remained a mystery.

And it was not until the 3rd of December, 1887, nearly two years afterwards, that the mystery was unravelled, and in a remarkable way, by a dog. John Slack, a shepherd in the employ of the Duke of Rutland, was walking across the moor with his two dogs, when one of the dogs began to "wind." He rebuked the dog, which, instead of noticing him, started off towards the centre of the moors. The shepherd followed, and after walking about a mile, he came upon the skeleton remains of a man. He was lying on his back, with his right hand across his chest. His hat was a little distance away, and near it was the skull, almost covered with green moss. The legs were literally bare of flesh, and the body was considerably mutilated. Horri-

fied at the shocking spectacle, the shepherd fetched the police.

The remains were those of poor old Mr. Hodkin There was no doubt of it, for one of the boots was in precisely the same state as described by the landlord of the "Peacock," and the relatives could say that the hat and clothing were his. Besides, in one of the pockets of the coat was a portion of a Wesleyan preacher's plan, and Mr. Hodkin had himself been a preacher on the same plan. The place where the skeleton was found was far from any highway, and to reach it the poor man must have waded through bog and brook, and at length, worn out with exhaustion, had lain him down in the snow, and had slept the sleep of death. It was then that Mr. Peate, a gamekeeper, remembered that on the wild night of February 17th, 1886, he thought he heard cries of distress, and saw practically obliterated footmarks, but was unable to trace them, and next day they were all snowed up.

These instances are sufficient to show with what severity the wintry blasts come over this part of the Peak.

In times of rapid thaw, when the snow has been washed down from the hills by heavy rains, the lower parts of Bradwell have often been flooded, but there are no fatalities to record on that account. Not so, however, in the surrounding district, when the Derwent, the Noe, and the Ashop have been in flood.

EDALE PEOPLE WASHED AWAY IN FLOODS.

About the year 1830 William Wigley, of Otterbrook, Edale, and Elias Kinder, of Cotefield, Edale, were fetching with horses dragloads of timber out of the Woodlands, and when crossing the river, where there was a ford at that time. Just below Hay Lee, to get on the road leading to Hope Brink and Edale, there was a terrible catastrophe. A great flood came rushing down the Woodlands, both horses, timber, and men being overpowered and washed completely away. The bodies of both men were found some time afterwards at Grindleford, ten miles distant. One of them was quite void of clothing with the exception of a leathern belt round his body, containing seventy sovereigns. The money was found intact.

A few years later a young woman named Elliott was one night going to Hollins Farm, Edale. She had to cross Hollins Bridge, near the Cotton Mill. It was a dark night, the river was in flood, but the young woman never arrived at the farm, and was never seen again. It is supposed as her body was never recovered, it was that she was washed down the river, and expected it was washed down the river, right through the country, and away to sea.

PRESENT-DAY FREEHOLDERS.

For centuries Bradwell has been noted

for its many owners of freehold property. Indeed, in the olden times, when only owners of property voted at Parliamentary elections, it was looked upon as a little community of freeholders. Consequently it received from candidates the attention commensurate with its importance. There have been some lively times when candidates for Parliamentary honours have addressed the electors from the hustings in the old Town Gate.

Throughout this work the names of voters at various periods are mentioned, and in closing it may not be out of place to give the names of the property owners at the present day. Now, of course, every householder is a voter, but the following list of property owners—male and female —will serve to show how the lands and houses, for the most part, remain with descendants of the old families, although some have been acquired by others who have made their abode here since the railway opened out the district.

Here are the property owners of to-day in alphabetical order:—

Samuel Adams.
Francis Allen.
John Smith Andrew.
Thomas Andrew.
Joseph Ash.
Elizabeth Ashmore.
Thos. Shaw Ashton.
Charles Alfred Bancroft.
Alicia Barker.
Robert Barker.
Mary Bamford.
Sarah Bennett.
George Bird.
Herbert Bocking.
Aaron Bradbury.
Abner Bradwell.
Albert Edwin Bradwell.
Ebenezer Bradwell.
Herbert Bradwell.
Fanny Bradwell.
Hannah Bradwell.
Harriett Bradwell.
John Bradwell.
Mary Bradwell.
Spencer Joshua Bradwell.
Walter Isaac Bradwell.
William Bradwell.
Wm. Bradwell, junr.
Hannah Bradbury.
Charles Bramall.
Samuel Bramall.
William Bramall.
John Hy Bramley.
William Brierley.
George Wm. Broadbent.

Edward Knowles Heaps.
George Harry Hemsoll.
Joseph Hibbs.
Samuel Hibbs.
Henry Hill.
Isaac Hill.
Maria Hill.
Mary Hill.
Thomas Hill.
Herbert Hodkin.
Walter Hodkin.
Harriett Howe.
Mary Jackson.
Arthur Jeffery.
Benjamin Barber Jeffery.
Jeshua Jeffery.
Joshua Geo. Jeffrey.
Samuel Fox Jeffery.
William Johnson.
Frances Kiddy.
Henry Birkett Leighton.
Elizabeth Lindsay.
John Longden.
Martha Longden.
Ann Maltby.
Isaac Maltby.
Seth Maltby.
Sir Frank Mappin.
Abigail Marshall.
Hannah Marshall.
Alfred Middleton.
Allen Middleton.
Charles Middleton.
Clarinda Middleton.
Daniel Middleton.
Elijah Middleton.

Frederick Walter Burnand.
Arthur William Burrows.
Cheetham Cooper.
Horatio Wyatt Cooper.
George Cooper, jun.
John Cooper.
Luther Benjamin Cooper.
Thomas Cooper.
Robt. W. Coupland.
Robert Craig.
James Hy Cramond.
John Edwin Dakin.
Samuel Dakin.
Stephen Dakin.
Thos. Percy Dakin.
Joseph Dalton.
William Darvill.
Edwy Maltby Darneley.
Arthur Drabble.
Bertram Elliott.
George Hy. Elliott.
Joel Elliott.
John Elliott.
Samuel Elliott.
Mary Ann Elliott.
William Elliott.
Wm. Albert Elliott.
Hannah Eyre.
Marmaduke Hallam Eyre.
Percy Robt. Hallam Eyre.
William Eyre
Dennis Evans.
Seth Evans.
George J. Fisher.
Delia Fiske.
Samuel Fiske.
John Ford.
Joseph Ford.
William Hy. Fox.
Armanda Gent.
William Gyte.
Arthur James Hadfield.
Francis Hall.
Isaac Hall.
Jacob Hall.
John Hall.
Hannah Hall.
Rachel Hall.
Harriett Hall.
Cheetham William Hallam.
Ethelbert Hallam.
Alice Hallam.
George Hallam.
Hannah Hallam.
Harvey Hallam.
Montague Hallam.
Samuel Hallam.
Stenton Thomas Hallam.
Thomas Hallam.
George Hague.
Wm. H. Harrison

George Middleton.
Hibberson Middleton
James Alfred Middleton.
John Middleton.
John Middleton.
John Bennett Middleton.
Mary Middleton.
Philip Middleton.
Samuel Middleton.
Thomas Middleton.
Thomas Henry Howe Middleton.
William Middleton (Smalldale).
William Middleton.
Louisa Miller.
Alfred Morton.
Abram Morton.
Ann Stafford Morton
Hannah Morton.
Luther Morton.
Sarah Allen Morton.
Walter John Morton.
Hannah M. Needham.
Robert Needham.
Edmund Nicholson.
James Nuttall.
Allen Oates.
Elias Palfreyman.
John Palfreyman.
Wilfred Palfreyman.
Ann Pearson.
Mortimer Petty.
Richard Mortimer Petty.
John Thos. Pinder.
Benjamin Plant.
Hannah Randall.
John Robinson.
Mary Shallcross.
Thos. Frith Sheldon.
Ada Shirt.
Benjamin Somerset Shirt.
George Wm. Shirt.
Nathaniel Somerset.
Walter John Somerset.
Ashton John Shuttleworth.
Frederick Stedman.
John Stevenson.
Durham Stone.
Robt. Tanfield.
Robt. Tanfield, jun.
Thos. Hy. Tanfield.
Nicholas Tym.
Henry Walker.
George Walker.
John Walker.
Olive Walker.
Mary Walker.
Mary Alice Walker.
Zechariah Walker.
Alice M. Wragg.
Durham Wragg.
Wright.
Thurlow Joseph

ADDENDA.

ROMAN BROUGH.

Through the kindness of C. E. Bradshaw Bowles, Esq., J.P., editor of the Derbyshire Archæological Journal, the following plates of Roman Brough, and also the Ancient Oven, have been lent to the Author. In this connection reference may be made to the explorations of Brough (Chapter II).

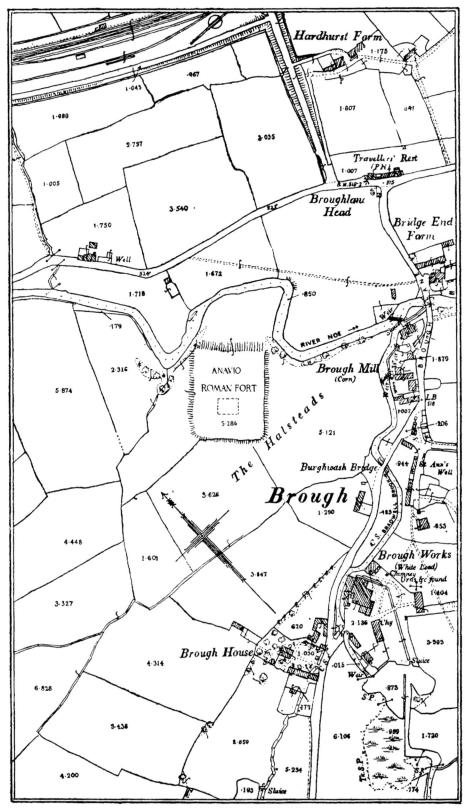

MAP OF THE SITUATION.

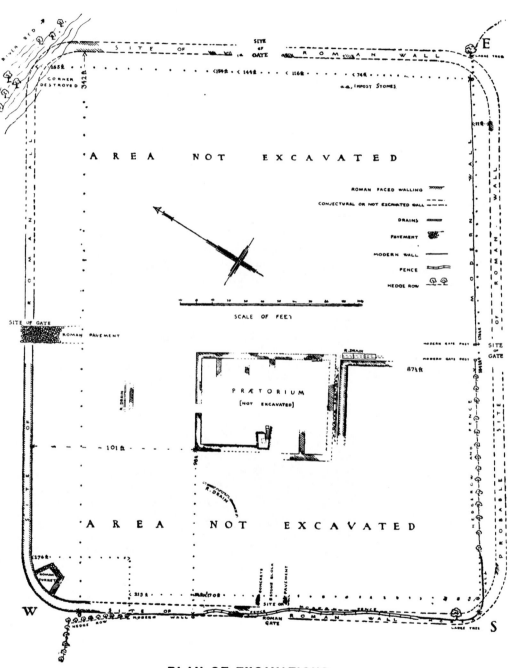

PLAN OF EXCAVATIONS.

WEST CORNER OF MAIN WALL

NORTH-WEST WALL OF PRAETORIUM.

UNDERGROUND CHAMBER OR WELL.

ANOTHER VIEW OF UNDERGROUND CHAMBER.

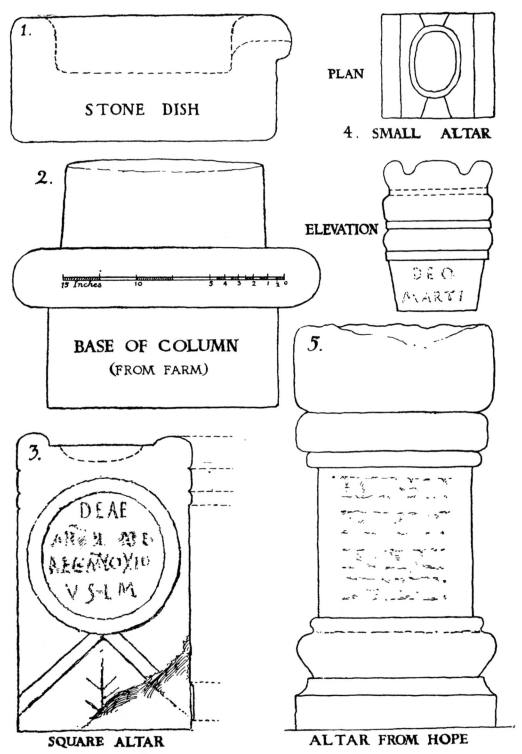

STONE DISH

PLAN

4. SMALL ALTAR

2.

15 Inches   10   5 4 3 2 1 ½ 0

BASE OF COLUMN
(FROM FARM)

ELEVATION

DEO
MARTI

5.

3.

DEAE
ARCIAE
NEMOXIA
V S·L M

SQUARE ALTAR

ALTAR FROM HOPE

ROMAN WORKINGS IN STONE AT BROUGH.

INSCRIBED TABLET, DATE MIDDLE OF SECOND CENTURY.

IMP·CAESARI·AEL·HADRIANO
ANTONINO·AVGVSTO·PIO·PP
COH·I·AQVITANORVM
SVB·IVLIO·VERO·LEG·AVG
P·R·PR·INSTANTE
CAPITONIO·PRISCOPRAE

KEY TO INSCRIPTION ON TABLET.

**REMAINS OF ANCIENT OVEN DISCOVERED IN CHARLOTTE LANE,
BRADWELL.**

"Now of the Peak I've said all I intend.
May health and pleasure wait on—every friend
At Tideswell, Grindlow, Grange and Abneylow,
Wardlow and Windmill, Hucklow and Foolow;
At Bretton, Bradwell, Middleton, and Leam,
Castleton, Baslow, Hathersage, and Eyam."

(Furness.)

Other Derbyshire titles available from Country Books

BLACK'S 1872 TOURIST'S GUIDE TO DERBYSHIRE
With engravings, map and period advertisements
Enlarged facsimile of the 1872 Derbyshire edition edited by Llewellynn Jewitt — a name which needs no introduction to local historians in the county. The contents of the book include: a general description of Derbyshire; area; population; position; history; antiquities; eminent men; geology; manufactures; agriculture; railways and canals; map of Buxton; map of Chatsworth and vicinity; plan of Haddon Hall and 25 engravings on wood and steel.
Paperback 210 x 148mm 351 pages
Country Books ISBN 1 898941 22 X Price **£8.95**

TRUE BRIT
THE ADVENTURES OF PETER FIDLER OF BOLSOVER 1769-1822
by K Gordon Jackson
A well researched book on the first 'white man' to map inland Canada. Fidler was employed by the Hudson Bay Company to chart the land for use as trade routes for the hunters and trappers. He married a Cree Indian, Mary, who acted as his interpreter.
Paperback 210 x 148mm 214 pages B&W photos
Country Books ISBN 1 898941 48 3 Price **£7.50**

NOTES FROM A PEAKLAND PARISH
An account of the church and parish of Hope in the county of Derby
by William Smith Porter MD
A facsimile of Notes from a Peakland Parish first published in published in 1923. It of especial interest to the local historian and those researching their family trees.
The church and the parish of Hope; Vicars and churchwardens; Free school of Hope; Parish charities; Parish registers 1599-1750; Churchwardens' book of accounts with a complete list of briefs; Inhabitants of the parish in the 15th-17th centuries; Landowners in the parish 1570; Easter roll of 1658; Agincourt roll; Spanish Armada and local levies; Volunteers enrolled at Hope in case of invasion 1803; Inhabitants of the parish who served overseas in the Great War 1914-1918
LIMITED EDITION OF 100 COPIES
Hardback 210 x 135mm 148 pages 10 B&W photos
Country Books ISBN 1 898941 43 2 Price **£25.00**

THE TAP DRESSERS: A PERSONAL ACCOUNT OF A WELLDRESSING VILLAGE
by Norman Wilson
The ancient and mysterious custom of well dressing is an astonishingly beautiful spectacle that can be seen to no better effect than in the Peakland village of Youlgrave. Yet for most of the thousands of visitors who flock to see it each year, that is all it can be — a spectacle. Who creates these magnificent but fragile works of art and why? what inspires the community spirit and why is the tradition so unique to the Derbyshire Dales? these are questions that for many wondering visitors have hitherto remained unanswered. In The Tap Dressers, This most comprehensive account of the fascinating tradition is a must for those who, having come to admire the spectacle, yearn to know more; it will appeal no less to those who know nothing of welldressing but who, in a time of bewildering change, find reassurance in the continuity and certainty of our rural heritage.
Paperback 210 x 148mm 144 pages Colour and B&W photos
Country Books ISBN 1 898941 47 5 Price **£7.50**

STAGS & SERPENTS
THE STORY OF THE HOUSE OF CAVENDISH AND THE DUKES OF DEVONSHIRE
by John Pearson
The story of four centuries and fifteen generations of one of the most talented and powerful families in English history. From Bess of Hardwick to the present day the Cavendishes have played central roles in politics, architecture, science and the encouragement and patronage of the arts. The great houses of Hardwick and Chatsworth are their chief monuments today. A history – in miniature – of England from Elizabeth I to Elizabeth II.
Paperback 220 x 150mm. 336 pages. Mono photos.
Chatsworth House/Country Books ISBN 1 898941 58 0 Price: **£9.99**